W9-ACA-795

The World and
How We Describe It

The World and
How We Describe It

Rhetorics of Reality,
Representation, Simulation

Barry Brummett

PRAEGER

Westport, Connecticut
London

Library of Congress Cataloging-in-Publication Data

Brummett, Barry, 1951–
    The world and how we describe it : rhetorics of reality, representation, simulation / Barry Brummett.
       p. cm.
    Includes bibliographical references (p.) and index.
    ISBN 0–275–98019–7 (alk. paper)
     1. Rhetoric.   2. Semantics.   3. Language and culture.   I. Title.
    P302.B86 2003
    808—dc21   2002037061

British Library Cataloguing in Publication Data is available.

Library of Congress Catalog Card Number: 2002037061
ISBN: 0–275–98019–7

First published in 2003

Praeger Publishers, 88 Post Road West, Westport, CT 06881
An imprint of Greenwood Publishing Group, Inc.
www.praeger.com

Printed in the United States of America

The paper used in this book complies with the
Permanent Paper Standard issued by the National
Information Standards Organization (Z39.48–1984).

10 9 8 7 6 5 4 3 2 1

For Greg Brummett and Kevin Brummett

Contents

Preface   xi

1. Reality, Representation, Simulation   1

2. A Construction Project: Why the Key Terms Converge   25

3. Reality, Representation, and Simulation in Structures
   of Experience   45

4. Reality, Representation, and Simulation in Lived Experience   71

5. A Rhetoric of Reality in the Novels of William Gibson   97

6. A Rhetoric of Representation in Rec.motorcycles   123

7. The Simulational Self in *Groundhog Day*   137

Bibliography   147

Index   153

Preface

Decades ago, as a novice teaching assistant in graduate school, I accepted an offer to teach a course at the Minnesota State Penitentiary. Although a learning experience for me, it was a disaster from the very start. Among the least of the troubles I encountered in trying to teach angry prisoners, sullen guards, and frightened undergraduates was the continued claim by the inmates that prison life was *reality*. The rhetorical value rather than the "reality" of such a claim was apparent to me from the start. After all, I got to return home to a comfortable if modest apartment after class; was that not real, too? But I understood the rhetorical claim inherent in the inmates' assertion, that what they faced there was somehow "more" real, more authentic, more grounded. It was clear even then that the claim did political and social work for the inmates and for the rest of us.

Fast forward to the twenty-first century, and it is not hard to find a rap or hip hop video in which an angry young urban poseur shouts, "I'm gonna *represent*!" By this he (it's usually he) means he intends not only to "keep it real" but also to "tell it like it is" (to use a much older foreshadowing of *represent*), to make plain the conditions of injustice and poverty of which he sings, and perhaps above all to show-to speak for-himself and his. Again, the usage is rhetorical: one represents how things "really" (*that* again) are to make a claim about how one has been or expects to be treated, and often the claim is made in explicit opposition to *mis*representations about oneself and one's group made by others.

Only recently has the term *simulation* come into common usage, although it has been in the dictionary for a long time. Simulation has in some sense always been possible, for as long as people could "make believe" or fantasize. But new digital technologies have exponentially increased the possibilities for rich, detailed, engrossing fantasy and for communal make-believe. The Internet in particular, with its virtual communities, electric shopping malls, games, and pornography is seen as a site of simulation, and thus as either an escapist fantasy land or a new utopia. Simulation today is not a clear nor is it a simple concept. It is a site of struggle; as some will think of it as an experience of delusion and retreat, others will think of it as desirable alternative realities or as preparation for better experiencing "reality."

This book studies how those three key terms, *reality*, *representation*, and *simulation*, are used rhetorically. I am not concerned with what they "really" are so much as with what people claim they are, with struggles over those claims, and with the political, social work that those claims perform. This book, in other words, is about the rhetoric of three key terms in contemporary discourse.

Many people are inclined to think of reality, representation, and simulation as if they were real themselves, as if the terms referred objectively to concepts if not actual experiences, objects, or properties with clearly agreed-upon characteristics. The book begins by reviewing in general what people mean when they use each term as if each had clear referents. But I quickly move to the claim that clear distinctions among the terms cannot be maintained, that they overlap and merge into each other. A second chapter explores some reasons in principle and in practice why each term is more unstable than people generally suppose, finding reasons in perception, language use, and aesthetic experience for the instability and mergers of the terms. Making a rhetorical term, we next consider four dimensions of rhetorical meaning that are involved when people use the three key terms. The discourse of critics, scholars, and social observers who are concerned with the three terms is examined in the next two chapters. Chapter 3 examines permanence and change, and commodification, as dimensions on which the meanings of the three terms vary. Chapter 4 examines subjectivity and aesthetics as dimensions invoked when people use the key terms. In each case, the book explores the kind of claim being made when people say reality, representation, or simulation.

Our three key terms are also manifested in rhetorical usage in popular culture. The last three chapters of the book examine the rhetorics of reality, representation, and simulation in everyday experience, particularly in popular entertainments. Chapter 5 presents three science fiction novels by William Gibson as arguing a rhetoric of reality. Chapter 6 shows the workings of a rhetoric of representation in an Internet news and discussion group. And Chapter 7 shows how the film *Groundhog Day* relies on a rhetoric of simulation. In each case it is clear that social and political rhetoric is embodied in a claim of reality, representation, or simulation.

Chapter 1

Reality, Representation, Simulation

At the start of a currently popular television show in which host John Edward channels the dead relatives of his studio audience, the television viewer is assured, "What you are about to see is *real*." Any school child knows that the American colonies rebelled against England's taxation without *representation*. Gamers sit for hours in front of computers running *simulations* of alien attacks on Earth. In these three terms of *reality*, *representation*, and *simulation* people describe what they take to be important dimensions of everyday *experience* (which we may take to be the overarching category). Indeed, it may be difficult to imagine a kind of experience that does not fall into one of those three categories.

This book explores the ways that people use these three key terms—*reality*, *representation*, and *simulation*—as rhetorical devices with political and social effect. What each term means is the subject of the whole study, and not easily explained. But to get us started, some brief indications of each term's usage might be sketched out; Reality is what happens when I stub my toe on a stone; it is immediate, material experience. Representation is my telling you about my stubbing my toe; the telling of it is not the same thing as the stubbing of the toe, it is a re-presenting of the stubbing to you in signs and symbols. Simulation is my stubbing a toe on a stone in the seventh dungeon level of the latest *Academics of Doom* video game; it is a self-contained fantasy that is none of the above, not real or a representation of the real but an experience within a world apart from the world.

Reality, representation, simulation—to begin a scholarly study with such a title seems impossibly ambitious; one may as well write of *The Human Condition*. But my purpose here is not so broad as it might seem, for I do not want to know what those things *are* so much as how those terms are *used*. People certainly do write and speak as if there were such things as reality, representation, and simulation. People treat the terms as if they were clearly referential and as if those referents were clearly distinct. But what kind of political, social work do people do when they write and speak in those terms? What kind of *claim* is being made, or accusation leveled, when such a term is used? How do the dimensions and parameters of meaning facilitated by each term work in the management and distribution of power? These are questions of *rhetoric*, the manipulation of signs and symbols for influence and effect. When someone claims that they are living an experience of reality while a rival is lost in a fantasy or is playing games (simulation), claims are made that empower and disempower people politically and socially. When someone speaks or writes discourse that claims to represent groups of people, the claim of representation itself asserts power. This study attempts to explain the dimensions of meaning that are enabled by each term, and to show the kind of rhetorical power engendered by those meanings.

These three key terms are given in order of cultural familiarity. *Reality* is of course an ancient concept, even among those who denied any such thing, such as ancient Greek Sophists or Eastern mystics; at least they had a concept to deny. *Representation* is also of long usage, and has especially gained currency since the ascendancy of semiotics as a foundational method for the humanities in the twentieth century. *Simulation* as a term is fairly new, popularized by the advent of first electric and now digital technologies and the fairy worlds they can create.

A parent may love all of his children and yet spend more time with one or two, especially with the more difficult ones that need explaining to the neighbors. Likewise in this book, I will spend more time with *representation* and still more with *simulation* as relatively more problematic and more likely to repay close critical examination. Although I will by no means ignore it, in a sense *reality* is old enough to play by itself.

So this book studies not what the three key terms *are* but what they *mean*, and how they are used rhetorically. This chapter reviews a range of the usages of each term, while not claiming to exhaust the full meaning of any of them. Part of my purpose is to reassure you that it is not a straw person to inquire into how each term is used rhetorically; such usage is in fact common all around us every day, and as we shall see, the terms are used as if they were distinct and unproblematically referential. So we begin the book in this chapter by a review of some of the ways that each term is used, with some of the broadest meanings implied in each.

It may be useful first to consider a scheme by which the three key terms may be compared on the dimension of dualism. *Dualism* is a philosophical tenet, disseminated in the modern age beginning with Rene Descartes, that divides the universe of experience into mind and body, into (respectively) the subjective and the objective, the "in here" and the "out there." In answer to the question of what is the most basic reality, or where may one search for the surest knowledge, dualism is the assumption that the answer is found in a choice between mind and body, subject and object. Mediating mind and body are language, mathematics, and other languages or sign systems; these are means of informing the subject about what goes on in the world of objects. Dualism is not which choice one takes, but rather the assumption that the choice is forced (Brummett, *Reading*, 503–4).

Clear distinctions among reality, representation, and simulation require a commitment to dualism, and each term may be understood in terms of the relative importance it grants to dualism's three key terms of mind, matter, and signs (which mediate between mind and matter). A preference for, a focus upon, reality holds matter to be of primary importance and mind of secondary importance. The key thing is for the mind to understand the ways things really are in the world. Signs come in third as merely the tools that link mind and matter. A preference for and a focus upon representation holds signs to be of primary importance and both matter and mind of secondary importance. The key thing is for signs to be so carefully devised that they accurately re-present the world to the mind. A preference for and a focus upon simulation holds the mind to be of primary importance, with representation second and reality a distant third place. The key thing here is the mind's own hermetic experience, disconnected from any kind of reality, aided by the excellence of representations that re-present reality barely if at all. It may be useful to keep this scheme in mind as we consider our key terms.

REALITY

Reality is treated popularly as an unproblematic term; never mind that it is not so clear and simple, as this study will demonstrate. It may well be that among avant-garde artists and black-swathed academics, reality is, like God, not believed in. But the concept of reality is certainly believed in even among those who regard it agnostically. Those in or out of the academy who would use reality as merely a concept, a foil, a basis of comparison for whatever is not real, are surely in a minority in the wide world. Your average Josephine on the street would agree with Mark Slouka that reality is "immutable, empirical, neither historically nor culturally relative" (160) and that it is a fact of life. Set aside your deconstructionist sensibilities for a moment here, gentle reader; when we piously avow that we don't believe in an objective, absolute reality, what is it that we say we don't believe in? That is the concept in question here.

Reality in popular usage is what *is*, that which cannot be wished away, gotten around, or ignored except at cost. It is the Great Recalcitrance, it is inevitable Death and uncopiable Life, it is primal pain and pleasure, sight and sound and the other senses, and the hard world that excites them. Related terms that express the same meaning are the *world, facts, nature*. Reality has a kind of precession, gravity, and singularity that undergird other dimensions of experience. One can manipulate reality by kicking a stone, but one cannot make reality by making the stone. One can make synthetic stone and one can make concrete, but out of irreducible materials that at some point are given to us, found in the great storehouse of reality. When we admonish our foolish friend to "get real" we are recalling her to the bedrock of hard material experience that is reality and from which one's mind (but never the body) may wander in lies and fantasy—that is to say, in representation and simulation.

REPRESENTATION

Once we get beyond "simple reality" and into representation, things get tricky. We might begin etymologically by noting that the term suggests a re-presentation: that which presents again (to awareness, in discourse, for consideration) something which is in some sense absent. A representation is not the same thing as its reference; as Michael Stephan reminds us, "a picture cannot in material terms be the object it represents" (111). Susanne K. Langer agrees in claiming that neither a sign nor a symbol is the same thing as that which it means, and it is certainly not a copy of what it means: "[a] picture is essentially a symbol, not a duplicate, of what it represents" (*Philosophy*, 68).

A representation is not a copy of something (a true copy, a duplication, may be sometimes understood as a simulation; see the following). Instead, a representation is some sort of material or cognitive occurrence that is different from that which it represents. Kendall Walton uses the term *matching* instead of copying, and notes that representations do not match but rather introduce what he calls "fictional" propositions about their objects (88). By "fictional" he does not mean false but rather in the order of discourse or signs.

A representation always entails an absence since one speaks, writes, or gestures in place of what one means. Even if I refer to an object in the room, the representation in my utterance *lacks* the object and stands in its place. Related terms that may express the same meaning are *sign*, *symbol*, *language*, *discourse*, *image*, *picture*, and *icon*.

Things that are called or treated as representations are, of course, quite widespread in everyday conversation and usage. Language is perhaps the paradigm case of representation. I. A. Richards's well-known definition of rhetoric as "a study of misunderstanding and its remedies" is clearly keyed to a sense of language's ability or failure to represent our thoughts to ourselves and to others (3). Representations may also be the linguistic form taken by internal thought processes; Gregory Currie argues that "imagining, belief and desire are attitudes we bear to representational contents symbolized in a language of thought. So imagination as I understand it is the concept of a representational state" (152).

Increasingly in our world, images are understood as representations. Larry Day argues that "painting is an art of representation. It always represents a subject, the artist's sensibility, idea, experience, and so on" (43). Rene Berger speaks of television as giving us the world beyond the here and now in this way: "A new fundamental change has taken place with modern audio-visual technology. Freeing us of the need to go somewhere to see it, television has taken its place in our homes, captivating our internal forum that its programs occupy from morning to evening, and often the entire night long" (3). Bell hooks writes of television's power to represent African Americans through images (1).

Representation has been well and thoroughly theorized. The term is often found in scholarly works today, especially those informed by critical or cultural studies and by postmodern points of view. John Stewart's anthology *Beyond the Symbol Model: Reflections on the Representational Nature of Language* is one example of a recent, thorough treatment of the subject. In *Representing Reality*, Bill Nichols connects our first two terms in a study of documentary film, and how such films lay claim to reflect the way the world really is. Kenneth Burke's work was written some years ago but is evergreen in its constant usefulness for scholars. Representation is a theme running across several of his works. He discusses the importance of the representative anecdote in several places in *A Grammar of Motives*, and representation is problematized in his landmark essay, "What Are the Signs of What?" in *Language as Symbolic Action* (359–79).

A key thinker in the problems of representation, Langer employs the well-known distinction between *signs* and *symbols* (*Philosophy*, 29) as two broad categories of communicative instruments. A sign is a meaningful entity that refers the observer to immediate time and space; in other words, it announces something closely connected to it in real experience; but a symbol, she argues, reminds the user of something and also implies an attitude toward that thing (30–31). This reminding of that which is not in the here and now is the clearest act of representation, which is unique to people: "Man, unlike all other animals, uses 'signs' not only to *indicate* things, but also to *represent* them" (30). The sight of a food bowl announces to a dog some possibility of food here and now, but to people that bowl may re-present a meal taken years ago. Langer claims that the subset of " 'signs' usedin this capacity are not *symptoms* of things but *symbols*" (31).

Let us consider Langer's claim that symbols, in representing rather than merely announcing, introduce attitudes into the minds of users. Representation must invoke complex cognitive processes in which a word or image invokes that which is not present: "signs *announce* their objects to him, whereas symbols *lead him to conceive* their objects" (*Philosophy*, 61). The introduction of personal or cultural biases, attitudes, and predispositions is thus integral to representation. Langer's point is that in going through the extra work of re-presenting what is not here and now, symbols inevitably entail perceptions and attitudes; they invoke culture and history. People are often unaware of these perceptions and attitudes, and thus many if not most representations can seem as if they are neutrally re-presenting the world to us. Michael J. Shapiro notes in that regard that "the mark of what is called a 'realistic' representation is that it is uncontentious" (4).

These references to absence, or what is not here, and to the inclusion of cognitions not originally a part of the reference, imply an irreducible poignancy for representation from which many of its most interesting characteristics flow: it gives us something but can never exactly give us something, it must add to or take away from meaning insofar as it involves human conceptualization. This poignancy places representation in the field of epistemology and morality, as we shall see in later chapters. Representation is epistemological because it is, as Rene Berger argues, an analogue of reality, shadowing reality but not precisely copying it: "[I]mages have always had and retained an *analogue status*, that necessarily postulates a reference to a known, or at least recognizable object. . . . [T]hey retain the same fundamental status that places them within the *order of representation*. Iconography, whether sacred or profane, remains provisional ontology" (18). Thus, as Massimo Negrotti observes, "representation plays a key role in relating the human mind to the world" (11)—how perfectly the relation holds is, of course, a key concern. Negrotti notes further that "representations are mental constructs whose consistency with the world depends, according to different psychological or social circumstances, on the strength of our subjectivity, or cultural models, or the world" (13). Because representations are epistemic, the judgment of their epistemic efficacy is often moral. Representations (and representers) are held accountable for their epistemic veracity; in representation we enter the realm of the Truth and of the Lie.

Ernst Cassirer expresses that representational poignancy in this way: "For all mental processes fail to grasp reality itself, and in order to represent it, to hold it at all, they are driven to the use of symbols. But all symbolism harbors the curse of mediacy; it is bound to obscure what it seeks to reveal" (7). Anne Norton refers to this poignancy as "the lie in representation, that it is what it is not, [which is] also properly a recognition of its truth. Representation depends on contradiction" (149). Paul Virilio describes the poignancy in terms of "dissimulation [which] was unquestionably *central to representation*, as the more powerful techniques of perception became, *the more the cancellation of reality would spread*, from people to large-scale objects and finally to whole regions" (*Art*, 131). Norton notes that representations give up something of what is represented as they add the "authority" embodied in discourses of representation themselves: "The act of representation invests the image with surplus value, if you will; it is its supplement. What is lost is the voice of the represented. What is added are the texts of authority" (167). As a voice of authority, representation is clearly a claim of *power*.

SIMULATION

What do people mean today when they speak of simulation? We will spend more time considering how this term is used than we did for reality or representation, since it is newer, more unfamiliar, and perhaps less conventional. In general, we may begin by saying that a simulation is an experience that seems like reality but in important ways neither is nor represents reality. Clearly, such a gloss will need unpacking.

Jean Baudrillard, one of the preeminent theorists of simulation, thinks of it as "substituting signs of the real for the real itself" (*Simulations*, 4). Note the shift away from reality and representation implied in that expression: signs are treated as if they *were* reality and are no longer taken to *represent* reality. Daniel J. Boorstin anticipated Baudrillard's formulation if not his terminology in discussing a world he perceived to be filled with pseudo-events. For Boorstin, his world and ours is "a world where people talk constantly not of things themselves but of their images. Yet it is by these circumlocutions that we unwittingly express our deepest unspoken beliefs. Belief in the malleability of the world. Belief in the superior vividness of a Technicolor representation to a drab original" (204). Both Baudrillard and Boorstin describe artificially, technologically created experiences that seem like reality but are not, nor do those created experiences refer to reality. There is a sense of simulation as fraud here—a very good simulation may make one forget that "real reality" is elsewhere, yet the fraud may always be exposed by switching off the set, leaving the theater, or being whacked on the head.

Note also that for both scholars, simulations may seem like reality, but they are in fact made up out of signs, which are usually the stuff of representations. The best simulations may be thought of as representations that are so technically perfect that they come to seem like reality, and may in fact be indistinguishable from it. Thus, the representative value of such signs is lost. In simulation, one loses a pre-occupation with how or whether signs represent. David Gunkel expresses this idea by saying that virtual reality ideally effaces itself as a sign at the same time that it is expected to represent reality (47–48).

It may be useful to track a single kind of experience as it moves from reality to representation to simulation. At this writing I am shopping for a house. This involves going to tour actual houses in *reality*. My agent has also directed me to a Web site where I might take "virtual tours" of houses without leaving my home. The images I obtain by way of that site are *representations* of real homes (never mind that "virtual" usually means a simulation; here it is clearly intended to represent real houses). Let us be clear that the Web tour is made of nothing but signs, which I access for their representational value. But one could also imagine someone accessing the Web site who had no intentions at all of buying a house and no interest in the particular homes represented. Such a person wants to take these signs at their sheer face value, not as representations but as a real-like experience on their own terms. This person wants the entertaining experience of a *simulation*, and will obtain it by wandering around homes in cyberspace. Note that for our simulational tourer, it matters not at all whether the homes on the Web are real; thus, the representational value of the signs gives way to simulation.

It may be worthwhile to distinguish simulation from representation more clearly. C. K. Ogden and I. A. Richards, years before the terms became fashionable, made this distinction between simulation and representation: "Simulative and non-simulative languages are entirely distinct in principle. Standing for and representing are different relations" (12). A language that stands for an experience may be taken as that experience; it is in the place of reality and must do as a more or less satisfactory copy of it.

Baudrillard makes these distinctions between representation and simulation: "This would be the successive phases of the image: —it is the reflection of a basic reality—it masks and perverts a basic reality—it masks the *absence* of a basic reality—it bears no relation to any reality whatever: it is its own pure simulacrum" (*Simulations*, 11). Michael Heim makes the point that images in simulations do not represent a reality as they would representationally; instead, they constitute one: "Virtual images are not like the images in paintings which we can mistake to be an outside entity and which the graphic image represents. In VR, the images are the realities" ("Design," 70).

Some experiences that are often taken to be kinds or variations of simulations are *virtual reality, fantasy, make-believe, games, myths, fantasies,* and *fiction*. For instance, Kendall Walton uses the terms "reflexive representation" and "fiction" in ways that may help us see what a simulation is; it is in fact a representation, but of itself: "A doll directs players of the game not just to imagine a baby but to imagine the doll itself to be a baby. So it generates fictional truths about itself; it represents itself. Let's call it a *reflexive* representation" (*Mimesis*, 117). Walton also writes of "make-believe" in simulational terms, as an experience that is a realistic experience apart from reality, when he argues that "make-believe is a pervasive element of human experience." (7). Langer describes both myths and fantasies as being like dreams, all three being experiences composed of symbols but with no literal references (*Philosophy*, 171).

The experience of virtual reality (VR) is often taken to be the paradigm of a simulation. David Gunkel practically equates the two, while distinguishing both from representation: "For what is at stake in VR is not a new form of mediated representation, but a specific kind of computer-generated simulation that deconstructs the metaphysical system that institutes and regulates the very difference between representation and reality" (46). Sherry Turkle sees "virtual communities" as "a culture of simulation" and argues that "in cyberspace . . . perhaps already millions of users create online personae who live in a diverse group of virtual communities" (89). Virtual reality is compared to the idea of cyberspace by Victor J. Vitanza, who sees VR as more simulational in its verisimilitude: "the easy difference between cyberspace and virtual reality is that in virtual reality we can *actually believe* we are *in* it" (4). For Vitanza, simulation is what comes closest to standing in for reality.

But Michael Heim complains that a distinction needs to be made between simulations and virtual reality, that some of what people call the latter are really the former (*Virtual*, 3–6). He argues that "some people consider virtual reality any electronic representation with which they can interact," but he objects to so broad a definition: "once we extend the term *virtual reality* to cover everything artificial, we lose the force of the phrase" ("Essence," 22). In a virtual world, Heim argues, technology does not represent but instead emulates reality: "Virtual worlds do not seek to re-present the primary physical world, nor to borrow integrity by imitation or photorealism. What emerges from virtual worlds are new functional habitats that emulate the engagement of real worlds" (*Virtual*, 89). Heim is saying that while a simulation may seem like a particular real experience (e.g., a simulation of Versailles), a VR seems real but not a particular "real" reality (e.g., a "realistic" tour of the Warlock's castle). Heim notes, for instance, that "a virtual world builder must . . . eschew literal references" (*Virtual*, 96), emphasizing simulation's lack of reference to reality. Heim's distinction between simulation and VR is not universally followed, of course.

Across the different ways of defining simulation is a conviction that it is very widespread, especially in Western culture and most especially in the United States. Even forty years ago, Boorstin complained that "in the last half century a larger and larger proportion of our experience . . . has come to consist of pseudo-events" (12) and that "the American citizen thus lives in a world where fantasy is more real than reality" (37). Boorstin believed that simulational pseudo-events would "overshadow" reality because the former are more dramatic, are created for dissemination and drama, are repeatable, are made in someone's financial interest, are more intelligible and reassuring, are more sociable and easy to witness, are the standard of being well informed, and because they spawn other pseudo-events (39–40).

Today, Mark Poster argues that "the terms 'virtual reality' and 'real time' attest to the force of the second media age in constituting a simulational culture. . . . The culture is increasingly simulational in the sense that the media often changes the things that it treats, transforming the identity of originals and referentialities. In the second media age, 'reality' becomes multiple" (85). Other observers agree that simulation is widespread. Norton argues that "the passion for simulacra, for art, contrivance, and representation, shows itself in every aspect of American life" (29). Slouka complains that today, "it's hard to think of a sphere of human activity that hasn't been simulated" (115). Moreover, Slouka sees these simulations as organically connected: "The culture of simulation is all of a piece, and whether we find our forgeries in a computer, a newspaper, or the culture at large makes little difference" (117).

The dimension of experience most often cited as simulational in Western culture is entertainment, especially as conveyed in the electronic media. Michael Parenti argues that the entertainment media create their own simulational worlds when they "invent a reality much their own" (4). Following Parenti's observation that simulation depends on following a model of experience, Baudrillard argues that "mass mediatization . . . is no ensemble of techniques for broadcasting messages; it is the *imposition of models*" (*For*, 175). A "model" in this sense is a pattern for the enactment of a separate world, a simulation, much as the rules of chess are a model for the creation of a simulation which is the experience of playing chess.

Although she does not refer to it explicitly as simulational, Langer describes music in similar terms. Music is "non-representative," she argues (*Philosophy*, 209). That is, it does not refer to a specific occurrence in reality. However, it is a symbolic "exposition" of a certain kind of experience, specifically, of feelings or emotion (218–21). Langer argues that "because the forms of human feeling are much more congruent with musical forms than with the forms of language, music can *reveal* the nature of feelings with a detail and truth that language cannot approach" (235). But since music does not refer to any specific emotion one might have, such as a reaction to a particular sunset, it must be creating a simulational experience of emotion, "non-representatively."

Television is often described as being simulational because it shows audiences a world it creates, not a world that objectively exists elsewhere. Steven Johnson calls television a parasitical form of discourse in that sense, and argues that "the new parasite forms take the images of contemporary television at face value—as a real, vital, unavoidable component of everyday life" (30–31). One important way in which television creates simulations is that the worlds it shows audiences are not objective reporting (representing) of reality, but are new, electronically induced realities. In support of that idea, Benjamin Woolley argues that "television is not a window on the world; it does not simply show its audience pictures of events that happen to be taking place elsewhere. Rather, it actually has a role in determining what the audiences see and how they make sense of it" (11). John Fiske argues that television characters or "figures" such as Murphy Brown are simulations in their own right: "A figure, as I use the term here, is a human simulacrum, one that simulates a person, and its simulation is what a person has become in hyperreality" (68).

Among the entertaining experiences of simulation to which observers point are computer games, which according to Nicholas Negroponte "represent a business that is larger than the American motion-picture industry and growing much faster as well" (82–83). Players enter a constructed reality while in the game, and the more real it appears, the better. Norton argues that significant sectors of professional sports are simulated: "The most interesting sports . . . are those that derive their interest from their falsity. Roller Derby and wrestling are what they are not. . . . Each is regarded . . . as an imposture, a simulacrum of a sport" (31). One might go beyond her argument to claim that sports of any sort are simulational, creating worlds apart from reality.

Travel, argues Boorstin, is now so full of what he calls pseudo-events that we no longer see the reality of the places to which we go (79–80). Instead, museums and other attractions draw us into their contrived worlds and separate us from the reality without (101–2). Disneyland is pointed to as a paradigm of simulation, a model for an increasingly simulational culture generally. The point is made most famously by Baudrillard in arguing that "Disneyland is a perfect model of all the entangled orders of simulation" (*Simulations*, 23) and that "Disneyland is presented as imaginary in order to make us believe that the rest is real, when in fact all of Los Angeles and the America surrounding it are no longer real, but of the order of the hyperreal and of simulation" (25). Nigel Clark argues that "Disney-style simulacra are now ubiquitous in many contemporary cities" (121–22).

Norton, responding to Baudrillard, claims that "Americans in Disneyland do not mistake it for reality" but instead celebrate "their collective capacity to produce a world more rational and more rewarding than that which Providence supplies them" (21). Norton's quibble may be prompted by her general unwillingness to speak of simulation, preferring instead to write of different orders of representation. But her explanation of the appeal of Disneyland is similar to other scholars' explanations of the appeal of simulation, in part, specifically that it reflects the drive to master Nature by creating separate, manageable worlds: "The passion to surpass the God of Nature in the making of a world manifests itself in every aspect of the life of Americans" (21).

Computers are often described as the engine of simulation in contemporary culture. Activities grounded in computers are thus preeminent scenes of simulation. Stefan Helmreich argues that "Artificial Life scientists consider computers to be worlds in a variety of sense. . . . Increasingly, they mean that computers are literally alternative worlds or . . . universes" (65). Paul Virilio argues vigorously that computers have created new, separate worlds:

Where the *far* horizon of our planet's antipodes has finally an *apparent*, or more precisely, 'trans-apparent' horizon, through the special effects of audiovisual techniques, the urgent necessity of another limit, a new frontier, suddenly makes itself felt—one that would no longer be geographic but infographic; the *mental image* of far distances hidden by the curve of the glove yielding to the *instrumental imagery* of a computer that can generate a virtual otherworld. (*Art*, 142–43)

Similarly, Woolley speculates of the separate space created by the Internet, "Could this be where the denizens of the global village truly belong? Could this be a *new* reality?" (17). Celia T. Romm likewise argues for the reality of the self-contained world of e-mail. "In many organizations, e-mail is becoming the major vehicle for communication," (2) she observes. E-mail creates "virtual communities" in her view, some of which overlap and some of which do not overlap with "real" communities (4–5). She concludes that "it can be claimed that e-mail networks provide users with communities that are more socially 'real' than the national, professional, or local communities to which they formally belong" (224).

   There seem to be two general themes that people (sometimes, the *same* scholar expresses both views) emphasize in defining the essence of simulation: one, that a simulation has no outside reference (it is *arepresentational*), and two, that a simulation is inherently a *copy* (often, it is added, a copy with no meaningful original). Let us review these two essentializing moves and see how they are actually synergistic.

SIMULATIONS WITHOUT REPRESENTATION

   In defining the essence of simulation, a number of theorists focus on the insular, hermetic nature of simulation. The actions, objects, and events comprising simulation do not function as signs in the usual sense of having referents. A simulation in this view is made of signs without representation; they refer only to themselves and to the world that they create.

   This sense of a world apart, of a closed world, is expressed in Margaret Wertheim's claim that "by making a collective space where the self can experiment and play with others, cyberspace creates a parallel world that in a very real sense is a new cosmos of psyche" (58). Slouka agrees with the idea of an insular world in cyberspace: "While the deconstructionists could only argue that nothing exists outside of us . . . the cyberists had machines that could *make* it so" (36). One way in which technology does that, according to Slouka, is through giving the human user highly interactive feedback that creates a sense of reality: "It was this element of feedback, more than anything else, that provided the alchemy of cyberspace, that seduced the imagination into accepting the fantasy as real. The place was alive, capable of responding to your commands, inhabited by the voices of real people" (49).

   Perhaps the classic expression of the arepresentational view of simulation comes from Baudrillard: "Simulation is no longer that of a territory, a referential being or a substance. It is the generation by models of a real without origin or reality: a hyperreal. The territory no longer precedes the map, nor survives it. Henceforth, it is the map that precedes the territory—PRECESSION OF SIMULACRA—it is the map that engenders the territory" (*Simulations*, 2). Of course, a map without a territory is a set of signs with no referents. In simulation, the map precedes, engenders, and generates the territory, in the sense that a map of Middle-Earth is part of the mechanics of generation of the simulation which is Tolkien's *The Lord of the Rings*. In that sense a simulation is a set of signs that creates its own reality but refers to no other reality outside itself.

Roy Wagner has developed a theory of figurative language as "symbols that stand for themselves." His theory fits the arepresentational view of simulation. Wagner compares the representational view of language, in which "a microcosm of symbols is deployed to code or represent the world of reference. The world of phenomena is self-evident and apart" with his own arepresentational view of figurative language, in which "naming becomes a matter of analogy; symbol and symbolized belong to a single relation" (14). Unlike ordinary language, which is usually representational, "figurative usage . . . because it makes a kind of prism of conventional reference, cannot provide a literal field of reference. It is not formed by 'indicating' things, or by referencing them, but by setting pointers or reference points into a relation with one another," an arepresentational characteristic shared by all tropes or figures of speech (6). For instance, "metaphor is at once propositional and resolution; it stands for itself" (11). Representational language is a "microcosm" that represents the macrocosm of the world; "but if we treat 'name' as relationship, the microcosm of names is no longer a microcosm; it becomes immersed in a macrocosm of analogic construction" (15), which describes figurative language in terms of self-contained simulations.

Michael Heim offers a way to understand simulation as essentially arepresentational in arguing that "an essential attribute of any system is the sense of immersion that it produces. . . . Immersion is the you-are-there experience you get when listening to an expensive stereo system" (*Virtual*, 17). Virtual reality or simulation in its strongest sense, he contends, "implies full sensory immersion—not keyboards and monitors" (47). Note that keyboards or monitors would maintain a sensory and psychological link to a world outside the simulation, whereas full immersion would create the "holodeck" sense of a fully self-contained world or experience that does not refer to a reality outside of it.

John Fiske notes that the arepresentational view of simulation refuses the usual binary of reality and representation. He discusses "hyperreality and the simulacrum, both of which are 'implosive' concepts. *Implosion* refers to the collapse of the organizing differences that were characteristic of a stably structured world. So 'hyperreality' implodes the binary concepts of reality and representation into a single concept" (2). Fiske also argues that "hyperreality . . . gathers into itself the conceptualization of both 'reality' and its representations, both the real and the imaginary, and becomes a concept whose power is greater than the sum of its components" (75).

Just as several theorists offer entertainment through electronic media as examples of simulation in our culture, so do they specifically identify entertainment media as a site of arepresentational simulation. Neal Gabler describes entering the simulational world of entertainment as a closed loop, an "escape from life into life" (6). In this way, Richard L. Dukes describes computer and video games as "autotelic," engaged in for their own sake and with no reference to any frame outside themselves (7–8). Rene Berger notes that synthesized images "are images that for the first time no longer refer to the world as we know it . . . but that mold themselves on our formative techno-imagination just as this contributes reciprocally to molding them" (18). Steven Johnson describes this as a matter of "data making sense of other data" (32), which seems to describe an arepresentational loop. Nigel Clark is clear about that, in claiming that "in place of a sequence of audiovisual scenes which propose to represent episodes from a 'real' world, today's media operate as a switching devices [sic] between multiple channels, delivering streams of images that are non-linear, discontinuous and, to all intents, a-representational" (122). John Beckmann describes the viewing self within the world of television in similarly arepresentational terms: "Television and computer screens have become my replacement windows on the world. Their flickering vistas do not offer me apertures of transcendence, or even escape. Ultimately, I'm led back to my monstrous and ever hyperaccelerating self" (7).

Steven Johnson notes the proliferation of "endlessly self-referential" television shows which are now taken to be the cutting edge of the medium; they are about nothing outside of the worlds they create (25–33). Because of that Johnson claims that "television has begun to offer its viewers different lenses through which to view the 'real' content, which turns out to be another television show" (36). An example might be the fatuously titled show *Real World* on MTV, in which camera crews follow a mélange of young people thrown together in a house for several weeks. What is shown, of course, is nothing like the real world but is the world television created in the first place. The crowning glory to this arepresentational simulation is the "documentary" special, *The Making of the Real World*, in which television covers itself creating an insular world.

One form of televisual simulation is an institution one might assume to have representation as its raison d'etre: news reporting. But as Paul Virilio claims, "The fourth estate . . . can function outside any effective democratic control, since the public at large does not get to hear any independent criticism of the media" (*Art*, 1). In this sense, news organizations often report what other news organizations report—or they report events created specifically to be reported. Thus, a closed arepresentational loop is created.

Even nonelectronic forms of entertainment can be simulational if they enclose the participant in a world with no outside reference. Walton argues that one mark of a "fiction" is that we cannot cross between "worlds" to affect developments or actions there (192–95). He thus describes reading a novel or watching a play as a kind of insular, hermetic, arepresentational simulation. Frances Dyson says that "the past thirty years have seen the proliferation of 'non-places': the bland shopping malls, indistinguishable airports, megalithic office blocks, gated communities, theme parks, old-worldly villages, and managed and coifed 'wilderness' areas that, functioning as signs rather than places, immerse the user in a self conscious form of ritual bearing little relation to any actual time or location" (29). Mark C. Taylor describes Las Vegas in similar terms, as if it were a simulational movie: "As the car is left behind and pedestrians roam the set, the cinemascape changes. No longer separated from the screen by a thin film of glass, viewers are consumed by a spectacle that knows no bounds. In this way, today's Strip creates an immersive environment in which the virtual becomes real and the real becomes virtual" (202).

SIMULATIONS AS COPIES

A second view of simulation sees it as essentially a copy or series of copies for which either there is no original or the original is unimportant or indistinguishable from copies. David Gunkel notes that etymologically, simulation is grounded in the Latin *simulare*, to copy or imitate (51). Victor J. Vitanza includes the copy in his definition of "*simulation*: A pretense to, feigned attempt at, or imitation of an action" (6). Massimo Negrotti equates simulation with copies: "The disposition to imitate, to mimic, to copy, to simulate, in a word to reproduce the world, is . . . a human disposition" (1). A copy in this sense tries to be as good as an original, and if it achieves that goal then the meaning of the distinction between copy and original is lost. Of course, if that distinction is lost, then the simulation may be multiplied as often as desired with no attenuation of immersion, quality, involvement, or effect. A really good simulation is thus the best copy, a copy so good that one cannot tell whether it is "real" or a copy. Gunkel explains that the copy point of view does not deny the difference between representation and reality, but it tries to obviate it through excellence of reproduction: "Under the conceptualization of the essential copy, virtual reality does not challenge the Socratic formulation that distinguishes the real from its derivative imitations, but operates within its logic, striving to produce more accurate and nearly perfect reproductions. In this way, VR is understood as a medium of almost perfect imitation" (47). Simulation is an experience in which the copy is just as good as reality, even preferable because it is reproducible and thus repeatable. As Gunkel argues, "simulation, therefore, not only inverts the relative positions of imitation and reality but also disperses or dissolves the very difference that would hold them in dialectical opposition" (55). John Fiske articulates the position that copies are of the essence of simulation in arguing that "the simulacrum . . . merges the 'copy' with the 'original,' the 'image' with the 'referent' " (2). Slouka describes the computer, one of the prime sites of simulation in our culture, as "a sort of deluxe copying machine" (27). By this definition, most consumer goods are simulational—or, together they constitute a simulational consumer culture. It is meaningless to look for the original of the off-the-rack shirt one wears or the music CD one plays.

Baudrillard, in describing "the real" as essentially that which has reproducibility, claims that "the real is produced from miniaturized units, from matrices, memory banks and command models—and with these it can be reproduced an indefinite number of times" (*Simulations*, 3). For a simulational reality, then, Baudrillard says that "the very definition of the real becomes: *that of which it is possible to give an equivalent reproduction. . . .* At the limit of this process of reproducibility, the real is not only what can be reproduced, but *that which is always already reproduced*" (146). Using this logic of copies, Baudrillard argues that polls are essentially simulational in reproducing public opinion: "It is no longer necessary that anyone *produce* an opinion, all that is needed is that all *repro-duce* public opinion, in the sense that all opinions get caught up in this kind of general equivalent, and once more proceed from it" (126).

Photographs are sometimes described as simulational copies. Michael Shapiro argues that photographs, although they may be created as representations, are of-ten *treated* as "an unmediated simulacrum, a copy of what we consider the 'real' " (124). Note that photographs are described as simulation because they are, or if they are, considered as essentially copies of a reality. John Berger notes the effect of photographs on original works of art: "When the camera reproduces a painting, it destroys the uniqueness of its image. As a result its meaning changes. Or, more exactly, its meaning multiplies and fragments into many meanings" (19). If this happens often enough, if a famous painting is largely known as a photographic copy, then "the uniqueness of the original now lies in it being *the original of a re-production*" (21). In this way, of course, Berger echoes the well-known arguments of Walter Benjamin in discussing the work of art in an age of mechanical reproduc-tion. Both writers note, with varying reactions, the simulational effect of turning reality into a series of copies. Paul Virilio argues that reproducibility is of the na-ture of photography, and that this simulational trait separates the viewer from orig-inal real experiences: "The camera would forever after come between [the spectator] and all things; the miracle of industrial cinema lay in reproducing this primordial communication breakdown by the million" (*Art*, 9). Televisual photos or images also are described by Fiske as simulational because they are highly copyable: "As a simulacrum, the individuality of the [television] figure can be infi-nitely reproduced: Murphy Brown may simulate Hillary Rodham Clinton, Zoe Baird," and so forth (72). In other words, the proliferation of a character type can be seen as simulational.

Virtual reality is, as we have seen, often taken to be a paradigm of simulation. David Gunkel describes VR as essentially a copying of reality: "The 'essential copy' comprises a technique of imitation that attempts to close the distance sepa-rating the copy from its formal referent by producing an image or icon so accurate that it could be confused with the real thing." When applied to VR, "what makes VR so compelling is that it promises to supply an even greater sense of realism and consequently confusion, for VR removes the frame that distinguishes and quaran-tines the space of imitation" (47). One can see the copying, infinite reproducibility of simulation if one considers the video game, in which the same game may be ac-cessed over and over. Even the "death" of a character does not end the game; one merely calls up another copy and begins anew.

A SYNTHESIS OF THE TWO VIEWS OF SIMULATION

One need not decide between the arepresentational and the copy views of simu-lation. One expression that merges the two views comes from Baudrillard, who re-fers to the "pure sign" as one which has no meaning because it duplicates itself rather than represents: "For the sign to be pure, it has to duplicate itself: it is the du-plication of the sign which destroys its meaning" (*Simulations*, 136). A sign with no meaning outside itself is, of course, arepresentational (and thus simulational). But in representing nothing outside itself, it duplicates itself; thus, a copy creates an arepresentational simulation. Another example of how the two views may be merged is in Joshua Gunn and David E. Beard's recent work "On the Apocalyptic Sublime." Here they argue that an important new form of discourse, the apocalyptic sublime, engrosses the public in endless preoccupation with whatever the latest hot news item is. Examples of the apocalyptic sublime, such as coverage of the 2001 war against the Taliban, show both a closed loop—a disconnection from reality as reporters interview other reporters and show Pashtun-speaking protesters waving made-for-television signs in English—but also endless copies of that "coverage," as anchors who have nothing to say must repackage the same "nothing" that they said an hour ago.

Another way to understand how the copy and the arepresentational perspectives are synergistic is to see how they merge in scholarly descriptions of an important cultural practice. I have been struck by the extent to which *religious practice*, or more specifically *ritual*, is described in simulational terms as both creating an arepresentational world or experience unto itself and as being essentially eternal repetition and copying of gesture. Insofar as the two dimensions of ritual are linked, we may understand the two views of simulation as integrated.

Generally speaking, students of ritual and religion describe religious experience as wholly apart from everyday reality. Mircea Eliade, for instance, argues that religious experience is "the manifestation of something of a wholly different order, a reality that does not belong to our world" (*Sacred*, 11). A religious retreat or hermitage is similarly described by Eliade as "*a world apart*, a world in miniature" (*Sacred*, 153). Langer has studied ritual as a kind of symbolic experience for its own sake, with little external, practical significance: "speech is the natural outcome of only one *kind* of symbolic process. There are transformations of experience in the human mind that have quite different overt endings. They end in acts that are neither practical nor communicative, though they may be both effective and communal; I mean the actions we call *ritual*" (*Philosophy*, 45). The clearest example of ritual is, of course, religious practice. However, as Eliade (in pejorative terms) notes, even nonbelievers participate in rituals that may be derived in form from religion: "the majority of men 'without religion' still hold to pseudo religious and degenerated mythologies" (*Sacred*, 209).

Scholars of ritual note that it transforms experience entirely. In this way, they emphasize the arepresentational nature of ritual as a simulation. Writing of a kind of ritual, Langer argues that "magic, then, is not a method, but a language; it is part and parcel of that greater phenomenon, *ritual*, which is the language of religion. Ritual is a symbolic transformation of experiences that no other medium can adequately express" (*Philosophy*, 49). Langer's description of ritual and its subset, magic, as language, as signifying practice, should be a hint to us of its resonance with simulation, which as we noted earlier seems like reality but is made out of signs.

One dimension of the arepresentational character of simulation is that the participant herself is transformed, her identity is changed, and in that way her own signification is erased. What one's signs mean no longer has any bearing outside of the ritual itself—the transformed participant's identity has meaning only at that moment in terms of the experience itself. As Eliade notes, "religious man *wants to be other* than he finds himself on the 'natural' level and undertakes to *make himself* in accordance with the ideal image revealed to him in myths" (*Sacred*, 187). Eliade calls our attention to the fact that "access to spirituality finds expression in a symbolism of death and new birth" (*Sacred*, 192). In that rebirth during the ritual one's signifiers float away from reality and have meaning within the context of the experience itself.

Ernst Cassirer describes "intellectual forms" such as ritual very broadly as arepresentational in these terms: "Instead of measuring the content, meaning, and truth of intellectual forms by something extraneous which is supposed to be reproduced in them, we must find in those forms themselves the measure and criterion for their truth and intrinsic meaning" (8). Note the insular, arepresentational view of "these spiritual forms" (8). Cassirer is clear that they create their own realities, using language that very much echoes that of scholars discussing simulations: "Thus the special symbolic forms are not imitations but *organs* of reality, since it is solely by their agency that anything real becomes an object for intellectual apprehension, and as such is made visible to us. The question as to what reality is apart from these forms . . . becomes irrelevant here" (8).

Further exploring the reality created by ritualistic, religious, mythic forms, Cassirer stresses the extent to which they create a world apart, in the here and now, separate from any external reality. Mythical thought "is captivated and enthralled by the intuition which suddenly confronts it. It comes to rest in the immediate experience; the sensible present is so great that everything else dwindles before it" (32). Individuals experience ritual as wholly apart from reality; the latter is as if it does not exist: "For a person whose apprehension is under the spell of this mythico-religious attitude, it is as though the whole world were simply annihilated; the immediate content, whatever it be, that commands his religious interest so completely fills his consciousness that nothing else can exist beside and apart from it" (32–33). The gestures and objects of ritual are denied representational value: "In mythic conception, however, things are not taken for what they mean indirectly, but for their immediate appearance; they are taken as pure presentations, and embodied in the imagination" (56). Another way in which ritual is arepresentational is in the way in which the sacred is immanent in, not represented by, the components of ritual: "Every part of a whole is the whole itself; every specimen is equivalent to the entire species. The part does not merely represent the whole, or the specimen its class; they are identical with the totality to which they belong" (91–92). For instance, "the rain is not just represented but is felt to be really present in each drop of water" (93).

Eliade makes the same argument: "the sacred tree, the sacred stone are not adored as stone or tree; they are worshipped precisely because they are *hierophanies*, because they show something that is no longer stone or tree but the *sacred*" (*Sacred*, 12). In the Eucharist, similarly, Christ's body and blood are not (at least in Catholic teaching) represented by the bread and wine, but are totally present in it. Signs become reality, and indistinguishable from it, in this view of ritual.

The example of the Eucharist also illustrates the ways in which some scholars of ritual describe it in simulational terms by depicting it as the infinite reproduction of copies indistinguishable from the original. Catholic theology holds that the bread and wine one receives today are copies just as good as, indistinguishable from, Christ's body and blood; thus they are the body and blood. The Eucharist then becomes a ritual gesture that is performed repeatedly, infinitely. Think of the Eucharist, then, as an analog to the video game that is always the same game, infinitely repeated and repeatable, copy after copy.

One aspect of an infinite copying is that time changes, too. If the ritual one experiences at the moment is a perfect copy of, and indistinguishable from, rituals going back and before one in time for centuries, then time has changed, perhaps even stopped. A ritual, and thus any simulation, is as Eliade puts it, "abolition of concrete time" (*Myth*, 85) and the creation of a new moment of experiencing time. As Eliade argues, "Religious participation in a festival implies emerging from ordinary temporal duration and reintegration of the mythical time reactualized by the festival itself. Hence sacred time is indefinitely recoverable, indefinitely repeatable" (*Sacred*, 69). Note how much Eliade's description of ritual time sounds like the replaying and replaying of simulational video games: "Everything begins over again at its commencement every instant. The past is but a prefiguration of the future. No event is irreversible and no transformation is final" (*Myth*, 89).

Eliade describes the infinite reproduction of religious practice in noting that "religious man feels the need of indefinitely reproducing the same paradigmatic acts and gestures" (*Sacred*, 91). This "repetition" (107) may be found in the presence of the same prayers, vestments, icons, and sacraments repeated over and over for centuries. For the person wrapped up in ritual, "his life is the ceaseless repetition of gestures initiated by others" centuries ago (Eliade, *Myth*, 5). Eliade describes the result of endless copying as the creation of a world apart, in our terms, a simulation, thus illustrating the essential unity between the arepresentational and copy points of view: "insofar as an act (or an object) acquires a certain reality through the repetition of certain paradigmatic gestures . . . he who reproduces the exemplary gesture thus finds himself transported into the mythical epoch in which its revelation took place" (*Myth*, 35).

Scholarly views concerning ritual thus provide us with a way to merge the arepresentational and the copy theories of simulation. But at this point let us pull back to a broader view and consider the whole range of key terms in this book. Although many use reality, representation, and simulation in discourse, and speak as if there really were such things, the following section will show that clear distinctions among the terms are untenable.

HOW THE KEY TERMS MERGE AND DISSOLVE

Philosophically, conceptually, "in reality," it is impossible to maintain clear distinctions among the three key terms. One example serves to introduce the difficulties. Imagine a pilot trainee experiencing a flight "simulator." A visual display re-creates the air up there, the cockpit moves as she moves the controls, outcomes of successful or disastrous flights are achieved, and so forth. The very latest technologies ensure that the experience seems to be "just like" actual flying. Although most people would call the experience a "simulation," consider the difficulties of maintaining that description in any exclusive, absolute sense. The simulation makes use of representations: of an airplane, or the sky and land, of other aircraft, and so forth. On the one hand, these are not representations of a specific, real flight—but on the other hand, if they did not represent real flight at some level they would not be used for training. One might say the whole simulation is constructed of representations; why then not call it a representation? But for the trainee with sweaty palms and tight muscles who is in danger of plunging the "airplane" into the "ground," the experience itself seems much like reality. Indeed, the better the simulation, as we have noted, the more of a reality it appears to be. And the simulation is no less real an experience as a flight 35,000 feet in the air in the sense that both involve sensation of material things. Why not then call it a kind of reality? This hypothesis is not fanciful; Negroponte notes that "VR can make the artificial as realistic as, and even more realistic than, the real. For example, flight simulation, the most sophisticated and longest-standing application of VR, is more realistic than flying a real plane" (116–17). Note the interesting claim that anything, especially a simulation, can be more realistic than the real; a clear case of how people use the key terms even as they understand that they are confounded!

From this one flight simulator example, let us move to a closer consideration of the ways in which the three key terms, and what they mean, merge into one another. Here, at the close of chapter 1, we consider *that* the terms merge; in chapter 2 we consider *why*. We do this so as to move toward a clearer understanding of what these terms mean and how they are used rhetorically.

A number of observations could be made that attest to mergings of the terms. Many have simply argued for the difficulty of determining the nature of the three key terms. Heim says, "Let us recall for a moment just how controversial past attempts were to define the term *reality*. Recall how many wars were fought over it. People today shy away from the *R* word" ("Essence," 26). Others have argued that social changes make distinctions increasingly difficult to make, as in Rene Berger's observation of "a progression toward the emergence of a new complexity. The imaginary as experienced is indissociable from the formation of the world toward which it is tending and simultaneously of its own formation toward which the world is tending" (19–20). Berger thus sees representation (the imaginary) as inseparable from the formation of rew realities (the world). In such a new world, Howard Rheingold points out that "not only do I inhabit my virtual community; to the degree that I carry around their conversations in my head and begin to mix it up with them in real life, my virtual communities also inhabit my life" (71)—which then is real and which is virtual?

Scholars have noted the difficulties of maintaining these distinctions, even as many of them continue to speak in terms of them! Note the contradiction of the "real artificial" inherent in Helmreich's report that artificial life creators "said that

their self-reproducing algorithms were *real* artificial life-forms; no mere representations or counterfeits of life, these algorithms were artificial creatures ultimately
realized as material entities in the voltage patterns deep within computers" (5). Nor
are artificial life scientists the only ones to confound reality and simulation;
Douglas Rushkoff reports that "psychedelic explorers are convinced that they are
experiencing something real, and bringing back something useful for themselves
and the rest of us" from their chemically induced simulations (38). Walton claims
that "we cannot easily say why something does or does not count as representational" even as he continues to use the word (*Mimesis*, 2).

Other scholars note the confounded use of the key terms in what they study.
Poster argues that "the opposition 'virtual' and 'real' community contains serious
difficulties" (88)—by way of example he offers the nation as a community passionately taken as real but yet fundamentally imaginary. Robert Irwin notes that
"modern art" is often called nonrepresentational; yet he argues that it may well be
more representational than so-called representational art in that it tries to convey a
pre- or nonsocialized reality of fundamental perceptions (224). His observation
points out the difficulties of saying what is representational and what is real. This
kind of complexity leads Gunkel, for instance, to use Derrida's concept of the
"undecidable" as something that transgresses boundaries, and to suggest that simulations may be an example of the undecidable (53). Gunkel suggests challenging
the dualities involved between reality-representation or representation-simulation
so as to see how simulation is really working (51–52). Slouka likewise predicts a
coming inability to decide between reality and simulation: "We will find it increasingly difficult to separate real life . . . from virtual existence. Or worse, that we
will know the difference but opt for the digitized world over the real one" (5).

We see the complexity intertwining the three key terms in a couple of quirky, related examples. Baudrillard's well-known example of the simulated holdup is one;
he asks his reader to imagine how such a thing might differ from a real holdup and
how one would explain the difference, and of course the difficulties of separating
what is real from what is simulated become apparent (*Simulations*, 38–39).
Baudrillard's forcing of the term *simulation* onto an experience with real guns, real
taking of money, brings both key terms into question. And Baudrillard likewise
notes the entanglements of simulation and representation in arguing that "whereas
representation tries to absorb simulation by interpreting it as false representation,
simulation envelops the whole edifice of representation as itself a simulacrum"
(*Simulations*, 11). Similarly, Arthur Danto asks his reader to "imagine an entity
that is an artwork though it resembles exactly the Manhattan telephone directory
for 1978" (5). This *koan* entangles the reader in the difficulty of separating artistic
representations from reality.

It is difficult to maintain distinctions among the three terms because it is difficult to speak of each in isolation; they form a trialectic. Of Jean Baudrillard, Alison
Landberg astutely observes that "Baudrillard's argument clings tenaciously to a
real; he desperately needs a real to recognize that we are in a land of simulation"
(178). In other words, he needs the one term to give meaning to the other. Slouka
complains that "simulation games . . . suggest the extent to which reality, increas-

ingly displaced in our lives by the authentic reproduction, is beginning to lose its authority" (116)—but note that his discourse uses reality and simulation as polar opposites by which each defines the other. Rene Berger, on the other hand, opposes representation to simulation: "Is the era of representation, which has endured for thousands of years, in the process of giving way to the advent of a new era of simulation?" (5). Yet he needs both terms to describe the shift to simulation that he foresees.

The difficulty of keeping our three key terms distinct may be seen especially in the ways in which simulations have connections with and implications for reality. One way in which simulation and reality are confounded is that a good simulation can seem so real. As Richard L. Dukes notes, gamed simulations can occupy the whole perceptual field and become more important to the player, in the moment of play, than is reality (3). Or as Mark C. Taylor offers by way of example, "What is important about Las Vegas today is the way in which the real becomes virtual and the virtual becomes real in this desert oasis" (195). Las Vegas contains such good simulations that they are indistinguishable from the real Las Vegas.

Simulation and reality are confounded in that simulations may speak to, affect, or have relevance for reality. Indeed, Julian Hochberg defines simulations in terms of their real effects: "B' is a surrogate for B and for A because it produces the same effect as they do, that is, it *simulates* A and B" (21). The effects of simulation on reality may be traced in several ways.

Scholarly investigations into folk psychology are one interesting scene in which the relevance of simulation for real life may be discovered. Martin Davies and Tony Stone write of "folk psychology," or "common-sense" psychology, which attempts to answer the question, "How are normal adult human beings able to negotiate a particular psychological task domain?" They present two major contending theories: (1) Theory Theory, which holds that people have theories to guide them in making everyday decisions, and (2) Simulation Theory, which holds that people simulate what to do and what will happen in their minds (1–18). Alvin I. Goldman, writing in Davies and Stone's book, likewise calls attention to those two options in folk psychology.

As one example of Simulation Theory, Robert M. Gordon argues that people simulate mentally what others are thinking and doing, and how we might act in response, as a way to predict and order behavior (128–55). He claims that we use "*simulated* practical reasoning as a *predictive* device. . . . To simulate the appropriate practical reasoning I can engage in a kind of *pretend play*" (137). Thus for Gordon, simulation is how we plan what to do in reality, in everyday life. Along the same lines, Gary Fuller sees simulation as *empathy*, putting yourself in another's shoes, so as to predict how the other will act (19). Simulation thus underlies one's decisions about everyday action. Gregory Currie likewise argues that people have an "internal simulator" to make decisions and to "test-run candidate strategies." He claims that "what goes on in the simulator is a substitute for real action; it gives us, under optimal conditions, the information that action would give us about the success or failure of a strategy, without the costs of failure—but also without the rewards of success" (157). What one simulates bears directly upon reality:

"Simulation can be of the mental states of another, of our own contemplated behaviour, or of causal and other processes of more alien kinds, depending on how much information is required to run the simulation realistically" (158–59). For Currie, "the condition for the success of a simulation is that it should have a structural affinity, particular in respect of causal relations, with the process simulated" (159), that process of course being in reality.

Several scholars point to the effects of simulational dimensions of the entertainment media on reality. Fiske refers to "figures," characters in television or movies, as simulations through which political work is done: "Figures are simulacra that speak and take up positions, and thus social interests can speak through them, occupy positions within them" (70). Through devices such as figures, social roles may be molded. Michael Parenti likewise points to a long list of ideologies promoted by simulational popular entertainment today, expressed in beliefs such as "the ills of society are caused by individual malefactors and not by anything in the socioeconomic system" (2–3). Such implicit ideologies clearly give simulations real life impact.

Simulational entertainment affects social attitudes toward gender, race, class, and so forth. Nigel Clark notes that "women's bodies have had a longer history of subjection to inscription by idealized images. . . . [T]he female body has long been constituted through a dense accretion of simulation models" (117). One example that might illustrate Clark's point is the simulational nature of pornography, which then has a social effect in shaping how the female body is regarded. Murray Edelman sums up the point in terms of how entertaining simulations may affect what is done in reality: "Although the imaginary worlds we create do not *describe* the complicated, often confusing and murky world in which we live, they do powerfully *rationalize* policy outcomes in that world, helping people to adjust to their social situations and accept them" (127).

Simulations can affect reality insofar as they teach us lessons about it, as in the example of the flight simulator. Dukes notes that "gamed simulations . . . have as their object the gaining of new insights into the selected aspects of the real social world they mirror. These characteristics separate them from parlor games which do not make as determined an effort to represent reality" (2). Note Dukes's comment that simulations teach us about reality by representing it—surely a clear instance of the confounding of the key terms! Dukes's point will be familiar to any teacher who has used simulations as a classroom exercise to teach students about life. Researchers also may simulate so as to study life. Prietula et al., for instance, study the ways computational models designed to simulate organizations and groups tell us how real groups operate.

Representations are the mechanism by which simulations affect reality. Simulations not only point "forward" in a sense toward reality, urging particular policies and actions in the world, but they also point "backward" toward reality by their heavy use of representations. Simulations are, like reality, likely not directly accessible to the mind. Instead, we access them through representations. Even if signs in a simulation lose specific referentiality, they nevertheless often retain at least the ability to reference what is taken as the real. Brian Massumi notes that "the virtual, as such, is inaccessible to the senses. This does not, however, preclude figuring it, or constructing images of it. To the contrary, it requires a multiplication of images" (305), images which are representations. One example of such a simulation depending on representations is the virtual community. As Poster argues, "Just as virtual communities are understood as having the attributes of 'real' communities, so 'real' communities can be seen to depend on the imaginary" (90), thus confounding the distinctions among them. Writing within the "simulational theory" perspective of folk psychology, Currie refers to everyday decision making as simulative. The mechanism for that simulation is representations, for he claims that "in the simulator representations are transformed in a way that mirrors one or another strategy for getting from belief-world to desire-world" (157). Writing of the related process he calls make-believe, Walton notes that simulational imagination uses representations of the real: "Sometimes . . . imagining is a means of escape from reality, and we do frequently imagine what is not really the case. But even when we do, our experience is likely to involve the closest attention to features of our actual environment" (*Mimesis*, 21).

Technological simulations are built upon representations. Let us first remind ourselves that technology is a major force behind an increasingly simulational world. Several writers have noted the representational nature of technology, at least from the perspective of the user. Heim argues that "life's body is becoming indistinguishable from its computer prosthesis" ("Design," 65), the latter being a simulation of life, the former a reality. Simulations would not be of the engrossing, high quality that they are were it not for the realistic representations enabled by digital technologies. But Steven Johnson also reminds us that "for the magic of the digital revolution to take place, a computer must . . . *represent itself* to the user, in a language that the user understand" (14). Computers, he argues, are one representation after another (15); as I type this page I see letters appear on a screen, but those are but the first in a string of representations that ultimately end in a reality of electrical pulses. If I use the mouse, a symbol moving across the screen represents me, in part (21). And although one may speak of virtual community, Johnson reminds us that "for the most part, the social fabric of cyberspace is still stitched together by the gossamer thread of text" (71), which he has described as strings of representations. Or as Daniel Punday reminds us, "online discourse is above all *text* imported from other, socially and politically charged sources" (199).

Our concepts of reality are largely made of representations. Norton makes the familiar claim that "what we commonly take for the 'real' world is a convention" (37), and conventions are representations. Vitanza defines reality in ways that depend upon the mediation of representations: "*actuality (reality)*: our consensual perception of the world as mediated only through the senses" (5). Fiske tellingly reflects the inseparability of the three key terms in his description of media events: "The term *media event* is an indication that in a postmodern world we can no longer rely on a stable relationship or clear distinction between a 'real' event and its mediated representation. A mediated event, then, is not a mere representation of what happened, but it has its own reality, which gathers up into itself the reality of the event that may or may not have preceded it" (2).

The usual causal model in which reality comes first and is re-presented by signs and images is, in this line of thinking, brought into question. Negrotti questions the direction of that causal line: "The representation process implies that the subject conceives and perceives the external world as a separate reality, although he may easily understand that this is simply a useful convention" (9). Now, if simulation and reality both are made up of representation, they might easily become confounded with each other.

Analyses of painting and photography often note the ways in which a sense of reality is built upon representations. Kenneth J. Gergen argues that "even photographic images create the world they depict" (*Saturated*, 88) in the sense that social views of reality are made out of representations. For us today, for instance, we might say that the Civil War is what Matthew Brady depicted in his photographs because he depicted it in his photographs. Marx W. Wartofsky argues that what we think we see in reality is made up of representations: "We do not come to have visual concepts of the properties of the visual world *except* by such a process of creating representations of it" (279).

In this chapter we have explored three key terms, *reality*, *representation*, and *simulation*, at an introductory level. We have seen the difficulties inherent in maintaining clear distinctions among those terms at the same time that we have seen how widespread their use is. Together they comprise a network of terms that constantly threatens to collapse. In the next chapter we turn to some reasons why these terms, so widely used as if they had distinct meanings, cannot lay claim to any objective, separate status. In the next chapter, we will come to understand why the terms must be considered as rhetorical more than referential. In doing so, we will see how the experiences of reality, representation, and simulation themselves are indistinct and intertwined.

Chapter 2

A Construction Project: Why the Key Terms Converge

We have seen that the three key terms *reality*, *representation*, and *simulation* are widely used and that it is difficult conceptually, objectively, to maintain them as clearly distinct concepts. We began to explore some reasons for why this might be the case in chapter 1. This chapter offers more detailed and systematic reasons for why reality, representation, and simulation converge. The purpose in this chapter is to provide reasons for why we should finally reject these three as distinct actual experiences. That will justify our shift, beginning in chapter 3, to think of our key terms *as terms*, with rhetorical impact. It is difficult and perhaps impossible to distinguish among them in any objective sense because of the nature of *perceptions*, *language and symbols*, and *aesthetic experience*. In a sense, each of these categories is a crucible in which reality, representation, and simulation merge.

A key concept in this chapter will be the idea of *constructedness*. Perceptions are constructed rather than natural or necessary. Language and symbols are a major mechanism through which perceptions are constructed. And aesthetic experience is a complex structure of constructions.

Construction means that human neurological, physical, social, psychological, or cultural mechanisms have intervened to shape an experience. No experience is natural in the sense of being "just so," or necessary, or "that way" for everyone. Whatever is constructed might be constructed differently. Thus if we see reality, representation, or simulation as constructed then we must understand them as not necessarily distinct, objective experiences but as made into what they are; and what is made can be made differently. Whosoever constructs can also be influenced to construct differently, and thus the centrality of constructedness in this chapter will prepare us for seeing our key concepts as rhetorical creations in later chapters.

PERCEPTIONS

One might think of reality, representation, and simulation as different orders of experience—that term *experience* being the uniting concept among them. In other words, sometimes we are experiencing reality, sometimes we experience representations, sometimes we experience simulations. This understanding would then lead us to inquire into the nature of experience as underlying and formative of the three key terms, especially if we want to see why the terms merge.

In this section we turn to several scholars who claim that human experience is an experience of *perceptions* directly, and only secondarily of sensations. A perception, we shall see, is constructed rather than natural or necessary. By extension, reality, representation, and simulation must be constructed rather than possessing natural and necessary substances. If our three key terms name but constructed experiences, then distinctions among them must be conventional and changeable. The human perceptual process thus enables the experience of reality, representation, and simulation at the same time that it makes firm, objective distinctions among them difficult or impossible.

First, let us consider the argument that experience is constructed, and that it is constructed fundamentally at the level of perceptions. Many scholars argue that people do not consciously experience raw sensations, that by the time a sensation has made it through to consciousness it has been modified by cognitive, social, or neural mechanisms that turn the sensation into perception. These scholars argue that experience, the world, is constructed, and by that they generally mean that our apprehension of the world, of experience, is not simple apprehension of sensations but of sensations that have been constructed as perceptions. Susanne K. Langer argues in this vein that sensation is not raw but is constructed through meaning: "Sense-data and experiences . . . are essentially meaningful structures" (*Philosophy*, 266). What we take to be a "fact," and for our purposes we might say a fact of reality, representation, or simulation, "is not a simple notion. It is that which we conceive to be the source and context of signs to which we react successfully" (267). We perceive facts, or reality, as we do in ways that serve our interests, to create "success" in everyday experiences.

If the world of perceptions is constructed, it will be experienced as formed or patterned rather than random. In support of that point, Heim argues that "a world is not a collection of fragments, nor even an amalgam of pieces. It is a felt totality or whole" and thus a constructed whole (*Virtual*, 89–90). He goes on to claim that "the world is not a collection of things but an active usage that relates things to each other, that links them" (90), and that active linkage takes place as we perceive the world (90). Richard L. Gregory likewise claims that "perceptions are extrapolations of data—hypotheses—much as in science" (230). By perception he thus means a construction built up out of sense data; we perceive a thing to be a chair by pulling together and interpreting many sensations. I. A. Richards argues explicitly (and outrageously) that perceptions are constructed, specifically from past, similar experiences:

> I can make the same point by denying that we have any sensations. . . . A sensation would be something that just was *so*, on its own, a datum; as such we have none. Instead we have perceptions, responses whose character comes to them from the past as well as the present occasion. A perception is never just of an *it*; perception takes whatever it perceives as a thing of a certain sort. (30)

Richards stresses that the construction or patterning that creates perceptions is abstraction, or the sorting together of sensations that we deem to be similar. As Richards puts it: "A particular impression is already a product of concrescence. Behind, or in it, there has been a coming together of *sortings*" (36). C. K. Ogden and I. A. Richards express this point of view in claiming that "whenever we 'perceive' what we name 'chair,' we are interpreting a certain group of data (modifications of the sense organs), and treating them as signs of a referent" (22). An important part of the process of perception, they argue, is to note recurrences (a "group" of data) in experience and to construct abstract categories that treat every new experience as being of a particular type. Thus they claim that "experience has the character of recurrence, that is, comes to us in more or less uniform contexts" (55). We must interpret what we experience, but interpretations likewise are never unique but also recur: "An interpretation is itself a recurrence . . . a *psychological* context" (56).

Although we seem to form perceptions instantly, the conclusions we have reviewed so far suggest that a perception is a reworking of sensation into categories, sortings, abstractions, and patterns. Sensation emerges in consciousness in a constructed form, different from how it began. Perception, in other words, is the re-presentation of sensation. And although we are working to problematize representation and its brethren, let us for the moment use it in this stipulated way and examine the claim made by many scholars that experience is based on representation (of sensory data). Marx W. Wartofsky argues for the constructedness of representations in saying that "Nothing, then, is a picture or a representation in itself apart from being made as one or taken as one. There are no entities, then, which may 'objectively' be characterized in this way. Instead, things of a certain sort are constituted as pictures and representations by makers and viewers" (277). We noted in quoting Gregory earlier a link between scientific hypotheses and the abstraction required for perceptions. Following that lead now, we note that Benedetto Croce likewise draws a link between the abstractions of science and the categorizations of representation: "Science substitutes concepts for representations; for those concepts that are poor and limited it substitutes others, larger and more comprehensive; it is ever discovering new relations" (13).

One consistent theme across much scholarly work is that our experience of reality and of simulation is made up out of representations; this is sometimes expressed in terms of the "imaginary," as in Mark C. Taylor's claim that "as reality is virtualized, we gradually are forced to confess that the real has always been imaginary" (203). Note that if representations are made antecedent first to reality and then to virtualized reality (simulation), then reality and simulation are constructed because representations are always constructed. Robert Irwin argues the representation is never simple re-presentation of reality (in the sense of objective reporting) because perception changes our understanding of reality. For Irwin, representation is always socially and intersubjectively created (221–22). Croce describes as "true" representation that which goes beyond the "natural fact" to become a form of perception: "There is a sure method of distinguishing true intuition, true representation, from that which is inferior to it: the spiritual fact from the mechanical, passive, natural fact. Every true intuition or representation is also *expression*. That which does not objectify itself in expression is not intuition or representation, but sensation and mere natural fact" (8). This means that basic perception, being the experience of representations, is constructed. It is the constructedness of perceptions from representations that confounds reality with representations and simulations. Virilio makes the point in a jocular way: "Let's drop all the poppycock Westerners go in for when it comes to art or representation and consider for a moment a phrase of Paul of Tarsus's: 'the world we see is in the process of passing.' We might now add: 'We cannot see the world as it goes by' " (*Art*, 68).

Michael J. Shapiro argues that we experience reality not directly but through representations, and that representations do not mimetically copy reality but rather reshape it; he is in fact speaking of the formative power of perceptions:

Representation is the absence of presence, but because the real is never wholly present to us—how it is real for us is always mediated through some representational practice—we lose something when we think of representation as mimetic. What we lose, in general, is insight into the institutions, actions, and episodes through which the real has been fashioned, a fashioning that has not been so much a matter of immediate acts of consciousness by persons in everyday life as it has been a historically developing kind of imposition, now largely institutionalized in the prevailing kinds of meanings deeply inscribed on things, persons, and structures. (xii)

The idea is that if representations are the building blocks of both reality and simulation, then our most basic experiences, our perceptions, are constructed rather than natural. Neal Gabler expresses this idea when, after arguing that movies are simulational, he observes that Ronald "Reagan intuited that in a society where movies are the central metaphor, everything boiled down to perception and that therefore there was nothing but perception" (109).

A number of scholars investigating the nature of visual images specifically have argued for the constructedness of perception. The choice of visual images as a paradigm of the constructed perception is especially important given the advent of new technologies that can create highly realistic images, especially in the service of simulations. As Mark Poster notes, "Virtual reality machines should be able to allow the participant to enter imagined worlds with convincing verisimilitude, releasing immense potentials for fantasy, self-discovery and self-construction" (93). The argument has been made neurophysiologically; Katherine Hayles notes studies in biology that show that "the frog's visual system does not so much *represent* reality as *construct* it. What's true for frogs must also hold for humans" (131). The conclusion she draws is that "perception is not fundamentally representational" (136). Her usage would seem to contradict this train of argument, yet it does not. By representation she means simple reporting. Other scholars have been arguing that representation is a construction. Considering this difference, Hayles's thought if not her usage falls into line with this one.

People in general do not sufficiently consider that visual images are constructed; the idea that they faithfully copy reality is strong. Let us consider a scholarly voice in disagreement with the idea that images are conventionally constructed. Michael Stephan argues strongly that visual representations are not conventional and learned but are natural and mimetic (110–12). His position is that

our (cognitive) relations to the visual image involve unexhibited properties in the form of *life values* (our experientially derived knowledge understood in the light of our biology) and that our understanding of these relations, although primarily non-discursive, can result in cognitive transformations which lead to the image appearing to possess affective import, and so forth. (158)

If visual images seem "more 'real' than our typical perceptions of the world itself," according to Stephan, it is because "the artist . . . possesses the capacity to present us . . . with a 'snapshot' image of the phenomenal world in which things visual are heightened" (160). Note that even while arguing for the naturalness of images, Stephan comes close to seeing the artist's choices that constitute constructedness.

But many scholars do not agree with Stephan's theory of the visual image as naturally mimetic. John Berger argues for the constructedness of the image in saying, "An image is a sight which has been recreated or reproduced. It is an appearance, or a set of appearances, which has been detached from the place and time in which it first made its appearance and preserved. . . . Every image embodies a way of seeing" (9–10). As Shapiro notes, "the photograph is the quintessential form of ideological statement inasmuch as it is a form of practice that tends to be thought of as a faithful representation" (134).

A number of scholars have claimed that our sense of reality is constructed from images. Since we have been taking images as a paradigm of the constructedness of perception, of representations, any claim that reality is based on images thus identifies a key source of the confounding of our key terms. As Steven Johnson claims, "We are fixated with the image not because we have lost faith in reality, but because images now have an enormous impact on reality, to the extent that the older image-reality opposition doesn't really work anymore" (30). Frances Dyson attributes the power of images to "ocularcentrism," defined as "the belief that, of all the attributes of objects, visibility and extension are primary" (33). Slouka expresses the idea of ocularcentrism as "the enormous and abiding power of the visual sense" (122), while Gabler refers to "the sanctification of the television camera" (187). What can be seen is real, in other words.

This point of view may represent a shift in Western cultural thinking. As Gunkel notes, since Plato "the image has been understood as a kind of derived reproduction, the value of which is determined by proximity and similarity to the original or real" (46). But Fiske argues that ocularcentrism is growing more powerful today, identifying the image as generative of both simulations and the real: "Our age may be that of the visual simulacrum, where what is seen is what matters, and any distinction between an unseen ('true') event and its (false) representations no longer seems achievable. Much of the thrust of our cultural technology is to extend what can be made visible and to technologize a panoptic power that lies in the means of seeing as much as in what it sees" (133). John Adkins Richardson suggests that a shift of images away from simple representation toward the status of reality or of simulation may have begun with the old Dutch Masters: "One of the things that makes the art of the Netherlands alluring is the very fact that its realism is fantastical. Ironically, some of the most impressive examples of VR in evidence today are, in fact, as far removed from truth as was the gleaming atmosphere that permeated Jan Vermeer's interiors" (164).

The power inherent in images as guarantors of reality is so strong that Slouka is moved to warn that "the threat inherent in image-manipulation techniques is the threat of authoritarianism" (125). Gergen points to the aesthetic side of reality construction in noting that "films can catapult us rapidly and effectively into states of fear, anger, sadness, romance, lust, and aesthetic ecstasy" (*Saturated*, 56). Film's power as a series of constructed representations that nevertheless seem to be reality is also reflected in Virilio's sarcastic reference to film as "the truth twenty-four times a second" (*Art*, 20).

If perception is constructed, if representations are constructed, if our sense of reality and of simulation is built upon constructed representations and perceptions, then long-standing distinctions between world and knower, object and subject (what Langer described as the Cartesian dualist "division of reality into thoughts and things" [*Mind*, 7]) must dissolve. Let us recall that our three terms were shown to be grounded in that dualism in chapter 1. Thus dissolves the ability to maintain distinctions among our key terms. Shapiro argues that "what is increasingly recognized is that objects and events are inseparable from the process of apprehension (indeed the imaginative process) within which they are formed" (7). The result is a collapse of the subject-object distinction. As Beckmann claims, "We have, in effect, fallen outside of ourselves, as the once hard distinction between remote and local states becomes even further dispersed, and the exposure intervals between time and space, inside and outside, mind and body, imaginary and real are no longer quantifiable factors" (3). Thus, for Beckmann, "the virtual dimension has triggered a decisive cognitive rupture with the very notion and relevance of the Newtonian conception of space" upon which dualism depends (4).

Virilio notes that the collapse of subject and object distinctions stemming from constructed representations must affect even our sense of the reality of self: "Smashing the being's unity to smithereens, the fractional dimensions of cyberspace enable us to transfer the content of our sensations to an impalpable DOUBLE, suppressing, along with the old inside/outside dichotomy, the *hic* and *nunc* of immediate action" (*Art*, 148). Thus the body itself may become the site of perceptual and representational constructions, as Stahl Stenslie argues: "Future communication will go beyond the interface as we know it. Not into an absurd 'up-loading of the body' or the disappearance of the body in information, but rather in the re-emerging of the body as interface; an unpredictable, unreliable, unstable, and emotional interface" (19).

We have seen how the constructedness of perception underlies the constructedness of images and representations, which confounds a distinction be-tween reality and simulation. The centrality of perception to human experience has meant that we have already seen some hints of how our two other main categories in this chapter, language and symbols and aesthetic experience, also underlie connections and confusions among our three key terms. We turn now to the role that language and symbols specifically play in confounding distinctions among those terms.

LANGUAGE AND SYMBOLS

Language has traditionally been regarded as the preeminent form of representation, and has been held to a standard of accurately mirroring reality (Locke). Richards describes that view as leading to the "superstition" that words have only one meaning: "A chief cause of misunderstanding . . . is the Proper Meaning Superstition. That is the common belief . . . that a word has a meaning of its own (ideally, only one) independent of and controlling its use" (11). The language of simulation has been regarded as a different sort of symbolization, one that constitutes rather than represents a world. But those distinctions begin to fail once some models of symbolization and signification are understood. We will note here that although our focus is on language, as Richardson reminds us, everything in culture is meaningful, even gestures and other nonverbal signs (26).

We might begin with Ogden and Richards's famous triangle model of meaning, in which symbols refer directly to people's thoughts (references) and only indirectly to real things (referents): "Between the symbol and the referent there is no relevant relation other than the indirect one, which consists in its being used by someone to stand for a referent" (11). Ogden and Richards thus challenge semiotic systems like that of de Saussure, who inquired into the object to which a word referred. But Ogden and Richards object that "he does not ask whether it has one, he obeys blindly the primitive impulse to infer from a word some object for which it stands" (4). Because, for Ogden and Richards, "the direct relation of symbols is with thought" (9), symbolization (representation) is not directly about reality but is about how we think about reality. As Langer put it in denying a merely referential role for language, "Symbols are not proxy for their objects, but are *vehicles for the conception of objects. . . . [I]t is the conceptions, not the things that symbols directly 'mean'* " (Philosophy, 60–61).

The direct linkage of symbols to thinking is decisive. When people think about the symbols we use, Ogden and Richards propose, we must construct a context that generates their meanings (55–57). Thinking about representations through contexts means that we are constantly abstracting from immediate lived experience by sorting experience into categories, a point made by Richards: "Do we ever respond to a stimulus in a way which is not influenced by the other things that happened to us when more or less similar stimuli struck us in the past? Probably never" (29–30). What symbols do for Richards, as for Langer (*Philosophy*, 115), is to transform sensation into conception more than to simply communicate or convey an unproblematic reality.

It is clear that we are back where we were in discussing perceptions as sorted, abstracted sensation. Now, we are looking at language specifically as a primary means by which sensation is transformed. Langer makes that connection for us. Langer argues for the constructedness through language of what seems to be sensation when she says that "our sense data are primarily symbols" (*Philosophy*, 21). Langer argues that "the human brain is constantly carrying on a process of symbolic transformation of the experiential data that comes to it" (*Philosophy*, 43) and that this "need of symbolization" is "basic" in the human (41). For her, perception constructing is symbol using. Cassirer agrees in claiming that it is "the work of naming [that] transforms the world of sense impression, which animals also possess, into a mental world, a world of ideas and meanings" (28).

Richards expresses the centrality of abstraction and sortings in language through his metaphorical theory of meaning. "Metaphor is the omnipresent principle of language" (92), he argues, because the sorting together of two disparate things is exactly what we do when we use any common symbol such as "cup" to put together an assortment of often quite different experiences. Language is therefore constitutive of reality, for Richards: "Words are not a medium in which to copy life. Their true work is to restore life itself to order" (134). Langer agrees in arguing that "metaphor is the law of growth of every semantic. It is not a development, but a principle" (*Philosophy*, 147). Each word thus does what a metaphor does in bringing together that which is not together in reality. As Richards claims, "Words are the meeting points at which regions of experience which can never combine in sensation or intution, come together" (131).

Symbols are thus not merely reflections of reality, and cannot be; but that means that our notions of reality are themselves constructed through symbols inherently involved in our processes of abstracting and sorting. As Shapiro puts it, "the real, or the what of our knowing, is inseparable from how it resides in our modes of representation" (8). Richards teaches us that we live a foot off the ground, at a constant and ongoing level of abstraction, thus confounding the difference between reality and representation. Langer agrees in calling symbolization "the most characteristic mental trait of mankind. It issues in an unconscious, spontaneous process of *abstraction*" (*Philosophy*, 72). Ernst Cassirer makes the same point in arguing that "the apparently singular fact becomes known, understood and conceptually grasped only in so far as it is 'subsumed' under a general idea" (26). He claims that our concepts are constructions rather than mirrors of reality: "What are concepts save formulations and creations of thought, which, instead of giving us the true forms of objects, show us rather the forms of thought itself?" (7). Note that in describing concepts as forms of thought that reveal our forms of thought, Cassirer puts concepts in (arepresentational) simulational terms. As a result of the creative work of symbols, for Richards, "it is no exaggeration to say that the fabrics of all our various worlds are the fabrics of our meanings" (19). As Langer put it, "The fact is that our primal world of reality *is* a verbal one. Without words our imagination cannot retain distinct objects and their relations, but out of sight is out of mind" (*Philosophy*, 126).

An important theme sounded by several theorists is the idea that language takes its meaning from other language, other discourses. The representation that is language is thus representing other representations, if anything. Gergen argues that "to write or speak is not, then, to express an interior world, but to borrow from the available things people write and say and to reproduce them for yet another audience" (*Saturated*, 105). Richard Rorty pleads that "we have to understand speech not only as not the externalizing of inner representations, but as not a representation at all. We have to drop the notion of correspondence for sentences as well as for thoughts, and see sentences as connected with other sentences rather than with the world" (371–72). Fiske makes the same point in saying that "no discourse event is ever complete in itself but always carries traces of the other, competing, discourse events that it is not" (4–5). Richards argues that at a fundamental level, even the meanings of individual words are taken from a whole utterance, that meanings "are resultants which we arrive at only through the interplay of the interpretative possibilities of the whole utterance" (55).

The other discourses from which language gets its meaning are of course grounded and contextualized. They are social, and so theorists have argued that language gains meaning from the different passing social uses to which they are put. Gergen writes, "As Wittgenstein proposed, our words are not pictures of what is the case. Words are not maps of reality. Rather, words gain their meaning through their use in social interchange" (*Saturated*, 102).

If language gains its meaning from social interchange, then the rough and tumble of social interchange will infect and affect the ability of language to represent. Representation will unavoidably be *stylization*—not merely pointing to referents but pointing with an attitude. This means that, as Ogden and Richards remind us, "signs are not pictures of reality" (79), or as Richards says, language "is no mere signaling system" (131). Signs and symbols are constructions of reality; they give us reality already always wrapped up with social and political meanings. The implications for reality are clear, as Fiske tells us:

There is a nondiscursive reality, but it has no terms of its own through which we can access it; it has no essential identity or meaning in itself; we can access this reality only through discourse, and the discourse we use determines our sense of the real. Although discourse may not produce reality, it does produce the instrumental sense of the real that a society or social formation uses in its daily life. (4)

We noted toward the end of chapter 1 that simulations and representations may affect reality, thus implying the constructedness of reality and muddling clear distinctions among the terms. We see now that the stylization, the attitudes, the social and political implications carried in symbolization, is a major reason for the effects of representation in changing reality. "What are the signs of what?" asked Kenneth

Burke, in turning on its head the usual theory of meaning in which language is a sign of the world (359–379). Our sense of reality may instead be a sign of certain ways of symbolizing, he argued.

Others have followed Burke's lead. Shapiro uses some of Burke's terminology in proposing a distinction between "pious versus impious modes of representation, the former having the effect of reproducing or reinforcing the prevailing modes of power and authority and the latter tending to challenge them" (xii). For Shapiro, pious representations uncritically reproduce reality from a perspective of the dominant ideology: "Persons' perspectives are pre-scripted in the sense that meanings, subjects, and objects are sedimented in the dominant and thus most readily available discursive practices. When we reference an object in an available discourse, we reproduce it unreflectively" (19). Pious references hide the fact that they are creating rather than copying a sense of the real, Shapiro argues: "Ideological scripting can be viewed primarily as a discursive mode that naturalizes and universalizes [discursive] practices, so that it appears that the world is being described rather than contrived" (21). It is the business of pious representations to hide their role as creators of reality: "The misrecognition involved in ideology . . . provides the kind of naturalized construction of the social reality that obscures a historically acute recognition of the constructed nature of the 'real' while making everyday life appear coherent and unproblematic" (24). Shapiro calls this a process of "dissimulation," in which "power or relations of domination pose as something else" (28). Although we are unaware of the role of pious representations in reinscribing received senses of the real, impious representations may challenge our sense of reality. Shapiro uses photography as an example of how that might occur: "There are some photographs that tend to arrest the subconscious process by which we assimilate the copy to the real. As a result, they allow other than the usual or canonical interpretive codes to enter into the interpretive economy of the contemplation of the image" (124), thus changing how we think of the reality pictured.

We began this chapter by looking at the ways in which the perceptual process collapses our three key terms, and we have added to that understanding the idea that language and symbolic processes are a specific instrument by which the perceptual process works. In considering images and photography, we have already gone beyond language and into art. We are now ready to add to this argument one last step, to consider the ways in which aesthetic experience also undermines clear distinctions among reality, representation, and simulation.

AESTHETIC EXPERIENCE

Aesthetic means several things. The word certainly refers to beauty and art, so we might say that we are having an aesthetic experience when we hear music or view a sculpture. What happens in such an experience of art is another step in the process of construction which we have been following. An aesthetic experience is a constructed experience to which one brings heightened awareness, a sense of order, form, and pattern, a sense of difference and similarity, an appreciation of color and texture, an awareness of movement, and so forth. It is the enriching *addition to* an experience of these ways of paying attention that makes an experience aesthetic. An aesthetic experience may or may not be planned intentionally as such; the sublime might overtake one without conscious intention for it to do so.

One might sit in front of a painting and not have an aesthetic experience if one is living only at the level of perceptions or only within the categories given by language ("Here is a painting. . . . Here is the *Experiment with the Air Pump*"). It is when one "wakes up" and begins to make the experience more complex, enriched, patterned, appreciative, that one has an aesthetic experience. By the same token, intense, appreciative attention to a simple, found stone can constitute an aesthetic experience. It is a more complex and structured experience than is simple perception or even language use; it incorporates both of those. Thus, an aesthetic experience is a third step from perception to language to aesthetics in the progressive construction of experience.

In other work (*Rhetoric*), I have developed an understanding of the aesthetic that I should like to use here. There I argued, following the theories of John Dewey, that the aesthetic experience depends in part on the socially conditioned reading strategies and modes of perception of the individual. This may be but an academic way of saying that "beauty is in the eye of the beholder." But following the theories of Kenneth Burke, I also argued that socially conditioned attributes of aesthetic material itself set the parameters within which aesthetic experience works. Putting Burke and Dewey together, one might say that a given material object such as a novel or a film facilitates a wide (but not infinite) range of experiences, and that from that range the reader or viewer makes her aesthetic experience—with social constraints for both the material and the making of the experience overarching all. Now, this section proposes that the constructedness of that kind of experience, which is woven throughout everyday life, is a reason for the confounding of reality, representation, and simulation.

We begin by examining the work of those scholars who consider aesthetic experience and perception, or cognition, to be closely connected. Aesthetic experience, for Ronald Schenk, is fundamental to perception; he sees "beauty . . . as that which makes everyday consciousness possible" (27). Schenk argues that "aesthetic or image perception is not just sensate perception, nor fantasy, but a combination of what we usually separate as inner and outer perception" (26). Our apprehension of the world (outer) and our cognitive processing of it (inner) make the constructed whole of the aesthetic. Schenk points to aesthetic experience as a complex *combination* of perceptions. We immediately see the effect of that truth on our key terms, for it means our reality must likewise be constructed from the aesthetic. Schenk is clear that our sense of reality itself, of what things are, comes into being through aesthetics: "Things are because they are beautiful" (51). "The world as object, split off from the subject, is the fallen world. Imagination is the redeeming act of unification through creation," Schenk argues, assigning to the human aesthetic experience the power of creation (123).

Croce's aesthetic theory also sees aesthetics as a complex form integrally connected to perception. He begins by arguing that perceptions of reality as well as of our own memories and of images are all "intuitions," by which he means the impo-

sition of a form or pattern upon raw sensation: "This means that the distinction between reality and non-reality is extraneous, secondary, to the true nature of
intuition" (3). Constructedness dissolves the objectivity of reality for Croce, in
other words, at the level of basic perception (or what he is calling intuition). "The
distinction between real images and unreal images . . . does not at the first moment
exist" for Croce, it is a constructed distinction added on to "pure intuition" (4).
Thus, every perception and intuition are continuous with art and aesthetic experience (14). Although we distinguish "the *real* from the *unreal*, real imagination
from pure imagination," it is all conventional for Croce, created by aesthetics (28).
When people have difficulty separating constructed "real" from "unreal" intuitions, they must rely upon the rhetorical process of deciding based upon probabili-
ties and verisimilitude:

Where the delicate and fleeting shades between the real and unreal intuitions are so slight as
to mingle the one with the other, we must either renounce for the time being at least the
knowledge of what really happened . . . or we must fall back upon conjecture, verisimilitude, probability. The principle of verisimilitude and of probability in fact dominates all historical criticism. (28–29)

Other writers also agree that aesthetic experience cannot be separated from the
viewer's constructive perceptual processes, and that the experience of making the
world is thus inseparable from the experience of appreciating it. Several writers focus on the constructed nature of visual aesthetics. Julian Hochberg claims that "in
general, *visual information simply cannot be defined except in terms of the sensory
and perceptual characteristics of the viewer*" (21). Michael Stephan argues that visual art involves the viewer actively in several ways, and this involvement is what
distinguishes art from the "banal image" (160–62). He is speaking of aesthetic experience as a constructed experience of a higher level than basic perception of the
"banal." Robert Irwin asks, "What other reality does painting have except the ones
we give to it by acting as if its representations, interpretations, and illusions were
somehow real? All of these should more correctly be thought of as games of
intersubjective meaning construction" (217). Note that Irwin sees visual aesthetics
not only as constructed, but also as constructed through meaning, which connects
it with perceptual and linguistic processes. Note that Irwin's reference to
intersubjectivity grounds the aesthetic in language, which is also intersubjective.
Likewise, Richardson insists that art, style, and fashion are grounded in communities (1–2). Those intersubjective communities generate conventions that construct
aesthetic experience. Richardson argues that "pictorial representations rely upon
conventions that correspond to vision in only the most tenuous fashion" (167)—as
conventions, they must be constructed.

Some thinkers point to the power of aesthetic objects, specifically visual images, in setting the parameters for the construction of experience. Rudolf Arnheim,
for instance, says that it is "essential to get beyond the traditional notion that pictures provide the mere raw material and that thinking begins only after the information has been received. . . . Instead, the thinking is done by means of structural

properties inherent in the image" (xxvi). The artist, in other words, encodes certain preferred ways of seeing immanent in certain material that others will come to for an aesthetic experience, and the experience of that audience is shaped by the possibilities contained within that object. Murray Edelman puts it more simply in saying that "seeing is constructed and so reflects models that art forms provide" (2). Note that Edelman features the constructedness not just of art but of seeing itself, and for him the construction of seeing flows from materials provided by the artist.

One way in which aesthetic materials set parameters for experience is the way in which art creates a stage for make-believe. A number of scholars argue that make-believe is the key to aesthetic experience. "Fictions are artifacts primarily intended by their makers to get an audience to imagine certain things," says Gregory Currie (151). Make-believe may be engendered by any representations, claims Walton (*Mimesis*, 4); it is what they have in common. A prime site for such make-believe is media, for as Parenti tells us, "The entertainment media are the make-believe media; they make us believe" (1). If this is true, it would seem to make aesthetics constructive of simulation, since simulations in video games, flight trainers, and so forth are essentially make-believe.

Walton argues that the experience of literature depends on make-believe, for readers "participate in games of make-believe, using works as props" ("Spelunking," 38). He describes the process in more detail: "Appreciators simulate experiences of being attacked by monsters, of observing characters in danger and fearing for them, of learning about and grieving for good people who come to tragic ends, of marveling at and admiring the exploits of heroes" (46). The simulative nature of fiction was described by Jerrold Levinson as "the paradox of fiction," that we have strong reactions to discourse depicting worlds we know are not "real" (22–23). Walton describes that paradox likewise: "It is extraordinarily tempting to suppose that when one is caught up in a story, one loses touch with reality, temporarily, and actually believes in the fiction. . . . Yet it also seems that the normal appreciator does not (of course!) really believe in the fiction. The central metaphysical problem concerning fiction is thus mirrored in the very experience of appreciation" (*Mimesis*, 6). If the aesthetic is simulation and also at the heart of our perceptions of reality, then we can see how aesthetics confounds distinctions among the key terms.

Several scholars argue that subjectivity, or a sense of the self, is constructed in aesthetic experience. As we put perceptions and linguistically given categories together into more complicated aesthetic experiences, we become who we are in terms of those experiences. As Shapiro puts it,

Our resistance or possible distancing from the re-presenting of a particular reality is overcome to the extent that we fail to recognize we are created as a subject/viewer as the objects are rendered in a particular way. Failing to reflect on our constructed viewer mode of subjectivity in the painting, we are overcome by its sightlines; we fail to see that the painting's reality *for us* is an enactment, reflecting a reality-making process in which we are implicated as users of visualizing codes. (136)

Shapiro speaks clearly in terms of the constructedness of reality that takes place as we construct ourselves in aesthetics.

If subjectivity and reality are constructed through aesthetics, then aesthetics is epistemic, as are the processes of perception and language. Aesthetic experience for Schenk leads to knowledge; it does not merely apprehend but apprehends with understanding: "Following Heidegger, I see the Neoplatonic tradition as presenting the apprehension of the beautiful as a way of thinking, *aisthesis* and cognition coming together. Passing through the mysteries of beauty allows for thought that sees. In this way, knowing and sensing would not be different" (58–59). Note the similarities of Schenk's description to the epistemic role performed by language, in leading the speaker to knowledge of that which is perceived. Science is often taken to be the paradigm of the epistemic, and Schenk claims that "it is the scientist's aesthetic sense, not the knowledge of scientific method, that leads to discovery" (145). By that I believe he means that it is the scientist's ability to construct data into a meaningful understanding, to notice pattern and form where an amateur might see only chaos or random numbers, that creates scientific knowledge of reality. Schenk indicates how aesthetics dissolves our three key terms, for he asserts that reality is something constructed in aesthetic experience instead of being a given.

Schenk argues that "the aesthetic vision apprehends truth through connection with the world of appearance, rather than by distancing from appearance via objectification and deriving conclusions through methodology" (26). Aesthetic epistemology is based on assumption of human involvement with, joining with, the world in creation, as opposed to a view in which people stand apart from the world as object. Schenk explains the difference:

Knowledge through Aphrodite's vision reveals itself via a sensuous view of the world. In contrast to the Apollonian vision, distant and objective, her seeming conjoins with what is there. It is a view of simultaneous giving and taking, being affected by, while affecting. Aphrodite's knowing is one of sensuous delight, an *episteme* of eros. (42)

For Schenk, the aesthetic is epistemic through activation of human memory: "Knowledge as aesthetic perception would not be something remote, to be derived through method, so much as a matter of memory, a recollection of form already there" (59). Aesthetic experience leads us to knowledge of the forms underlying experience at large, in other words. Croce likewise emphasizes the centrality of form in saying that it is the "human spirit" which constructs aesthetic experience, bringing sensation to the level of consciousness, and it does this through the aesthetic experience of *form*: "Matter, clothed and conquered by form, produces concrete form. It is the matter, the content, which differentiates one of our intuitions from another: the form is constant: it is spiritual activity, while matter is changeable," changeable because constructed (6).

Following Schenk's and Croce's leads in aesthetic epistemology here, I propose that the structure of the aesthetic experience is one and the same thing as the structure of human memory. What happens when we store "real" experience in memory is that we leave out trifling details and reduce or condense the experience into a compact *form* ordering relatively few details of information. Your month-long trip to France becomes a few distilled, ordered memories. But that is precisely what aesthetic experience gives to us, in predigested form. A novel, a film, a painting gives us relatively few (compared to the richness of immediate lived experience) details of information hung on a scaffolding of form, structure, or narrative. When we have read the novel we have internalized the same structure that we would have had we really experienced what the novel describes. Alison Landberg describes the process: "The experience within the movie theater and the memories that the cinema affords—despite the fact that the spectator did not live through them—might be as significant in constructing, or deconstructing, the spectator's identity as any experience that s/he actually lived through" (180). I agree, because both "real" memory and aesthetic experience are highly formalized arrays of a few details. Note that Landberg identifies aesthetic experience as constructive of identity. Memory likewise is the site in which identity is stored. You *are* the set of memories of your trip to France, of your first day at school, of your wedding, and so forth. And thus you are also the person who through art has experienced the whale hunt, the broken heart, the Russian revolution, and so forth. If it is true that the structure of aesthetic experience is the same as the structure of memory, then both our sense of reality and our sense of self are constructed. Maintaining firm distinctions among reality, representation, and simulation becomes nearly impossible if this is true.

There is another important sense in which aesthetics is epistemic, and that is in the way that aesthetic experience creates templates for life to follow. The ancient Greeks held a mimetic view of art: sculpture, painting, dance, and so forth were thought to represent real life and would be judged on the basis of their fidelity in representation. Such a view reinforces a sense of reality as primary, representation as derivative but also distinct and separate from reality. But if experience is constructed in large part through aesthetics, then we should not be surprised to find that relationship reversed.

A number of scholars argue for a reversal of the traditional epistemic relationship between reality as primary and representation or simulation as derivative; and in that reversal we see how distinctions among the three are confounded. A number of scholars argue that life follows art. Gabler's recent book is entirely devoted to this premise, explaining his sense that life is becoming "art" or "performance" (4). But how does that happen? Notice the reversal found in Gabler's claim that "what the movies provided . . . was a tangible model to which one could conform life and a standard against which one could measure it" (57)—the aesthetic experience of movies is primary and life is judged according to whether it follows art! Gabler expresses that reversal elsewhere by saying, "Where we had once measured the movies by life, we now measured life by how well it satisfied the narrative expectations created by the movies" (233). Wartofsky makes the same reversal in arguing that even modes of representation taken to be the measure of accuracy are themselves constructed: "There is no intrinsically veridical, or 'correct,' mode of representation . . . that is not itself a product of the social and historical choices of norms of visual representation" (272). Thus, "it is we who create the very norms of veridicality by our pictorial practice" (273). If so, the constructions of aesthetics are primary. But also the hard and fast distinctions among our three key terms are weakened.

Life follows art because life conforms to narrative structures given by art. We have considered aesthetic experience as a higher level of constructedness than perception or language. Shapiro expresses these higher levels of constructedness in narrative terms: "Objects and events cannot be construed outside of the grammar, figuration, and plots which animate and connect them one to another" (8). Experience of things and events, in other words, comes into being only insofar as they are cast into narrative form, which means aesthetic form.

Wartofsky argues that visual perception in life likewise follows forms given in art: "Pictures—or rather styles of pictorial representation—exemplify canons of representation, by means of which we come to *see* the visual world as *like* the picture" (273). Wartofsky claims that the act of seeing is constructed from aesthetic experience: "Human vision is a cultural and historical product of the creative activity of making pictures" (272).

What we think of as "life" thus follows the structures of our aesthetic forms. Hayles even argues that our experiences of both technologies and of our bodies themselves follow the aesthetic templates of discursive patterns: "Discursive constructions affect how bodies move through space and time, influence what technologies are developed, and help to structure the interfaces between bodies and technologies" (207).That is why Gabler sees life and aesthetic structures as now inseparable: "The movies would come to approximate reality more closely than any previous medium, but . . . it would not be what we now call 'virtual reality,' some simulacrum of real life. Rather, total cinema would be the result of the entertainment cosmology leaping tracks from screen to life" (58). Gabler's refusal of simulation as a description for this situation bespeaks the confounding influence of the merger and reversal he sees between reality and its representation in film.

If life follows art, other interesting reversals follow, confounding clear distinctions among our key terms. Wartofsky notes correctly that "the classic story here, of course, is about Picasso's portrait of Gertrude Stein. When told that it did not look like her, he answered: 'It will' " (277–78; Edelman, 12). Gabler notes that with the rise of "reality programming" such as real crime shows, "real-life entertainments don't have to be harvested from reality" (85)—they are entirely aesthetic contrivances, reality generated by aesthetic forms of television. Under these circumstances, people see media images as real, and they act upon or copy them (Parenti, 7–8). Virilio gives an example of how life follows art in that way: "So after creating it in the first place, television then fueled the violence it was supposed to be elucidating to the public—just by the mere presence of TV cameras at the scene of the confrontations, murder, and looting" (*Art*, 12). It is in that sense that Gabler can claim that "life has become a show staged for the media" in which "pseudo-events . . . proliferated to such an extent that one could hardly call them events anymore because there were no longer any seams between them and the rest of life" (97). Baudrillard anticipated Gabler in arguing that "*It is now impossible to isolate the process of the real*, or to prove the real. Thus all hold-ups, hijacks and the like are now as it were simulation hold-ups, in the sense that they are inscribed in advance in the decoding and orchestration rituals of the media, anticipated in their mode of presentation and possible consequences" (*Simulations*, 41).

One reason why it may be hard to separate the real from representations or simulations is because of the verisimilitude of aesthetic constructions, expressed by Gergen in terms of artifice: "The ultimate question is not whether media relationships approximate the normal in their significance, but whether normal relationships can match the powers of artifice" (*Saturated*, 57). That verisimilitude gets better every day with technological advances. Because of the aesthetic attraction and power of media, their images generate our desires for certain kinds of "reality." As Parenti notes, "it is not simply a matter of demand creating supply. Often it is the other way around: supply creates demand" (199). But the power of aesthetic experience to define the real is not only a recent phenomenon. John Berger argues that the venerable art form of oil painting does this: "What distinguishes oil painting from any other form of painting is its special ability to render the tangibility, the texture, the luster, the solidity of what it depicts. It defines the real as that which you can put your hands on" (88).

As one final illustration of the power of aesthetic experience to confound reality, representation, and simulation, we consider the observation made by several scholars that politics, which would seem to be preeminently a battleground for real power distribution, is becoming simulational. The citizen of the future will be, as in Chris Gray's book title, a *Cyborg Citizen*. The argument in general is that electoral politics, especially as seen in the media, is neither real nor does it represent real things going on in the world, but is entirely about itself. Politics is literally theater, a constructed experience judged for its aesthetic value. Presidential debates, for instance, are not really about what a candidate would do about Taiwan or the budget or world trade—instead, the debates are about what a candidate would do in the debates themselves and whether the candidate's performance is artistically pleasing. Boorstin identifies such debates as perfect examples of "pseudo-events" (41–44). In these spectacles, Norton claims that "candidates appear . . . not as authors but as texts, not as productive but as commodities" (113). Carl Boggs identifies the commodification of contemporary culture and the rise of corporate power as a reason for *The End of Politics*, although he does not connect this trend explicitly to simulation in other cultural developments. If politics, so often taken to be a bastion of the real, is moving toward simulation because of aesthetic influences, then we see once again why our three key terms must be confounded.

One reason why politics has become simulational, in this view, is that it has moved into the realm of signs and representations. People now struggle over signs rather than over the "real" condition of streets in front of their homes or schools down the block. As Baudrillard claims, "Power . . . for some time now produces nothing but signs of its resemblance. And at the same time, another figure of power comes into play: that of a collective demand for *signs* of power—a holy union which forms around the disappearance of power" (*Simulations*, 45). In that view, major figures in Washington struggle for victories that are no more real than was

Mr. Smith's going to Washington—turning in the best performance, as defined by media standards, is key.

Claims that such events as political debates are simulational rather than real are largely based upon "television's power to convert events into entertainment" (Gabler, 83). The power arises because of the media's simulational insularity; what it presents as reality is in fact contrived aesthetics. Parenti argues that "the media images in our heads influence how we appraise a host of social realities, including our government's domestic and foreign policies" (4). Edelman is explicit in identifying not only the media but the aesthetic dimension of media as generative of today's politics: "The models, scenarios, narratives and images into which audiences for political news translate that news are social capital, not individual inventions. They come from works of art in all genres" (1). Thus, "the conduct, virtues, and vices associated with politics come directly from art, then, and only indirectly from immediate experiences" (2). One result of the aesthetic grounding of politics is that narrative values of sporting events have been chosen to generate media political creations, according to Edelman: "The mass media and the strategies of many candidates have largely converted election campaigns into media events, treating them as sporting contests and obscuring the emptiness of the ritual" (135).

Media coverage of politics is really media demonstration of aesthetic prowess, says Gabler: "The purpose of a presidential campaign was now not just to provide a striking set of images and events for the media to cover but to show the media how efficiently and effectively the politicos had created these images and events" (107). As Gabler tells us, "the media weren't really covering politics at all. They were covering themselves covering politics" (105). Because of that, Gabler claims, politics is becoming nothing but a media event (99–117). Boorstin likewise argues that media create rather than report politics: "Our 'free market place of ideas' is a place where people are confronted by competing pseudo-events and are allowed to judge among them. When we speak of 'informing' the people this is what we really mean" (35).

Baudrillard argues that the simulational nature of media coverage of politics can be clearly seen in polls and referenda; and here he grounds it in explicitly aesthetic terms: "The mass medium *par excellence*, and the most beautiful of them all, is the electoral system: its achievement is the referendum, where the response is implied in the question itself, as in the polls" (*For*, 170–71). Elsewhere he argues that

We live by the mode of *referendum* precisely because there is no longer any *referential*. Every sign, every message . . . is presented to us as question/answer. . . . Now texts and referenda are, we know, perfect forms of simulation: the answer is called forth by the question, it is design-ated in advance. (*Simulations*, 116–17)

Polls are thus not really about what the public thinks but about how the polls themselves are designed. For Baudrillard, "The polls are located in a dimension beyond all social *production*. They refer only to a simulacrum of public opinion" (*Simulations*, 125–26). The result is that among politicians, "the representatives no longer represent anything because they control so well the responses of the electoral body" (131). Anne Norton, although she does not use the same simulational language of Baudrillard, also points to the constructedness of polls, which create rather than reflect:

Survey research is an exercise in representation. . . . These nested representations, which transubstantiate speech to words, words to numbers, people to words and numbers, and parties to percentages, necessarily alter the things they signify. People appear in these surveys, divested of characteristics they regard as significant, marked by traits they were unconscious of or uninterested in. (38–39)

The aesthetic simulationalization of politics occurs in large part through investing media events with political import. If an ordinary shred of "real" experience can possibly be dramatized, especially if it can be invested with a plot device based on conflict or struggle, then it can be constructed as political. This is the point Baudrillard makes in observing:

There is a tidal wave in Pakistan, a black title fight in the U.S.; a youth is shot by a bistro owner, etc. These sorts of events, once minor and apolitical, suddenly find themselves invested with a power of diffusion that lends them a social and "historic" aura. New forms of political action have crystallized around this conflictualization of incidents that were hitherto consigned to the social column. (*For*, 175)

CONCLUSION

In this chapter we have inquired into the reasons why reality, representation, and simulation may be hard to distinguish clearly and objectively. Our basic perceptions and language are constructed, and thus all three of our key terms are constructions. Aesthetic experience is an even higher, more complicated level of construction. What is constructed may be constructed in different ways, and so we see why the three key concepts cannot be treated as if they named objectively distinct realms of experience.

What then are we to make of our three key terms? For we saw in the first chapter that they are widely used, and used as if they meant something! It is time to make a rhetorical turn. The rest of this book treats our three key terms *as terms*, with rhetorical power to do social and political work. We will explore what it means for someone to refer to reality, representation, or simulation as if they had clear and distinct referents. We will look not at what the terms name or what they are, but instead how they are used.

Chapters 3 and 4 pursue the project of explaining the rhetorical dimensions of our key terms. Between them they explore four dimensions of the rhetorical meanings of reality, representation, and simulation—without, of course, claiming that these are the only four dimensions that might be named. Although it is an artificial and dualist distinction, the chapters will be divided between exploring dimensions of meaning that point to "external" structures and those dimensions that point to "internal" experiences. The reader is invited to treat that division as purely arbitrary, as an organizational convenience to be put aside through reintegration at the end. Chapter 3 investigates "external" *structures of experience* within which people act and by which we may feel we are constrained—specifically, our understandings of the sources of *permanence and change* and of *commodification*. Chapter 4 investigates two dimensions of *lived experience* likely to be felt as personal or "internal" by people—specifically, *subjectivity* and *aesthetics*. Within each chapter and section, we shall examine the kinds of claims that people make in regard to that dimension of experience and how reality, representation, and simulation are rhetorical claims or strategies with political and social impact.

Chapter 3

Reality, Representation, and Simulation in Structures of Experience

To understand what people mean when they use our three key terms of reality, representation, and simulation, it is helpful to think in terms of some key categories of experience. One overall dimension of experience is those socially shared structures of experience into which we are born, which at least seem to be external to us. I bypass for the moment here a consideration of whether structures of experience are in some sense "really" external. Since we are exploring how our key terms are used in discourse, consider it enough for the moment that most people think, act, and speak of them as in part implicated in an external realm. So I am asking about dimensions of what seems to be given, socially or materially grounded experience; and I am asking about how reality, representation, and simulation are used as terms or concepts on those dimensions. Furthermore, two such dimensions will be explored here, although of course I do not claim that structures of experience have only two such dimensions. This chapter explores what reality, representation, and simulation mean and how they are used on the dimensions of *permanence and change* and of *commodification*. When I say "reality is . . ." or "there is a sense in which simulation is . . ." I am not making a claim for what those terms "really" are or really mean but for how they are used. The reader is invited to mentally insert the clause "reality is (in widespread usage)" into every such expression.

PERMANENCE AND CHANGE

When we apply a label of reality, representation, or simulation to an experience, what are we saying about the permanence or changeability of that experience? What level of stability or mutability, dependability or shiftiness, is implied by such a usage? Part of what is being asked by this question is to what extent and on what level an experience can be struggled over. If *reality*, for instance, implies absolute stability and lack of change, then consider the political work that is done by identifying racial categories or claims of gender characteristics as real. If it is "just a fact" that male athletes are stronger and faster, then that is a claim that existing sports performance differences are real and thus immutable. The claim privileges whole domains of experience as exempt from rhetorical struggle, thus privileging (as reality) whatever understanding is currently in place about those experiences. On the other hand, if race or gender is but a representation, or even a simulation, and if those categories denote more fluidity, then consider how that opens up those categories for struggle and change. So the element of permanence or change implied in a claim of reality, representation, or simulation is well worth examining because of the political work that they do.

Reality. What is the rhetoric of reality in terms of permanence and change? Mark Slouka uses several typical descriptors for reality in arguing that it is "immutable, empirical, neither historically nor culturally relative" (160). Let us examine those three key descriptors one by one. *Immutability* is a claim of permanence. The sense that reality is immutable is widespread, but exactly what that means needs some consideration. In one sense, it is clear that reality is highly mutable: one minute the skies are clear and the next moment it is raining. One changes a real match by striking it, and one can change real paper by holding the match to it. The mirror gives us daily evidence of the mutability of our bodies. Yet there is also the sense that reality is what can be counted on because it is immutable. My alma mater once received a huge gift to its endowment in the form of ironclad securities, and the Provost was quoted as marveling, "It's so real"—by which she meant that it was not likely to disappear, that the funds were in the form of reliable investments and thus not likely to lose value, in short, that the new-found wealth would not change.

I believe we can understand the immutability dimension of the rhetoric of reality in several ways. First, reality is whatever is *most* immutable. Even if one envisions a world in which everything changes, reality is what changes the least. A rock will change, but slowly; an opinion can change in the next moment.

Second, although reality is changeable, it is only changeable at the hands of other reality. I can change a match but only by striking it against reality; neither thinking nor talking about it will change it. Only reality trumps reality. Indeed, reality trumps every other order of experience, as in Slouka's gleeful claim that "reality had a bad attitude" in its ability to break into technofantasies (36). The dominance of reality over other orders is a source of power in Baudrillard's claim that "when it is threatened today by simulation (the threat of vanishing in the play of signs), power risks the real, risks crisis" (*Simulations*, 44). Note reality is used there in the sense of a bedrock guard against fantasy. Kevin Robins uses this sense of immutability when he rails against devotees of cyberspace and simulation that "we are living in a real world, and we must recognize that it is indeed the case that we cannot make of it whatever we wish" (137). Wishing here is in the order of representation or simulation, and it has no chance if reality vetoes it.

Third, to say that reality is immutable means that it is predictable. If I set a plate in the sink and do a slow turn, I can predict that the plate will be there when I look again because it is a real plate. Predictability means that if reality changes it does so by following laws that do not change. This is not to say that anyone always can predict reality; but failure of prediction comes about because of our failed predictive instruments, or the complexity of reality, or the intervention of other reality, not because of some mutability in reality itself. What is real is predictable but not necessarily predicted. This premise underlies the hope of predictability in all science, which knows that it cannot predict everything at the moment, but works on the assumption that everything is nevertheless predictable in principle. Science dares to predict because it predicts what reality will do (I am reporting how reality is spoken of, not necessarily making such a claim myself).

Paradoxically, the immutability of reality sometimes means that although predictable in principle it cannot be predicted in practice because reality is so complex. Were reality mutable, its complexity could be tamed and simplified through the intervention of language, logic, or other organizing systems. But the complexity and thus inability to predict the real resulting from reality's complexity is ironically a guarantee of its immutability. In this sense Katherine Hayles notes that "artificial life" simulations are often claimed by their creators to be real precisely because the simulations generate their own unplanned complexities, unlike models (representations) that are intentionally simplistic (233–34). Likewise, people are not predictable and not systematizable because through embodiment our actions are always "improvisational" and "tied to the circumstances of the occasion and the person" (197)—in that sense the messiness of human action is a guarantee that we are real rather than cartoon figures or simulations in a video game. Heim likewise argues that the contingencies of the world are its guarantors of reality:

Real environments in the primary world do not present themselves for our amusement nor can they be switched on and off like the situations in movies or television shows. Real environments are anything goes and messy. They have no pause, no fast forward, and—most important—no rewind. Our actions can affect what happens next. So anything that simulates a real environment must have something of that spontaneous, improvised feel of real environments. (*Virtual*, 11)

Slouka's claim that reality is *empirical* is likewise widespread. One sense of this usage is that reality is the world, or in the world, rather than a dimension of one's thought, imagination, or fancy. Reality is what we do not make up. By empirical, Slouka follows the widespread view of reality as grounded in material experience, in the body (as an object of the mind, not as the mind itself), and thus in the order of objects. This usage puts reality in opposition to discourse, aesthetics, imagination, and thought. Thus Slouka refers to "the shock of the real: the nakedness of face-to-face communication, the rough force of the natural world" (3). Robins urges people to remember that we live in a "materially straitened and socially divided world" and that thus "we remain in need of politics" (137); his argument subordinates the political dimension of talk and thought to the reality of material limits and social difference. Slouka's and Robins's usage is typical in that the dimensions of reality interlock: the material and objective is likewise immutable and predictable, while the subjective and cognitive is not. Empiricality thus denotes permanence.

To speak of reality as empirical implies a precession of reality, that reality is the order of experience that always comes first and that other orders are only commentaries on reality. Rene Berger puts reality in a position to comment on and finally to judge reality, for "simulation, no matter how refined it may be, is always considered an approximation; it is not, nor can it be, confused with reality. . . . This means that once its mission has been accomplished . . . it yields to experience which alone decides ultimately" (15). It is in this sense that Michael Heim accuses Slouka, Sven Birkerts, and others of being "Luddites" who see reality as primary and computers as secondary, as intrusions upon reality (*Virtual*, 37). Heim's description may be just; note both the temporal precession of reality and a distaste for its lately arrived substitute, cyberspace, in Slouka's comment that "it is possible to see, in a number of technologies spawned by recent developments in the computer world, an attack on reality as human beings have always known it" (4). The real is that which anticipates the pretensions of simulation and can unarguably reassert itself because it comes first. Temporal priority is one way to argue permanence, as in the sense that God is permanent because God has always been.

An important part of the empirical precession of reality is the uniqueness of the real. Paul Virilio makes this point in arguing that "you can easily imitate appearances, but not reality" (*Art*, 29). By this he means that one can imitate or duplicate the appearance of something—a photograph, an artificial scent, a CD of music—indeed, capitalist economies are based upon the ability to do just that. But one cannot imitate a reality—what one would get would be another reality. One cannot "imitate" a stone in this usage without getting another real stone, which is a reality rather than the appearance of a reality. Another word for imitate is *copy*; Virilio's usage thus opposes copies to reality, and let us recall that one characteristic of simulation is its repeatability. The real is the unique original.

Such references to the real, or the "authentic," echo Walter Benjamin's sense of original "art," as opposed to mechanically reproduced images such as film or photographs. Ronald Schenk speaks in this way of authentic art as unique (and thus real): "An image is ugly when it is not well crafted, when it makes its own unique, intrinsic being" (29). Daniel Boorstin likewise searches for "authentic" events in that which is spontaneous and therefore unique, concluding that "the world of crime, even more than that of sports, is a last refuge of the authentic, uncorrupted spontaneous event" (254). Clearly, he wrote before the appearance of today's "real" crime shows and hyped celebrity trials on television.

The descriptor *empirical* is not unproblematic. Mircea Eliade reminds us that religious thought might see the real as that which is not material but is instead spiritual. The spiritual is often spoken of as opposed to the empirical. Nevertheless, the sense of reality as having precession is what is key. Religious experience falls within Slouka's empirical category for that reason, and precession is often behind claims that spiritual experience is real. Eliade claims that "when the sacred manifests itself in any hierophany, there is not only a break in the homogeneity of space;

there is also revelation of an absolute reality" (*Sacred*, 21). Note that in his usage, spiritual reality precedes the material and breaks through it. What interests us is the rhetoric of reality, not whether that reality is posited as material or spiritual; in either case, it is in Slouka's terms "empirical" as an inalterable and undeniable experience with precedence over other orders of experience.

An important dimension of reality as empirical is that reality is what happens to the body and in the body rather than to or in the mind. Slouka argues that "as technological developments carry us ever more rapidly into the virtual future, we risk tearing ourselves loose from our own biological past—the basis, in the deepest sense, of all we know and are" (134). Death, in this sense, is the great and final arbiter of reality, for what death comes to—the body—is the grounding for what is real. The body changes, but usually it does so slowly. What happens to the body, however, has happened forever. If I break a leg it will heal, but I will be permanently the one who broke a leg. Whereas representations and simulations are erasable, making the body a site of reality creates a rhetoric of permanence.

This usage of mind and body in a structure of precession and dominance is of course dualist in premising a distinction between a nonempirical subject or mind that is wiggling around "in here" and a hard and fast empirical reality "out there." Baudrillard, for example, argues that "ideology only corresponds to a betrayal of reality by signs; simulation corresponds to a short-circuit of reality and to its reduplication by signs. It is always the aim of ideological analysis to restore the objective process; it is always a false problem to want to restore the truth beneath the simulacrum" (*Simulations*, 48). Note in Baudrillard's usage the dualist distinction between a bedrock truth on one side and deceptive signs and simulations that are somehow not in the order of the real on the other side. Dualist usage is also found in Heim's claim that "there is a sense in which any simulation makes something seem real that in fact is not" ("Essence," 21). Note the insistence hiding in Heim's "in fact," by which he bifurcates a precessional reality and insubstantial simulations or signs. Note also that for Heim, what can be made (and thus changed) is only "seeming" or appearance and thus opposed to the real (which is by implication permanent). As noted in chapter 1, we see that the rhetoric of reality is grounded in Cartesian dualism.

Slouka's claim that reality is neither historically nor culturally *relative* holds up a hex sign to ward off the evil influences of the subjective, whether personal or social. This common usage does not deny the presence and effects of history and culture, but does deny that either can fundamentally influence whatever is reality. In this vein, one might argue that although different societies may say (represent) different things, at different times, about the relative strength or value of males and females, the "reality" is that human males are larger and stronger than are human females, by and large, and that this reality cannot and will not change. Of course, we see some of the political work done by asserting a claim of reality over a claim of relativity in that example. An assertion of reality, or a surrogate term, has often been used in this way, to assert power against those who see the change and instability implied by mere representations and simulations as foremost. Reviewing the last few decades, Gabler argues that "the great cultural debate . . . was one between the realists who believed that a clear-eyed appreciation of the human condition was necessary to be human, and the postrealists who believed that glossing reality and even transforming it into a movie were perfectly acceptable strategies if these made us happier" (243). The human condition in that sense is permanent, compared to the shifting shadow plays of the movies.

Stefan Helmreich notes that *nature* "has frequently served as a resource for legitimating social orders—for naturalizing power" (20). Nature is a term within the rhetoric of reality for warding off relativism. Slipping nature underneath any existing social order empowers that order precisely by attempting to make it not relative, not a construction built upon representations, but instead an order that is necessary because natural. But as we learned above from Eliade, reality can be spoken of as spiritual as well—and just as nonrelative and absolute: "Revelation of a sacred space makes it possible to obtain a fixed point and hence to acquire orientation in the chaos of homogeneity" (*Sacred*, 23). If such an order, sacred or secular, is not relative to changing time and circumstance, then it is permanent.

When people speak of the real, then, they speak of it as immutable, empirical, and not relative. Those who do not believe in such things nevertheless mean them when they offer alternatives to a world view grounded in "reality." On the dimension of permanence and change, reality is the domain of the former.

Representation. If reality is of the order of permanence, representation would initially seem to be of the order of change. Nothing can be easier than to change what we say. I can write "I am writing a book" or I can write "I am not writing a book." I can alternate each sentence, changing with equal ease. Representations are highly changeable in that technical sense.

Yet I am not completely free to change in that way, for strong social forces govern the rhetoric of representations. Although I am physically free to write "I am not writing a book," nevertheless it is a lie to do so, with potential social and psychological sanctions for doing so. So when we consider where representations lie on the dimension of permanence and change, we must consider their physical changeability but also the moral and epistemological pressures that contribute to their permanence.

Rene Berger makes an observation that clearly compares representations to reality on the dimension of permanence and change in saying that throughout history, "representations are part of a progressive passage from the solid to the fluid" (2). As a culture moves from a preoccupation with bison to a relatively greater preoccupation with paintings, drama, and poetry about bison, it moves from the "solid" real animal to the more fluid material of signs, of which representations are made.

Understanding where representations lie in terms of permanence and change requires an understanding of their epistemic function. The rhetoric of representation regards them as epistemic because they re-present another order. The epistemic process is traditionally spoken of as one of re-presenting the world to the mind of the knowing subject. That is not a source of joy to Slouka, for instance, who complains of the representational intercession of television between audience and reality: "we're being reduced to watching the world through the electronic windows of the television screen and the computer monitor" (74). Slouka's complaint seems premised on an assumption that television represents reality poorly. Re-presentation can be done well or poorly, but the consequences are as much moral as they are technical. For that reason, Arthur C. Danto notes that "we can criticize representations only from the perspective of truth and falsity or completeness and incompleteness" (12). The ability of representations to be true or false, complete or incomplete, depends upon their ability to change so as to be more or less true and complete.

One might even go beyond saying that representations are epistemic to claim that the epistemic is representational. One cannot know experience until one represents it in that view; the unsymbolized is unknown. Susanne K. Langer makes this point: "It may seem strange that the most immediate experiences in our lives should be the least recognized, but there is a reason for this apparent paradox, and the reason is precisely their immediacy. They pass unrecorded because they are known without any symbolic mediation, and therefore without conceptual form. We usually have no objectifying images of such experiences to recall and recognize" (*Mind*, 57). The implications of this stance are that "knowledge begins, then, with the formulation of experience in many haphazard ways, by the imposition of available images on new experiences as fast as they arise; it is a process of imagining not fictitious things, but reality" (*Mind*, 63). Fiske claims a similar world-presenting function for electronic representations: "Events do happen, but ones that are not mediated do not count, or, at least, count only in their immediate locales" (2). If we know the world only through representations, it becomes vital to get the act of representation *right*. Such responsibility arises only because representations can be changed so as to be more or less correct.

Croce makes the same argument for the importance of representations in manifesting aesthetic experience, saying that "it is true that the [aesthetic] content is that which is convertible into form, but it has no determinable qualities until this transformation takes place. We know nothing about it. It does not become aesthetic content before, but only after it has been actually transformed" (16). Michael Stephan likewise agrees that "our relations to the arts can be understood in terms of cognition, for the present best defined as the *act of knowing*, with the implication that different art forms suppose distinct *ways* of knowing" (1). Following C. S. Peirce, Stephan claims that "the whole purpose of the visual image is to present us with an *iconic* reminder of our experience of the world thereby eliciting its unique (non-linguistic) way of knowing" (2). Art in these views is one form of representation with the same implications of perilous change and more responsibility.

The traditional view of representation is of course highly dualist, using representation to link the "in here" of the mind with the "out there" of the world. Richard Rorty describes this traditional dualist view as the metaphor "of the mind as a great mirror, containing various representations—some accurate, some not" (12). Rorty describes the task of representation within the traditional discipline of philosophy:

To know is to represent accurately what is outside the mind; so to understand the possibility and nature of knowledge is to understand the way in which the mind is able to construct such representations. Philosophy's central concern is to be a general theory of representation, a theory which will divide culture up into the areas which represent reality well, those which represent it less well, and those which do not represent it at all. (3)

Rorty's observation that traditionally some representations match the world well, others less well, others not at all raises the issue of how such linkage is determined. The widely held position that representations are conventional, that their connection to the world is decided by social agreement and must thus be learned, places representation very much on the "change" side of permanence and change, since that which is conventional is so technically malleable. But Stephan takes the remarkable position that images at least are naturally representative and employ no social conventions at all. Thus, "we do not need to *learn* to see pictures" (2). For Stephan, "we understand the representational visual image because the nature of the light reflected from its surface sensibly corresponds, in certain essential respects, to how we habitually perceive the phenomenal world" (2). He argues that images suggest whole contexts of experience, yet for technical reasons cannot do so completely, thus creating artistic tensions that are part of their visual appeal (11–12). Stephan's position is in the minority; most scholars would seem to argue that all representations are conventional and must thus be learned. It is only because of their conventional nature that they can be manipulated so as to reflect the truth or not; in that way, representations are not only epistemic but the representer is accountable. In fact, Stephan's stance makes the representations that are images of the order of reality, material appendages of their real originals.

When representation is held to a standard set by social convention, it acquires some moral and social (but not technical) permanence and thus becomes an instrument of power and control. Anne Norton notes that "the privileging of representation in the American regime shows itself . . . as a privileging of convention. Convention is a curious, ambivalent amalgam. The word refers to an authoritative fiction. A convention is imposed. It is obeyed without reason; it usurps the will" (43). Indeed, it must usurp the will or it is not a convention: once one uses "dog" to mean anything other than what convention says it means, one is using only a private representation at best. Convention thus empowers people to insist on the ways in which representations are used: people are denied or allowed to represent two gay parents and their children as "family," and strict conventions govern whether a group of "insurgents" in a given country are "terrorists" or "freedom fighters." Massimo Negrotti points to the action that follows, indeed that depends upon, such representations: "everything we do depends on how we represent the world around us, including . . . how our actions cause changes in the world" (9). Control over representations then leads to the kind of "mastery" described by Norton: "Representation enables those still subject to nature to know themselves its masters. This is neither naivete nor delusion. It is representation that gives us mastery. The mastery that we acquire permits an imperfect overcoming, a partial evasion, of nature's rule of the body" (24). A representation in place, sanctioned by social convention, acquires a kind of permanence. Change of such representations comes with social cost.

Representations are also sites of power and control in the sense articulated by Foucault, that power is the ability to control how representations are used and which representations are used. Baudrillard sees "real" political struggle not, curiously, in the reality of raw experience and certainly not in simulation but in control of these street representations and the "immediate" interactions they represent: "the walls and their speech, the silk-screen posters and the hand-painted notices, the street where speech began and was exchanged—everything that was an *immediate* inscription, given and returned, spoken and answered, mobile in the same space and time, reciprocal and antagonistic" (*For*, 176). John Fiske agrees with Foucault that power lies in representation, but notes that whereas for Foucault the power abides in a static structure, for him control over representations is always a site of struggle (4)—thus, for Fiske, change is central to the power of representations because it is constantly being tugged this way and that by competing forces. Fiske lists these ways in which discourse itself, representations, are a site of struggle: "the struggle to 'accent' a word or sign, that is, to turn the way it is spoken or used to particular social interests. . . . The struggle over the choice of word, image, and therefore discursive repertoire. . . . The struggle to recover the repressed or center the marginalized. . . . The struggle to disarticulate and rearticulate. . . . The struggle to gain access to public discourse in general or the media in particular—the struggle to make one's voice heard" (5–6). This struggle is "the processes of discursive contestation by which discourses work to repress, marginalize, and invalidate others; by which they struggle for audibility and for access to the technologies of social circulation; and by which they fight to promote and defend the interests of their respective social formations" (4).

The key epistemic challenge for representation is that technically it is so completely malleable, yet it is also assigned the social, moral task of re-presenting another order, usually reality, to the mind. Thus, representations and those who make them are held morally accountable. I am accountable for what representation I apply to the canine creature by my desk, whereas the dog itself is hardly accountable for its (permanent) reality. This accountability is entirely a matter of change-ability, for only if representations can be changed to be more or less "true"—and the rhetoric of representation holds that they can—can anyone be held morally accountable for changing or not changing them. Choice depends on change, and moral accountability depends on choice. In that sense, Virilio identifies "mediatization," or the imposition of representations between people and "brute physical force," as a kind of "moral force" (*Art*, 30).

The basis for accountability is what Baudrillard describes as "the dialectical capacity of representations as a visible and intelligible mediation of the Real. All of Western faith and good faith was engaged in this wager on representation: that a sign could exchange for meaning and that something could guarantee this exchange" (*Simulations*, 10). The standard for accountability in this view is fidelity to reality. As Slouka puts it, "reality has been and continues to be the great touchstone for the world's ethical systems" (13). Kenneth J. Gergen describes this standard as a referential theory of language, in which language is held accountable for its ability to reference reality (*Realities*, 276–78).

We clearly see the moral accountability of representations and representers in Slouka's complaint that "Increasingly removed from experience, overdependent on the representations of reality that come to us through television and the prime media, we seem more and more willing to put our trust in intermediaries who 're-present' the world to us. The problem with this is one of communication; intermediaries are notoriously unreliable" (1–2). Kendall Walton makes an interesting distinction between believing and imagining, and locates the former squarely in the camp of representation. But because it is a representation it is also held accountable, and the belief is thus "not free" to change at will: "Beliefs, unlike imaginings, are correct or incorrect. Belief aims at truth. What is true and only what is true is to be believed. We are not free to believe as we please. We are free to imagine as we please" (*Mimesis*, 39). Note the insistence on relative permanence in Walton's argument. He goes on to say that "what is crucial is not whether what the author writes is true but whether he *claims* truth for it" (77). To claim truth is not only to identify something explicitly as a representation but to accept accountability for it as well.

Representations occupy an unstable middle ground between permanence and change. Their ability to change instantly and easily is coupled with the epistemic task traditionally assigned to them of representing the world to the mind; if one assumes the world (reality) is permanent, then the ability of representations to change so easily creates a poignant moral accountability for those who use them. Putting representations in charge of epistemology is thus like putting an alcoholic to work at a bar—the responsibility is great at the same time that potential for failure is inherent. On the other hand, we have seen that because of the political and social power wielded by representations, there is struggle over their usage. Social interests that are already empowered will work to maintain the permanence of representations that underlie or naturalize their empowerment.

Simulation. As we have seen in earlier chapters, simulation is often understood as a situation in which signs do not refer beyond themselves, thus creating a closed, arepresentational system. Signs, which are the instruments of representation, no longer represent. They themselves become the stopping place of attention and importance. Another way to express that idea is to say that simulation is a situation in which there is no reality other than representations—or—in which representations are the only reality. Kenneth J. Gergen describes a simulational situation as one in which "the object of understanding has been absorbed into the world of representations" (*Saturated*, 122).

A closed world is disconnected from The World. Simulations are by definition outside the world of time and space; since they are "not real" they are not bound by reality's expectation of permanence. Simulations are free to change in ways constrained only by technology and imagination. Virilio points to simulation's disconnection from reality when he argues that "cyberspace is a new form of perspective" in that it "does not coincide with the audio-visual perspective which we already know" from living in a material world of reality ("Speed," 1). Douglas Rushkoff describes simulation as "a world free of time, location, or even a personal identity" (37). Negroponte describes "digital neighborhoods" in similar terms, as worlds "in which physical space will be irrelevant and time will play a different role" (7).

Simulation cut loose from reality is a world of complete malleability in which, as Slouka says, "individual identity, physical space, reality itself, had turned plastic and malleable, mere constructs we might choose to buy into, or reinterpret, or discard altogether—as we saw fit" (26–27). The determinant of simulational change is human agency, what the person "sees fit" to do, not the changes of history or circumstance. Boorstin coined the useful concept of the "pseudo-event" to describe increasingly widespread practices among the news media and publicity industry. A pseudo-event is simulational in that it is a repeatable, manufactured experience. A pseudo-event is also clearly manipulated in that it is planned rather than spontaneous, created for the purpose of being reported or reproduced, ambiguous in its relationship to any "underlying reality," and a self-fulfilling prophecy (11–12). Manipulation is key to all these characteristics, demonstrating the centrality of change in simulation.

When one speaks of representations in a world that contains reality, the technical changeability of representations is held in check by the moral accountability contained in the expectation that representations will re-present reality. Some measure of permanence comes to be expected of such representations. But when reality is representations, there is nothing outside of themselves that representations must match, or to which they must be true. The technical changeability of representations then reigns supreme. That is the world of simulation, where change is of the essence. A completely changeable world is described by the Critical Art Ensemble as "the age of the recombinant: recombinant bodies, recombinant gender, recombinant texts, recombinant culture" (339). The recombinant is above all the changeable.

A simulational world is a relativistic world in which, as Kendall Walton notes, truth and reality are conventionally determined (*Mimesis*, 99). Any continuity in a relativistic world comes not from the bedrock permanence of reality but from social conventions. As Gergen argues, "The degree to which a given account of world or self is sustained across time is not dependent on the objective validity of the account but on the vicissitudes of social process" (*Realities*, 51), and social process means changeability. What happens within one simulation is relevant, especially in a moral sense, only to that simulation precisely because change is of the essence in simulation. Values and presumptions do not hold steady from one simulation to another. What is paramount in one simulation is to plunder a tomb; in another, to outrace an opponent; in a third, to inflict horrific violence. One could even imagine a simulation that valorized Christian charity—but only within that particular game. Slouka notes, and objects to, the relativizing of history and of self that comes from a simulational culture (34–35). As the anchor of reality rusts away and changeability reigns supreme, Gergen argues that a sense of the self becomes relativized as well: "As we begin to incorporate the dispositions of the varied others to whom we are exposed, we become capable of taking their positions, adopting their attitudes, talking their language, playing their roles. In effect, one's self becomes populated with others. The result is a steadily accumulating sense of doubt in the objectivity of any position one holds" (*Saturated*, 85). That "doubt" is the seedbed of relativism.

Key to the changeability of simulation is its grounding in technologies that allow the world to be changed. John Beckmann notes that "technology has always evoked new representations of reality" (12), and in a culture of simulation those representations outstrip reality, overrunning their referential function in their technical excellence. Boorstin for instance blames the rise of the "pseudo-event" on the *ability* to create them and the demand of new media for always-new content (14). That observation bespeaks signs that are of such high quality that they are no longer taken to be representations, mere sounds or stick figures, but can easily be confused for any reality that they might otherwise represent. Victor J. Vitanza observes that virtual reality "is a matter of technology that can create the illusion of actually being in another possible world" (3). That observation also bespeaks a technical ability to manipulate those signs at will. Simulation, in other words, depends on very good special effects. As Michael Heim notes, "Virtual reality is an immersive, interactive system based on computable information" (*Virtual*, 6), and he is clear that "the decisive factor in VR technology is the computer that handles the data (8).

The importance of technology in creating a highly manipulable simulation is noted by many scholars. Massimo Negrotti argues that the artificial is always technological, and keys simulation's reproductive prowess to the power of artificial construction (19). He argues, "The artificial is arguably related to technology. . . . [T]he art of constructing, or the ability to modify, nature becomes the art of reproducing it" (2). Paul Virilio compares the experience of a play versus that of the film, and identifies the cinematic technology as the device that enrolls the audience together into the same experience (*Art*, 8). As film becomes more simulational by making that shared experience more encompassing, it will be technology that drives the change.

Slouka traces the beginnings of increasing fascination with images and simulation to the beginning of the twentieth century (2), when emerging "technology . . . was the real force behind our journey toward abstraction" (3). For Slouka, the shared reality of "human culture depends on the shared evidence of the senses" whereas "a technology designed to short-circuit the senses . . . would take away this common ground and replace it with one manufactured for us by the technologists" (12–13). He grounds cyberspace in what he calls "technological absolutism" (21), which is paradoxical since it is precisely the changeability and mutability of technology that makes cyberspace possible.

We saw earlier how the body is a site of unchangeable material reality. In simulation, technology trumps the body. Mike Featherstone and Roger Burrows note in contrast that "the development of technology . . . offers the ultimate possibility of the displacement of the material body from the confines of its immediate lived space" into cyberspace (2). Baudrillard agrees in arguing that in a simulational culture the body disappears in relationship to code and the brains that process it (*Ecstasy*, 18-19). Personal memory likewise is made fluid by technology, as in Rene

Berger's comment that "today television is leading us to develop 'volatile memory' " (3).

Digital technologies based on information are especially generative of experiences removed from the material. A number of observers connect the rise of simulation in postmodern culture to the rise of digital technology. Signs and images can in principle be created that are so good they are indistinguishable from any reality to which they might refer. Such signs are taken as reality, and thus become simulational. Negroponte notes the measure of control that digital technology gives to the public as ordinary consumers of signs: "Being digital will change the nature of mass media from a process of pushing bits at people to one of allowing people (or their computers) to pull at them" (84). As Katherine Hayles argues, "The great dream and promise of information is that it can be free from the material constraints that govern the mortal world" (13). Virilio likewise notes the connection between developing technologies and shifts away from materiality: "With the telegraph, distances and territorial boundaries evaporate; with real-time technologies, real presence bites the dust" (*Art*, 57). Negroponte also argues that computers allow the reorganization of time (167–71). If it is true, as John Beckmann argues, that "we have already gone virtual" then "the limits of the physical realm have been eclipsed by the digital" (4). The digital technology removes simulation from the physical context of reality, as Margaret Wertheim argues: "cyberspace is outside the physical complex of matter-space-time that since the late seventeenth century has increasingly been held as not just the basis of reality, but as the totality of the real" (47).

Simulation comes about from a refusal of dualism; distinct categories of mind and reality no longer work. It is in that sense that Gunkel says that virtual reality challenges "the metaphysics of representation" (51). Baudrillard agrees: "This representational imaginary . . . disappears with simulation. . . . With it goes all of metaphysics. No more mirror of being and appearances, of the real and its concept" (*Simulations*, 3). Slouka explicitly uses the dualist language of "in here" and "out there" to locate simulation beyond that choice: "When you entered a cyberspace community . . . you were neither in nor out, here nor there, within the private world nor out in the public realm, entirely present (in real life) nor entirely absent" (50). This collapse of dualism occurs precisely because simulation depends on a shift in how representation works. When representations are no longer tasked with linking mind and world, when they become the closed world of simulation, dualism is no longer tenable.

The disenfranchisement of representation is a consequence of recent social and philosophical movements summed up by Gergen: "These movements—sometimes labeled post-empiricist, poststructural, or postmodern—no longer seek a rationale for precisely linking word with world. Rather, in each case the arguments raise a more fundamental challenge to the assumption that language can depict, mirror, contain, convey, or store objective knowledge" (*Realities*, 33). Postmodernity creates an arepresentational view of language, says Gergen: "language is not 'about the world'; it is not a simulacrum of reality, a mirror or a map. It operates according to an inner logic of its own, according to its own inventions"

(*Saturated*, 107). Gergen's statement that language is not a simulacrum of reality does not deny that it is ever a simulation, in our terms here; he simply wants to deny that it represents reality. Thus, "words are not mirrorlike reflections of reality, but expressions of group conventions" (*Saturated*, 119). What is conventional is changeable. When a simulational world leads one to deny dualism, then "reality" becomes a consequence of the conventions one follows. Gergen notes that "in the postmodern world we become increasingly aware that the objects about which we speak are not so much 'in the world' as they are products of perspective" (*Saturated*, 7). Baudrillard likewise grounds the rise of simulation in a postmodern collapse of referentiality in representation: "the age of simulation thus begins with a liquidation of all referentials—worse: by their artificial resurrection in systems of signs, a more ductile material than meaning, in that it lends itself to all systems of equivalence" (*Simulations*, 4). Note that Baudrillard uses a rhetoric of change twice, referring to the "liquidation" of reference ("meaning") in a shift to a system of mere, "ductile" signs.

As a product of postmodernity, simulation refuses the task of representation. Some, such as Danto, argue that simulational experiences such as art use representations but that such signs "play a role in the work as a whole that is not exhausted by their representational role" (13). In other words, a character in a play may ask, "Is this a dagger I see before me?" but the term *dagger* has a role to play in creating the simulation that goes beyond mere reference to a real weapon. Others argue more strongly that within simulation, it makes no sense to ask what is true or false, although the whole project of simulation itself may be attacked as untrue. Boorstin sees that the amoral "language of images" has replaced the moral, ethical "language of ideals" in an increasingly simulational culture (183). Images especially lend themselves to simulation over representation. This is because, as Boorstin says, "there is no way to unmask an image" (194); note the dualist tension in his desire to find out what an image really and truly is, or represents, which would be the result of "unmasking."

Of course, someone who insists on a dualist world in which representations are held accountable for re-presenting the world will condemn the easy, unfettered changeability of simulation; thus Slouka freely uses terms such as "lies" and "lying" to describe simulation (123–24). Simulation is for him a world of "illusions" (121). Slouka finds simulation morally reprehensible because he insists on looking at it from a dualist perspective in which language is to represent the world faithfully. Determined realists will for that reason often look askance at simulation. The whole process of simulation itself is seen as lies and deceptions. Richard L. Dukes makes this argument in saying, "The game itself makes no truth claims. It does not assert anything about some referent system. . . . On the other hand, real definitions make truth claims. They assert something about the referent" (7). This is the situation today, Boorstin complains, in which "the broadest of the old distinctions which no longer serve us as they did is the distinction between 'true' and 'false' " (213).

Boorstin condemns simulation because it collapses a distinction between a representation such as an image and reality: "An illusion . . . is an image we have mistaken for reality" (239). Paul Virilio likewise calls cyberspace "a synthetic illusion" (*Art*, 152). Richard Thieme complains that "without correlation with other data, no digital photo or document can be taken at face value. There's no way to know if we're looking at a copy of an original, a copy of a copy, or a copy that has no original" (50). Thieme means that an image, say on the Internet or in a newspaper, cannot be taken to be representational because we do not know its provenance. Contrary to his wording, that is precisely why such images can be taken *only* at face value rather than as a representation of a reality.

Complaints about the amorality of simulation come in many forms. Note the strong condemnation in David Gunkel's claim that "no matter how useful or perfect the VR representation is, it is still an imitation and, as such, necessarily remains a counterfeit and illusion. . . . [A] copy, no matter how useful or beneficial, is misleading and, therefore, essentially dangerous and potentially corrupt" (48). Fiske complains that "Baudrillard's theory of hyperreality and the simulacrum lacks a dimension that I consider crucial, that of struggle" (3). By that he means that Baudrillard's understanding of simulation has no place for struggle over what simulations are to be—a dimension that would presumably be found in reality, with its material constraints. For his part, Baudrillard sees a simulational age as "the era of non-response—of irresponsibility" (*For*, 170–71). John Adkins Richardson seconds that concern for lack of engagement by complaining that we live in an age of "spectatorial detachment from reality" which is "an ultimate form of estraingement" (182). Baudrillard refers moralistically to "the murderous capacity of images, murderers of the real" (*Simulations*, 10). Baudrillard's complaints about simulation are sometimes lodged specifically against the changeability it imposes upon everything in its purview, as when he refers to the endless copying characteristic of simulation: "Reproduction is diabolical in its very essence; it makes something fundamental vacillate" (*Simulations*, 153). Gergen complains that "it becomes increasingly difficult to distinguish between sincerity and simulation" (*Saturated*, 225), and note that sincerity is a term keyed to a dualist, representational model: one's smile is sincere if it represents a reality of friendliness.

The utter changeability of simulation makes it on the one hand a site of control and mastery, for there is little beyond technical constraints to keep one from changing and mastering the simulational world. Deborah Lupton argues that cyborgs and computers have often been seen as male because they are a site of control and mastery. Consider the simulational character of cyborgs and computers; they are or they create their own world on their own terms. Helmreich likewise calls attention to the centrality of control in simulations in his study of computer scientists: "One man reflected self-consciously that he built simulations because he wanted to get away from a world that felt difficult to control" (70). Among these scientists, "describing programmers as a genus of god was a frequent strategy. . . . This move permits programmers to have the same relation to their simulations as the God of monotheism has to His creation" (84). An imperialist image is used in addition to a theist metaphor, for Helmreich also reports that computer simulations are seen as colonial spaces, new frontiers for starting the world over again (92–96). The rhetoric of simulation in Helmreich's examples bespeaks the central of change, which nests within a rhetoric of control. One has control precisely of that which one can change. Stephen Perrella seconds this view in arguing that "the virtual dimension may be understood as an immanent manifestation of instrumental reason in late-Western culture. . . . [T]he virtual dimension unfolds as an escaped mutation of the State, whose tacit mandate includes military dominance, technological mastery over nature, and the pursuit of social progress" (235), the mastery of all of which can be obtained very easily within simulation. The easy manipulation of simulation especially leads to power when simulations comment on or seem an alternative to reality. Gunkel points out that "the duality opposing the real and the true to its other, the imitation or copy, is fundamentally a political matter. . . . The imitative arts and media have always been recognized as posing alternatives that threaten and promise to alter the status quo" (58).

If simulations give total control over their created worlds on the one hand, on the other they give very little control and mastery precisely because that world is "not real." The rhetoric of simulation is the rhetoric of a kingdom within a teacup, and whether simulation means power or lack of power depends on the size of the cup. Control over cyberspace is total but without excitement or substance, complains Ted Gup (250–53). Slouka sees cyberspace as without consequences (54), "a world without risk" and hence as an "ethical vacuum" (22). If one can kill an opponent repeatedly and yet the opponent springs up anew with each new video game, what happens to the moral implications of killing? Kendall Walton likewise notes that "there is a price to pay in real life when the bad guys win. . . . Make-believe provides the experience . . . for free" (*Mimesis*, 68), which means that there is no accountability for whether the "bad" or the "good" guys win. Featherstone and Burrows argue that understanding reality by studying simulational models is a false hope, for "the danger is that it merely continues the dream of reason, with its quest for total control, order, and pure unsullied communication" (16); note that for them, it is a "mere" control over a fantasy world. Anne Balsamo describes that control as illusory: "What these VR encounters really provide is an illusion of control over reality, nature, and especially, over the unruly, gender and race-marked, essentially mortal body" (229).

Baudrillard finds simulation wanting in that it misses the give and take of real human conflict: "a *simulation model* of communication . . . excludes, from its inception, the reciprocity and antagonism of interlocutors. . . . What really circulates is information, a semantic content that is assumed to be legible and univocal" (*For*, 179). Because real exchange is missing, who the characters in a simulation are or what they do becomes unimportant: "At this point it makes no difference at all what the parties in power are expressing historically and socially. It is necessary even that they represent nothing: the fascination of the game, the polls, the formal and statistical compulsion of the game is all the greater" (*Simulations*, 132). If simulations do not present us with real people, we are not responsible for what we do to and with them; nobody will complain if I rip the spine out of a video game opponent for a lark. Simulation in that view is too changeable; my opponent can be reborn with the press of a button; hence, I cannot be blamed for my actions.

Rhetoric and art have traditionally shared a preoccupation with using manipulable materials to create a self-contained world built of appearances. Rene Berger describes simulation's manipulation of appearances from a representational bias when he argues that

[T]he term simulation had long designated, and exclusively so, the *disguising* of an act under the appearances of another, in other words causing something that is not real to seem so. . . . The "pretense" attached to the notion of simulation thus implies that there is "true" behavior and then other behavior that, although not "false," is but a travesty of the former. Such a distinction then produced a value judgment that gave negative connotations to simulation. (14)

The changeability of simulation thus shifts it from the world of moral accountability in representations to a playful, ludic world of art or of rhetoric. If one does not expect the signs that make up a discourse or a world to mirror some reality, then the model of "narrative rationality" which modernist dualism imposes upon discourse breaks down (Gergen, *Saturated*, 132). Frances Dyson notes the shift to rhetoric as a master discourse in simulation: "the 'ontology' of cyberspace does not imply the being of some thing or another, rather it signals the attempts to assign being as an attribute to these new forms of media and communications. It signals, in other words, a rhetorical maneuver" (28). Slouka likewise notes, although disapprovingly, that "in America, reality's domain was always under siege, its power continually undermined by a people uncommonly good not only at manufacturing illusions but at believing in them," and he calls that process of creating illusions "rhetoric" (110).

Others note that a simulational world is an aesthetic one, in which the pursuit of sensual pleasure rules. Heim makes this argument: "Perhaps the essence of VR ultimately lies not in technology but in art, perhaps art of the highest order. Rather than control or escape or entertain or communicate, the ultimate promise of VR may be to transform, to redeem our awareness of reality—something that the highest art has attempted to do" ("Essence," 31). Gabler argues that "the deliberate application of the techniques of theater to politics, religion, education, literature, commerce, warfare, crime, *everything*, has converted them into branches of show business, where the overriding objective is getting and satisfying an audience" (5). The world of the movies is explicitly simulational, described by Gabler as shifting the audience out of reality: "the movies played in our heads and seemed to replicate our own consciousness. Conspiring with the dark, they cast a spell that lulled one from his own reality into theirs until the two merged" (50). Simulation is simply more aesthetically attractive than are reality and its representations. Baudrillard argues that simulation destroys truth in favor of beauty: "*There is no truth of the object, and denotation is never more than the most beautiful of connotations*" (*For*, 196). As Boorstin argues, in the language of representation, "The pseudo-events which flood our consciousness are neither true nor false in the old familiar senses. The very same advances which have made them possible have also made the images—however planned, contrived, or distorted—more vivid, more attractive, more impressive, and more persuasive than reality itself" (36). Heim argues that cyberspace is replacing nature as an attractive place of manufactured adventure and wildness, for instance (*Virtual*, 143–72).

We have seen a complex structure of permanence and change in the rhetoric of our three key terms. Reality is all permanence and simulation is all change. Representation straddles the rickety fence of technical changeability and moral permanence. So when people speak our three terms, that is what they mean on the dimension of permanence and change.

COMMODIFICATION

Late capitalism brings to the foreground a structure of experience that has always been present in human life to one degree or another: commodification. When something is commodified it is regarded as a good thing or service, and especially as a good to be traded, bought, and sold in an open market. Commodities array themselves according to desirability on a template provided by a standard unit of value, which one might call currency. Cars, massages, opera tickets, and battleships all thus become connected by reduction to their common denominator, money. And all other things being equal (which they never are), it is presumably more desirable (or more pleasurable) to own a battleship than opera tickets because the ship costs more than do the tickets.

Desire or pleasure is the primary motive fueling commodification, and thus it is widely encouraged as a supreme value in capitalist societies. Such cultures are inundated by messages advising people to consult their own desires, their pursuit of pleasures, in making decisions to purchase. The pursuit of desire is generative of individualism. Capitalism encourages consumers to think in terms of what each desires instead of what is good for the group, the environment, the cosmos, and so forth. Richardson notes the centrality of individual desire in capitalism: "every culture touched by capitalism's fruits tends towards individualism" (180).

A widely used distinction may be useful in this section: use value as opposed to exchange value. Use value is the practical, material benefit one derives from a good or service. A hamburger has the use value of tasting good and being nutritious. An aircraft carrier has the use value of providing military defense. Exchange value is the ability of a good or service to function as a currency, a medium of trade. Money is the object with the greatest exchange value in capitalist societies. The distinction works in principle but in practice is often confounded. Although money primarily has exchange value, it does have some measure of use value: you can open the battery compartment on your camera with a quarter, and one can slide a dollar bill around between door and frame to check for binding. Hamburgers have exchange value for procuring that other kid's tuna sandwich at lunch, and the presence of an aircraft carrier can be exchanged for temporary deference to national purpose and prestige, hence gunboat diplomacy.

When we consider reality, representation, and simulation in terms of commodification, one important factor is to consider the degree of use value or exchange value assigned to each term or examples thereof. We will want to think of each of our three key terms as instruments or agents of desire or pleasure. The centrality of each term as objects of value and their role in economies will be our concern here.

Reality. Reality is spoken of largely in terms of use value. This is how we know we are dealing with reality, in that rhetoric: if you can eat it, sit on it, drive it around, or build a wall with it, you have a hunk of reality. Another way to put this is to say that reality is the same thing as a commodity. John Berger expresses this point of view in saying that capital "reduced everything to the equality of objects. Everything became exchangeable because everything became a commodity" (87). Note that the world, reality, is conceived of in Berger's term as commodities.

There is also a sense in which reality's use value varies in inverse proportion to its exchange value. To the extent you have something you could use as a medium of trade, it is probably less useful and *less real* than something you could not trade. Rhetorics of reality are therefore a little suspicious of exchange value and of the entities that acquire exchange value (which then edge closer to becoming representations, as we shall see later). A rhetoric of reality sees exchange value mainly in terms of its ability to get stuff, to accumulate reality.

Objects and experiences in reality have a singularity, an aura about them in Walter Benjamin's terms (217–52). Although many real commodities are mass produced, ownership and use of any given commodity invest it with a sense of singularity. The more real something is, the more it seems as if one can have it as a possession. How many of us would freely exchange a shirt we are wearing for one just like it? The request to do so would seem peculiar, whereas we honor requests to trade instruments of exchange value all the time: "Can you make change for a dollar?" Shirts tend to use value, dollars tend to exchange value. The mass produced object that we buy, having thus become a commodity with use value, becomes *our* mass produced commodity, it picks up some of what Benjamin called aura (although not as much aura as has a truly unique object, which would be a work of art in his analysis). Mass produced or widely copied objects without any aura at all move into the realm of representations, as we shall see later. Reality is at least in principle ownable, and the ability to own something and to wrap an aura, a sense of singularity, around that thing is likewise a mark of reality.

Representation. When considered on the dimension of commodities, representations are spoken of far more often in terms of exchange value than use value. One reason why this is true is that anything with exchange value is a representation. The more purely an entity functions as exchange value the more it represents. Roy Wagner calls our attention to the ways in which money has come to stand "in front of things" as representations of them, at the same time that it is largely exchange value: "If God . . . was somehow mysteriously *behind* things, ethereal and working in wondrous ways, then for modern Westerners money, and symbols too, are somehow mysteriously *in front* of things, too elemental for easy or ordinary comprehension" (3). It is through representations that we apprehend reality; note that Wagner gives to both money and symbols that referent function.

Dollar bills represent a unit of exchange. Although they have some shreds of use value, they are almost entirely representations. A new, one-hundred-dollar, designer label shirt represents sophistication, savoir vivre, and style (whether those characteristics are true of the wearer is no more or less relevant than is the truth of any other representation). One can exchange those meanings for acceptance, belonging, praise in social circles, and so forth. The shirt also has the use value of keeping the rain off of your back. A ten-dollar shirt on sale at Walmart has the same use value, but what it represents in terms of style, class, and so forth is much less clear. Hence, what sort of admiration and status one could get in exchange for wearing it is not clear. In other words, it is not clear what it represents, in the way that a designer shirt represents style and class. Where you have exchange value you find representations.

If anything with exchange value is a representation, it may also be said that anything that is a representation has exchange value. Language consists of signs that represent because they have exchange value, and have exchange value because they represent. We use words with the understanding that they will represent something other than their physical selves, and we exchange those representations for tangible goods and services and for other words. We exchange "please pass the salt" to procure a seasoning at breakfast. The words "I love you" represent a certain state of affairs, and we offer up their utterance in exchange for the same words in return, for love itself, for a hug, and so forth, unless the one to whom they are spoken is not taking that currency in trade today. Representation and exchange are not conceptually the same thing, but the one strongly implies the other. Representation and exchange value vary together.

Many representations began life as real objects with use value. Gold, cowrie shells, elephant tusks, and other means of exchange may have started as real objects with use value. John Berger tracks one route by which real commodities become representations when he notes that "publicity turns consumption into a substitute for democracy. The choice of what one eats (or wears or drives) take the place of significant political choice" (149)—in other words, the purchase of what was once simply a bicycle with practical use value becomes a representation of one's ecologically responsible political views, which one can then trade for strokes at the next Sierra Club meeting. Anne Norton observes that "any commodity may serve as a signifier of identity, status, and allegiance. It presents itself as a mere representation of the position it signifies, no more. Yet often the signifier acquires the independence of currency, functioning as if it had value in itself" (6), value here meaning exchange value. Norton also notes that objects move from reality to representation as they move from being the fruits of their labors to representing people: "Each product that a man creates represents him in the world. . . . [I]t is in the thing produced and, more importantly, in the act of labor that men see themselves in the external world. They recognize themselves in representation" (47–48).

But reality has the greater gravitational pull over representation here, and, even if a representation is sought long and hard enough for its exchange value, it will begin to be sought for its own sake, thus acquiring use value. This occurs as the result of fetishizing the means of exchange; they tend to become ends in themselves rather than purely means. Think of the whole baroque structure of finance in the United States (stocks, bonds, mutual funds, futures, and so forth) as pure exchange value and often at several levels of abstraction: you can't eat a mutual fund but you can cash it in for money which you can cash in for turnips. These means, these instruments of exchange, easily become ends. People study all day so as to amass bonds, several magazines are devoted to the worship of mutual funds, and all with very little attention paid to the use-value goods that one might get by exchanging those instruments. The financial means have become ends, and thus exchange value has slipped over to use value.

Beyond the monetary examples above, we see this process of exchange value erosion in, for instance, religious objects. The cross began as an actual real object with a horrible use value. It was turned by the church into a representation with the power to be exchanged for acceptance into a religious body, a devotional mood or attitude, protection against evil, and other goods. Yet the cross, like the flag, like an icon of a saint, like the picture of the king, is tending to become an end in itself, a stylish decoration, a vampire repellent, that which is traded for in monastery gift shops, that which is fought over for its own sake—not for what it represents or can obtain. The use value of reality pulls back toward itself eventually.

Erosion of a representation with exchange value into a reality with use value happens in other ongoing everyday experience. Michael J. Shapiro refers to the way we might "fetishize" a photograph, which is surely a common experience: the photograph that represents a loved one comes to be valued as an object in and of itself. Fetishization describes the ways in which any representation such as a flag slips into being a reality with use value, and comes to be desired and struggled over for its own sake.

Simulation. An experience that is spoken of as a simulation is in a peculiar and complex position in regard to commodification. A simulation is described as a system of signs without a reality that they represent. In the language of commodities, a simulation is a system of representations with exchange value that represent, and can be exchanged for, nothing but other representations with exchange value. A simulational economy is thus an *ecstatic* economy in Baudrillard's sense, who defines ecstasy as a reduction to one dimension, specifically such as exchange value: "Ecstasy is all functions abolished into one dimension" (*Ecstasy*, 23). When in ecstasy, one is lost in that one dimension, consumed by it.

One interesting site of ecstasy in today's economy is of course pornography, which is all over the simulational Internet. Norton notes that "the effective presence of erotica and pornography prove the ascendancy of representation" (126). Pornography goes beyond just representation, though; the viewer lost in pornography is in a simulational world of representations without referents. The images themselves are engrossing.

That engrossment is true for many other dimensions of economic life today. A culture that stares at the television or computer screen all day is in an ecstasy of images. As Baudrillard puts it, "*Images have become our true sex object,* the object of our desire. The obscenity of our culture resides in the confusion of desire and its equivalent materialized in the image" (*Ecstasy*, 35). Whether one is gazing at images of the naked body or streaming lists of stock quotations, one is adrift in representations desired for their own sakes, in the language of simulation. As Slouka complains, "we're retreating inside because the world outside our homes has less and less to offer us" (78). When Baudrillard thus says that *"We . . . are in the ecstasy of communication*. And this ecstasy is obscene. Obscene is that which eliminates the gaze, the image and every representation" (*Ecstasy*, 22), he means that images and representations no longer represent, the gaze is no longer directed toward a real other.

We have seen arguments earlier in this book that our culture is becoming increasingly simulational. That process may be understood as a result of late capitalism. To understand the role that the dimension of commodification plays in that process, we must first examine the argument that capitalism encourages a shift of public attention toward signs—and thus, toward representations primarily keyed to exchange value. Benjamin Woolley notes that with the collapse of the gold standard (a real metal that money used to represent), money becomes representations with referents, in other words, simulations: "The abandonment of the gold standard has turned money into a purely abstract quantity, a symbol. A deficit is no different from a surplus, except that the mathematical sign for one is a minus, for the other a plus" (16). Norton agrees in noting that "currency has moved, under the ascendancy of representation, from a representation of gold, and then of silver, which might at any time be exchanged for the material it signified, to an empty signifier" (24); Norton does not like the term simulation, but an empty signifier is precisely that. Woolley locates the economy today in simulation because cyberspace, a world of signs, is where "money" is circulated: "Perhaps cyberspace, then, is—literally—where the money is. Perhaps it is also the place where events increasingly happen, where our lives and fates are increasingly determined; a place that has a very direct impact on our material circumstances" (16). Note Woolley's equation of a simulational culture with late capitalism's increasingly abstract representations of exchange value. Hayles refers to the reduction of all experience, even our bodies, to the forms of information, which are of the order of representations. She notes the role that capital plays in a simulational culture by arguing that "an information society is the purest form of capitalism. When bodies are constituted as information, they can be not only sold but fundamentally reconstituted in response to market pressures" (42). Of course, Hayles's observation applies equally well to our earlier discussion of pornography.

Baudrillard (bitterly) identifies capitalism as the driving force behind the destruction of referents common to simulation:

Hyperreality and simulation are deterrents of every principle and of every objective; they turn against power this deterrence which it so well utilized for a long time itself. For, finally, it was capital which was the first to feed throughout its history on the destruction of every referential, of every human goal, which shattered every ideal distinction between true and false, good and evil, in order to establish a radical law of equivalence and exchange, the iron law of its power. (*Simulations*, 43)

He is arguing that capital overreached itself: it turned everything into representation so that only the Grand Representation, money, would matter—but then found that a world of simulation can undermine the "real" power of capitalism. One response, which makes the world even more simulational, is to capitalize the world of representations: "We know that now it is on the level of reproduction (fashion, media, publicity, information and communication networks) . . . that is to say in the sphere of simulacra and of the code, that the global process of capital is founded" (*Simulations*, 99). In a practical sense, the trading of representations in an "information economy" is as important as or more important than the trading of iron, cars, or corn.

The information economy involves trading representations (money) to get back more representations (information). The entertainment sector of that economy involves giving up signs (money) so as to get signs (movies) in return. Slouka envisions a simulational world in which everything is commodified but also in which everything is artificial. In the world of cyberspace that is built only of signs, he argues, "As more of the hours of our days are spent in synthetic environments, partaking of man-made pleasures, life itself is turned into a commodity. Someone makes it for us; we buy it from them" (75). Boorstin describes this entertainment economy as the demand for illusions: "By harboring, nourishing, and ever enlarging our extravagant expectations we create the demand for the illusions with which we deceive ourselves"—nor is this a minor enterprise, but instead, "the making of the illusions which flood our experience has become the business of America" (5). Boorstin gives the examples of heroes as marketable commodities (48–49); but the truth of that observation depends on heroes becoming pure representations. Many of our entertaining heroes are in fact heroic only as screen actors whose deeds on camera, like John Wayne's, reflect no actual experience in the reality of war or the Western prairies. Another example of entertainment cited by Boorstin is travel, in which one travels so as to travel, so as to say that one has done it, rather than to engage the reality of any destination (85). So one might "go to Jamaica" or "spend a week in Cancun" and never leave a fantasy world of signs constructed around a resort.

A number of scholars describe the economy that results from these forces as an economy of signs, in which representations are exchanged with little regard for their real referents. Recall that in the language of representations, signs have some tendency to shift back toward reality, to acquire use value. But a simulational economy has broken signs free from reality; in this discourse one may become entranced by the signs themselves, but as in the world of a video game there is no "real" use to these signs because they are spoken of as simulational. The gravity of reality is broken in simulation as signs float into space. Baudrillard writes of "the political economy of the sign" which "institutes a certain mode of signification in which all the surrounding signs act as simple elements in a logical calculus and refer to each other within the framework of the system of sign exchange value" (*For*, 191). Such an economy would allow the exchange of signs with no thought as to their grounding in reality. As Hayles argues, "a defining characteristic of the present cultural moment is the belief that information can circulate unchanged among different material substrates" (1–2).

A resultant economy of signs would be one in which use value is subordinated to exchange value. We examine aesthetics in greater detail in the next chapter, but note that in an economy of simulational signs, art is no longer derivative, no longer a representation of reality, it is as real or unreal as anything else. Art becomes of the same order as wheat, cloth, or chicken.

Hence, a simulational culture is an aestheticized culture, engrossed by style. In such an economy, as Hal Foster argues, "use value is now largely a projection of exchange value [and] both are now largely subsumed by sign exchange value—and . . . *in this logic art works are no different than vacuum cleaners or basketball shoes*" (96–99), all of them being signs. Allucquere Rosanne Stone supports Foster's reasoning in noting the radical commodication of art in today's economy (18), and claims that "industrialization meant . . . a threat of the collapse of art's special status into a fetish or a commodity" (32). Stone notes that although capital turns everything into a commodity (with a use value), it deflects attention away from a thing's usefulness (otherwise, why would we have twenty pairs of shoes each?), which of course turns art into a sign with less connection to reality and to real usage (35). Of course, one way in which art is commodified is to reproduce it; as Benjamin argued, mechanical reproduction of art destroys its singularity and aura as an object and, as others have argued, moves it toward status as a representation within a simulation.

The idea of potentially infinite reproducibility is key to the idea of simulation, as we saw in earlier chapters. Reproducibility is also key to capitalism and commodification, in several senses. Currency is a representation that can be reproduced potentially infinitely, the only danger being inflation—dollars may be printed as fast as the presses may go. Commodities themselves are infinitely reproducible, the only constraint being raw materials.

The industrial process that is key to capitalism likewise requires infinite reproducibility of workers, machines, and processes, a reproduction that, as Frances Dyson notes in speaking of commerce on television and the Internet, overrides personal or cultural characteristics: "Cultural difference is absorbed, and an intense uniformity is produced via the rigorous programming that commercial interests demand" (29). Note also the destruction of the unique reality in simulational reproduction in Fiske's comment that "it is hard to conceive of a more convincing evidence of postmodernity than an automatic pen, for in destroying the direct relationship between a signature and an individual, it destroys a centuries-old guarantor of the final truth. When a signature is a simulacrum, postmodernity is rampant" (144). Note that Fiske describes a move from a signature that represents the reality of a signer to a signature that is an empty signature precisely because its reproducibility removes it from the authentic, real original. Such a signature is the embodiment of what Slouka called "the dream of the perfect fake, the undetectable forger" (109). He sees it as part of a larger process of "the general breakdown of the barrier separating original from simulation, fact from fake, [which] is visible everywhere; the slow bleeding of reality into illusion is systematic" (128).

One important dimension of the link between simulation and capital is the increasing presence of advertising in our lives, not just as representatives of products one can buy but as part of the visual and cognitive landscape. Advertising is also among the most widely experienced forms of art today. We experience advertising as systems of signs in an often closed simulational loop. Several magazines founded on aesthetic principles (e.g., *Architectural Digest* or *GQ*) are perused largely for their artistic advertisements. Thus Virilio notes, "Closely tied in with state propaganda . . . advertising certainly managed to saturate all spheres of power without fear or favor, from sport to science, philosophy, ethics, culture, humanitarian aid. . . . This is a population in which each individual is subjected on average to more than fifteen hundred ads a day in explicit, hidden, or subliminal form" (*Art*, 15), hence, "over the years the whale of television production has been gradually sliding into this *intermediate zone* governed exclusively by economic constraints" (16). Television and every other medium of communication have thus become saturated with capitalist advertising, in other words. When it is hard to separate what is meant to entertain us from what is meant to entice us to buy, then as Gabler put it, "entertainment and consumption were often two sides of the same ideological coin" (205), an ideology of capitalism.

We have seen in this chapter how dimensions of life likely to be felt as external structures are spoken of in terms of reality, representation, and simulation. Specifically we have examined the two dimensions of *permanence and change* and of *commodification*. How one experiences the changeability of the world, what one thinks of the value of things and experiences in the world, thus changes according to which key term one uses. A distinction between external and internal, objective and subjective, is artificial and clearly dualist—but with those reservations in mind, let us now proceed to two subjective dimensions of lived experience to further enrich our understanding of how reality, representation, and simulation are used rhetorically.

Chapter 4

Reality, Representation, and Simulation in Lived Experience

Many dimensions of lived experience are likely to be felt as personal, internal, and subjective. The two dimensions examined in this chapter are *subjectivity* and *aesthetics*. Whereas we may feel that permanence and change and the structures of commodification do not originate with us personally, and come from "outside" as imposed structures of experience, many people will feel as if the nature of the person as subject and as if aesthetic feelings are more personal and "inside" the self. Subjectivity and aesthetics are ways in which we experience cognitive and emotional centeredness, continuity, authenticity—or their opposites. The entirely artificial distinction between the internal and external continues in this chapter, then, with a discussion of how our three key terms of reality, representation, and simulation are expressed in terms of *subjectivity* and *aesthetics*.

SUBJECTIVITY

What does it mean to be a person, a subject? How do answers to that question change when one considers the subject as composed of or as comprising reality, representation, or simulation? Have different eras or do different types of societies tend to create people as real, as representations, or as simulations more than do others? When we say that we are experiencing reality, representation, or simulation, what are we saying about ourselves, about our experience of being a person? How does such a claim affect what we are claiming about ourselves? These are some of the key issues we explore in this section.

Reality. The "real" subject, or the person living in reality, is stable, essential, and immutable. The sense of personhood as a durable, centered locus of consciousness is the subject as it emerges in a rhetoric of reality. The physical body grounds this centeredness and marks the boundaries of the subject, however much it may be socially connected.

What marks the real subject varies from one era and society to another. Perhaps the clearest descriptor of its manifestation in modern, Western societies has been the often-used term, the *centered subject*. Centeredness means a stability of personality, consciousness, orientation, and motive in the individual subject despite the competing roles and characters we are called on to play in our shifting contexts. A real subject maintains the same core and awareness of a core in these shifting contexts. The subject is centered because real, and centeredness is validation of that reality.

A mark of the real subject is agency: the real subject is an origin of intention and motive. Real subjects may be hard pressed and sorely constrained, but the power of decision making originates and remains in them. Gergen notes that modern beliefs about the self make it the site of "beliefs, opinions, and conscious intentions" (*Saturated*, 6). This is how real subjects may be distinguished from representational or simulational subjects, who are made up or programmed by real agents. Pinocchio is not real until he decides for himself and originates moral action.

Real subjects partake of the kinds of permanence we observed in the previous chapter. They are predictable because empirical, but not always predicted as sources of decisions. Real people are complex and multidimensional. The difference between real people I know and characters in a video game is that the characters are unidimensional, drearily predictable, and transient, coming and going at each push of the reset button, but real subjects retain a core subjectivity that is not redefined relative to the moment.

Since the real features the physical, the real subject is grounded in the body. Alice, Jose, and Chan are each understood as the person housed in that body over there. The subject is understood to be the ghost in the machine, the consciousness inhabiting that body. The rhetoric of reality thus uses the material body as a locator for the subject. Some rhetorics of reality are spiritual and imagine an imperishable subject within the body, others are obdurately material and equate the subject with the operations of the brain within the body. Both views use a rhetoric of reality to describe the body, although with varying degrees of dualism. The more single-mindedly materialist the less likely is the view of a real subject to be dualist as well, as self and material collapse into one another.

Stone calls attention to the widely used "framework of the individual's self awareness in relation to a physical body. It is by means of this framework that we put in place the 'I' without whose coupling to a physical body there can be no race or gender, no discourse, no structure of meaning" (85). The rhetoric to which Stone alludes here makes race, gender, and other descriptors a matter of physical reality rather than social construction, and it thus calcifies those descriptors. The real subject is thus also really male or female, really Asian or African American, and so forth.

A centered, real subject has definite social roles to fulfill, but remains the same subject from role to role. Since the subject is stable, so are the roles, and so by extension is the social collective (although the effect is more attenuated the larger the group). The stability of the group nurtures the stable subject and vice versa. Slouka argues that traditionally in the West, "social roles had always been bound and kept in check by the constraints and limitations of the physical world. And this allowed, in most cases, for the development of a relatively uniform ego. Take away those boundaries . . . and the ego could refract wildly and at will" (60). Slouka is clearly speaking with approval of the stable subject, and just as clearly that stability is grounded in a rhetoric of reality through his reference to the physical world.

Although the real subject has social roles, in any choice between subject and society the subject is taken to be primary. Slouka fears for loss of the authentic individual as society becomes more simulational (93), and argues that people are at their best as real, unmediated individuals (104). As Gergen put it, "In Western culture the individual has long occupied a place of commanding importance" (*Realities*, 3). A rhetoric of reality sees the social as derived from contracts and covenants made by individuals coming together.

The nature of that social contract and the role of the individual within it is taken to have a "natural" manifestation. Sometimes the "natural" way to be is conceived of as monarchical or fascistic; the subject is "naturally" part of a state, in need of absolute leadership, and so forth. Others argue that democracy is the natural state for the real subject, and that democracy is grounded in a stable, physical reality. So Slouka argues that "unmediated reality . . . is a profoundly democratic thing; we experience the world . . . in subtly different ways, and this diversity is both the foundation of our independence and a bulwark against authoritarianism" (148). As we noted in our discussion of permanence, this prominence of democratic diversity is attenuated by the authoritarianism implied in a claim of material reality.

The real self is a mainstay of traditional capitalism. Capitalism depends on desire as a prime motive; consumers are to consult their own needs and preferences rather than those of a group, ecological concerns, spiritual requirements, or other bases for decisions. Capitalism depends on individualism: the real self as an origin of decisions generates the process of buying or selling. There is often a further implication that real selves, needing to feed, clothe, and shelter material bodies, primarily seek real goods with use value.

Representation. There are several senses in which one might see the self, or one's subjectivity, in terms of representation. One can see oneself as composed of representations. This is the sense in which the self is a tapestry of images and discourses, of memory unifying our many real experiences. One can be concerned with the representations of self and with the idea that whatever one's own "reality," what others see in us is representational. This is the sense in which we are concerned about our image, about the self as a text or set of signs that generate meanings for self and others. One can see oneself as a representative of something: of a nation, a demographic group, and so forth. This is the sense in which we remind our debate teams that while on the road they represent the University of Texas.

Gergen defines the self as "that process by which the person conceptualizes (or categorizes) his behavior—both his external conduct and his internal states" and structurally the self is "the system of concepts available to the person in attempting to define himself" (*Concept*, 22–23). Gergen's definition is remarkably representational. The self is not located in the body or in feelings or in kinesthetic awareness but in concepts, categories, and their systematic use, which are representative of internal states and of behavior. Norton likewise points to the role of representations in creating a subjectivity, for "representation is not merely a form of governance, it is also the means we use to create ourselves in a new world order" (3).

The self composed of representations is a connected network of memories: I am the one who went to Europe, who broke my leg, who fell in love. Those memories are encoded in the representations of image, text, and story that stand for the real things that happened to us. The self is not so much the real thing as a structure of representations of the real thing. Our selves in this sense are documentaries (not cinematic fantasies, for that would be simulational) of our own histories. The sense in which knowledge depends on and is encoded in representations discussed in the previous chapter expresses this kind of representational self.

Since the self is constructed of representations in a social context, the subject is also validated, confirmed, and identified through those representations. Norton argues that "the American reliance on representation as a form of authority extends beyond political institutions and into popular practices. Americans give the nation written form in the Constitution. They give themselves a written form in practice" which then represents each self (3). Representation thus becomes a confirmation of the self; we are subjects because of the practices that represent us; we are a nation because, look! we have a Constitution that defines us.

The idea of subject as achieving form through representations in social space may be especially true in cyberspace. Although cyberspace is often taken to be the site of simulation, anyone who has ever participated in a chat room or a newsgroup knows the extent to which the self becomes present to others only through representations. The subject in cyberspace is often an image constructed for others, which we consider later. Here I mean a subject constructed for ourselves and for our selves: a way to *be* in electronic space. Featherstone and Burrows note that "technologies . . . promise, literally, a new world in which we can *represent* our bodies with a greater degree of flexibility" (5), and the chief technology they cite is that which creates cyberspace: "with the potential development of the parallel world of cyberspace, the range of ways in which one can represent one's embodied subjectivity becomes much more carried and flexible" (12). Their usage here treats cyberspace as representative of a real subject, and highlights the flexibility that digital technology gives us in how we are represented. But the self that is constructed is representational, since our cyberspace fellows have no other access to us (as real selves).

So we have seen that one kind of representational subject sees the self as constructed of representations. Even if socially validated, such a subject is primarily personal. The stability of such a subject depends on the stability of the representations, which can be affirmed or subverted by our social contexts. One's fond memories of childhood may be undermined (and thus the subject is undermined) by family members' claims that "it never happened that way."

Another kind of representational subject brackets off the question of the real self. This subjectivity is the image of the self we construct for rhetorical effect in society. Representations are how we come before others. This has historically been seen as a function of language, which is how we represent our inner selves, our subjectivities, our minds, to others.

The image we construct of ourselves is subject to the same moral accountability we noted for linguistic representations in the previous chapter. Gergen notes that historically, "the problem of how people understand each other and the world about them once seemed relatively clear. Language expresses ideas and sentiments, it was held; to understand language is to understand the mind of the speaker" (*Saturated*, 81–82). Language gives "knowledgeable accounts of the world (including ourselves)" in Gergen's view (*Realities*, viii–ix). If it fails in that task, then we are taxed with misrepresenting ourselves.

Dyson notes that "subjectivity is performed as a new kind of text while the body becomes a permeable surface, adorned with signs and riddled with the inscriptions and prescriptions of culture" (30). Those signs and performances add up to the "text" of subjectivity presented on display to the world. Norton uses similar language to Dyson's in arguing that "Representation alters not only what we read but what we are. The body itself, the literary locus of acts, sensations, and tastes, becomes an inscribed surface, a written text" (127)—in other words, a self composed of representations offered up to others.

Representation of self is fundamentally social: we use socially held signs to show ourselves to others and we represent only because there are others in whose society we would find a place. We also use representations to understand how the world appears to others; we represent others to ourselves and thus build social bonds. The social cohesion at stake from self representation raises questions of true or false self display, with moral consequences. Virilio argues that

We have the . . . ability to distinguish between what we think is real and therefore true, and what another individual might consider real and true. Through language (gesture, vocal, graphic), this secondary ability allows us to *put ourselves in the other person's place, to see with his or her eyes,* to take advantage of his or her optical system . . . to *re-present* to ourselves people and objects we cannot see or cannot yet see, and to finally act accordingly. (*Art*, 7)

Gergen sees essential similarity between the formal theater and the role playing we engage in during everyday life, in which language, gesture, and other signs represent our selves to others. The raw subject has no traction with other people in social situations; instead, it must be couched in representational terms that fit with the social discourses in which others move. The representational self considered in social contexts is therefore sort of half in and half out of the physical body; representations are discursive, but reference the real individual. Stone describes this situation in terms of social apprehension: "The socially apprehensible citizen, then, consists of a collection of both physical and discursive elements. . . . By means of warranting, this discursive entity is tied to an association with a particular physical body, and the two together . . . constitute the socially apprehensible citizen" (41).

In one particular case of social representation, Norton makes the interesting observation that "the law is a vast construction of representations. One must be represented, whether by oneself or another. No one comes before the court as oneself" (143). The real self has no place before the court, but a representation of the self does.

The signs that we wrap around ourselves represent those selves to the world along socially determined categories. We construct images, we represent ourselves, as male or female, rich or poor, and so forth. Gabler notes that in the United States today, people offer up representations of the social class they wish to be identified with; such representations constitute a "class by style" composed of fashion, entertainment choices, posture, gesture, and so forth (193–94). This is the process described by Norton as "the consumption of representations" through which "one leaves one's mark upon the world" (51). One does not merely purchase or have about oneself goods, but goods that can represent the self to others according to clear socially constructed categories: "In what they own, in how they furnish their homes, in what they drive, and most of all in what they wear, Americans endeavor to represent themselves" (51). Norton is clear that these representations build subjectivities: "Through commodities Americans reveal their conceptions of their identities," and thus we see a link from subjectivity to commodification in our previous chapter (52). Norton points out that this is especially true for marginalized groups that may have trouble claiming representation in any other way: "Consumption thus became, for these groups, not merely a way but the principal, often the only, way in which they could represent themselves in the world or interject themselves into public discourse" (57). Clothing, music, or transportation choices thus become a way of presenting the self in a multicultural world. Note the connection between the images of self that we construct and the exchange value acquired by that image, in terms of our discussion in the previous chapters.

Simulation. We have seen how the self can be made of representations, or displayed for others and negotiated in representations. Those senses of the self assume the referential nature of representations: there is a reality somewhere to which the representations refer. As we have seen, a simulation is composed of representations that no longer represent, signs that have lost their referent function and are free floating. When we speak of simulational subjectivity, we are thus speaking of the subject constructed of signs with no grounding in reality. In a simulational age, the construction of the subject from signs that have no reference in the individual's material circumstance is widespread. It is the process described by Norton: "We make ourselves from the materials of books and films, television and popular music, newspapers and magazines" (11). A representation taken from a film cannot reference me, unless the film is about me. If I make my subjectivity out of such representations, they can have no real reference and my subjectivity is simulational.

Simulation is the realm of masks; in it, the subject is all mask, all appearance and presentation, all style and image. There is no reality for these signs to connect to. The signs of which the simulational self is made found in Norton's "books and films" have lost their referents. Such signs are all around us today, and

Featherstone and Burrows thus note that "in an increasingly hyper-aestheticized everyday life, it is through various fictions that we endeavour to come to know ourselves" (13)—of course, a self that is known through fictions rather than representational truths is a simulational self.

In the first section of this chapter we learned that real subjects are grounded in the physical body, but the simulational subject has lost that grounding. As Howard Rheingold notes, "People in virtual communities do just about everything people do in real life, but we leave our bodies behind" (65). The rhetoric of the simulational self as freed from the material body is remarkable and pervasive. Looking widely at our culture, Stone sees that "the changes that the concept of presence is currently undergoing are embedded in much larger shifts in cultural beliefs and practices. These include repeated transgressions of the traditional concept of the body's physical envelope" (16). Hayles observes the same cultural shifts but disapprovingly notes that "one contemporary belief likely to stupefy future generations is the postmodern orthodoxy that the body is primarily, if not entirely, a linguistic and discursive construction" (192). As an example of that orthodoxy she cites Hans Moravec's contention that human identity can be downloaded into a computer and the body dispensed with (xii). This dematerialization of the body she blames on our culture's reduction of everything to information, which leads us to consider the technologies of information that create our simulational culture (193).

Key to the simulational separation of the subject from the body is the *digital technology* that we have seen is key to simulation. Simulational technology makes linkages among subjects and between subjects and texts more important than their physical grounding in the body, extends the body into cyberspace where physicality loses meaning, and allows the subject to forget its materiality. Stone interprets "the history of technology . . . as a series of complexifications, knots and loosenings of the bonds and tensions between bodies and selves, mediated by technologies of communication" (86). The technology of simulation then enables the self, the subject, to float free from the embodied real subject. Stone sees computers as but extensions of the physical self (12), noting that famed physicist Stephen "Hawking doesn't stop being Hawking at the edge of his visible body" because of his extensive reliance on technological prostheses; Hawking merges off into the technology, in other words (5). Dyson uses the language of prostheses in painting this remarkable picture of the simulational subject: "The new postmodern subject, barely distinguishable from its prosthesis, existing in flows of information, suspicious that—as some technophiles claim—matter is nothing but data after all, enters a new theoretical order. Seeing, and the poststructuralist framework dominated by the mediated image, is replaced by being, and the supposedly unmediated experience of immersion" (31).

Dyson's subject merges with its "prosthesis" of representations. The bipolarity of seer and image, representation and thought, is merged in simulation's "unmediated" single plane of immersion in floating representations. The theme of simulational mergers between human subjects and technological prosthesis is also sounded in Hayles's review of the "posthuman view," which privileges information patterns over material embodiment, downplays the centrality of individual consciousness, considers the body as but the original prosthesis, and makes the subject seamlessly articulated with the machine (2–3). That leakage of the subject beyond the body must then be true for everyone who is taken up by technology into the world of an engrossing film or video game. Let us examine several characteristics of the physically grounded real subject that are erased, overturned, or decentered in the technologically engendered simulational subject. We shall examine *relationships*, *authorship*, *identity*, and *orientation*.

The real, physically grounded subject is limited in the *relationships* it can maintain. But technology links the subject to a huge, destabilizing number of relationships. As a result, as Stone argues, "the accustomed grounding of social interaction in the physical facticity of human bodies is changing" (17). Social connections out of physical contact are moved entirely onto the plain of representations, and from representations to simulations if those relationships are never understood to have a "real" basis. A simulational understanding of culture is expressed by Roy Wagner, who says that "culture is but analogy based on (and subversive to) other analogies, not in a tension of rigid oppositions or categories, but a mobile range of transformations worked upon a conventional core" (7). Nowhere does the real appear in Wagner's claim; let us turn to Kenneth J. Gergen to consider what happens to the subject in such an ungrounded, widely dispersed net.

Gergen's theory of the *saturated self* (*Saturated*, x–xi) relies in large measure on technologies that pull the subject away from grounded physical experience and the real social relationships that depend on that presence. Gergen links the increasing prevalence of the "saturated self," the decentered and unstable subject, to "the condition of postmodernism" (*Saturated*, 7). Postmodernity is a condition of decenteredness, of incommensurate roles and contexts in everyday life. Gergen argues that the postmodern self is fragmented and unstable because of the conflicting relationships that tug it this way and that: "This fragmentation of self-conceptions corresponds to a multiplicity of incoherent and disconnected relationships. These relationships pull us in myriad directions, inviting us to play such a variety of roles that the very concept of an 'authentic self' with knowable characteristics recedes from view" (7). Key to this postmodern self is changeability: "Under postmodern conditions, persons exist in a state of continuous construction and reconstruction; it is a world where anything goes that can be negotiated" (7). Gergen sees virtual subjectivities as quite apart from real ones in his observance of "selves as artifacts of hyperreality. As political events, health and illness, and world history slip from the realm of the concrete into the domain of representation, so a commitment to obdurate selves becomes increasingly difficult to maintain" (*Saturated*, 122). The obdurate self is permanent and stable; in hyperreal simulation, it destabilizes. These simulational identities do not necessarily replace real subjectivities, but they do acquire virtual lives of their own, proceeding on parallel but virtual tracks.

The postmodern saturated self is hyperlinked by digital technologies to other subjects until it stretches too thin to retain any unity: "Emerging technologies saturate us with the voices of humankind. . . . Social saturation furnishes us with a multiplicity of incoherent and unrelated languages of the self" (*Saturated*, 6). Gergen may be understood as saying that simulational, digital technologies bleed the subject off into relationships in many sites and many voices. Gergen is clear that technology creates the multiple relationships that decenter the subject: "What I call the technologies of social saturation are central to the contemporary erasure of individual self. . . . [A]n array of technological innovations has led to an enormous proliferation of relationships" (*Saturated*, 49). Technology simply offers multiple sites for relationship, so many that the self is fragmented. Gergen argues specifically that "television has generated an exponential increase in self-multiplication. . . . [T]he media . . . are vitally expanding the range and variety of relationships available to the population" (55). Every new program offers to the viewer engrossed by simulation a new role to play in virtual relationship. Note that these relationships are largely simulational, being conducted largely within the closed world of floating signifiers that is television.

Another characteristic of subjectivity is *authorship*, being the origin of messages, text, and voice. But as the Critical Art Ensemble observes, cyberspace dissolves any clear sense of authorship:

Notions of origin have no place in electronic reality. The production of the text presupposes its immediate distribution, consumption, and revision. All who participate in the network also participate in the interpretation and mutation of the textual stream. The concept of the author did not so much die as it simply ceased to function. (346)

In other words, what the material, real subject says is beyond question *her* discourse. Texts produced by simulational technology such as chat room contributions, a particular iteration of a video game, or a series of jumps among links in a hypertext are less clearly *yours* or *mine*, connected to and clear evidence of a single subject.

The material subject has real physical characteristics that engender *identity*, enabling identity to be signaled in the world. Simulational technology removes those characteristics; virtual subjects may claim to be gay or straight, old or young, but there is no reality to hold those representations in place. As a result, as Daniel Punday notes, "Individuals can leave their physical characteristics undefined in some types of online communication or can create virtual identities for themselves in others" (194). Disembodied subjects in cyberspace are, in Punday's words, "so obviously *only* discourse and cut off from the physical basis upon which conventional narratives of gender and racial identity are traditionally built" (208). Punday's point is not merely that cybersubjects are disembodied but that the body gives an identity that technological presence cannot. The identities one does assume in simulation are inauthentic and stereotypical, according to Punday: "conventional social practices shape this new noncorporeal space. When individuals define new identities in an online environment, they frequently rely on stereotypes built up in the real world or learned through mass media" (194).

Another characteristic of the material subject is physical *orientation* to time, place, activity, community, and context. Virilio points to the destabilizing effect of information technologies that remove the individual from a material grounding that gives orientation: "Together with the build-up of information superhighways we are facing a new phenomenon: loss of orientation. . . . A duplication of sensible reality, into reality and virtuality, is in the making. A stereo-reality of sorts threatens. A total loss of the bearings of the individual looms large" ("Speed," 1). The stereo-reality Virilio fears is a decenteredness, subjectivity in more than one channel.

Simulational technology offers so much disconnected information to the subject that unity of perception is impossible: Virilio explicitly contrasts the emerging simulational subject with the real subject as an effect of new technology, for cyberspace shatters "*man's unity of perception* and [produces] AUTOMATICALLY the persistence of a disturbance in self-perception that will have lasting effects on man's rapport with the real" (*Art*, 147). Hayles notes the disorienting disconnection between the material context of the body and the subject (that connection being *point of view*) in her observation of the ways in which self and technology merge in cyberspace: "instead of an embodied consciousness looking through the window at a scene, consciousness moves *through* the screen to become the pov [*sic*; point of view], leaving behind the body as an unoccupied shell. In cyberspace, point of view does not emanate from the character; rather, the pov literally *is* the character" (38). Point of view requires a separation between subject and any object of the subject's perception. But simulational technology removes that distance.

Once perspective is gone, so is the orientation, the centering of the subject. One way this happens is named in Stone's startling statement that "software produces subjects. When we engage with symbolic structures of sufficient complexity, to a certain extent we synchronize our own internal symbology with those structures. In this we are carrying out our own programs as social beings" (167). Baudrillard likewise sees the simulational subject as merging with the technology that creates simulations: "Our private sphere has ceased to be the stage where the drama of the subject at odds with his objects and with his image is played out: we no longer exist as playwrights or actors but as terminals of multiple networks" (*Ecstasy*, 16), and as terminals we are sutured into the world that as real subjects we would but observe.

As we have been observing, cyberspace is often a prime site for the discovery of simulational subjectivities with no real referents. An important dimension of the work of the virtual environment is that it destroys "real" boundaries among its constituent entities, since everything is mutable in simulation. Real subjects remain whole and oriented because they can view a stable world apart from themselves. But since a simulated subject merges with the simulation as described above by Stone and Baudrillard, it is coextensive with any "other" that might come along. Featherstone and Burrows thus observe that "the boundaries between subjects, their bodies and the 'outside world' are being radically reconfigured" in cyberspace (3). The simulational subject emerges when one is wholly engrossed in cyberspace rather than simply observing it; as Dyson says, it emerges when "one is in cyberspace, not watching it, one is a navigator, a netizen, not a viewer" (31). Dyson also claims that "virtual humans don't just enter cyberspace, they become cyberspace" in the sense that the subject, the virtual self, is indistinguishable from the instruments of simulation; cyberspace, in this example (39). Characteristics of the simulational environment undermine the possibilities of orientation, as noted by Mark Poster: "Virtual reality takes the imaginary of the word and the imaginary of the film or video image one step further by placing the individual 'inside' alternative worlds. By directly tinkering with reality, a simulational practice is set in place which alters forever the conditions under which the identity of the self is formed" (86).

We have seen how a technologically induced simulation changes several key characteristics of real subjects. The effect of a virtual environment is an unstable, multiple, decentered subject. This is most clearly seen in on-line communities, or cyberspace. Sherry Turkle observes that "in cyberspace . . . perhaps already millions of users create online personae who live in a diverse group of virtual communities where the routine formation of multiple identities undermines any notion of a real and unitary self" (89). The simulational self may be a special, temporary creation of cyberspace, as in Mette Hjort and Sue Lauer's observation that "in simulating, one's psychological mechanisms are being run 'off line.' This means at least that they are disconnected from some of their usual behavioral manifestations" (43). The simulated self is a subjectivity that is taken up and then put aside alternately. In this vein, Celia T. Romm notes that in many cyberspace communities, "members . . . develop 'virtual identities' that are completely removed from their real-life identities" (224). The real self will not do in simulational space. As John Beckmann argues, "To venture into cyberspace with your own personality is insufficient. You need to cultivate multiple yous, avatars, and partial derivatives. You need to construct a new surface, a new territory, on which to project your desires" (9).

The simulated subject is not only decentered, it is unstable and rapidly changing. We learned in the previous chapter that simulation is a site of nearly unrestricted change. So is the simulational subject, at least potentially. In contrast to the centered real subject, the simulational subject is decentered and fragmented; it has no core identity but what Gabler described as only collections of selves (227–28). The simulational self, made of unfettered free-floating representations that no longer represent, is also changing and multiple. This is the situation Gergen describes as the saturated self, and he notes that "like the concepts of truth, objectivity, and knowledge, the very idea of individual selves—in possession of mental qualities—is now threatened with eradication" (*Saturated*, x). Victor Vitanza specifically compares this simulational self to the real subject: "Being in real places demands that we maintain a stable self-identity. Being in virtual places, however, invites people to be fluid, unfixed, ever-changing, and multiple" (61). Stone lists a variety of ways in which the subject might be multiple and fragmented, including

- Many persons in a single body (multiple personality).
- Many persons outside a single body (personae within cyberspace in its many forms and attendant technologies of communication).
- A single person in/outside many bodies (institutional social behavior). (86)

Stone's reference to multiple personalities is echoed in Baudrillard's dismal vision of all of simulational society as schizophrenic: "In spite of himself, the schizophrenic is open to everything and lives in the most extreme confusion. . . . He becomes a pure screen, a pure absorption and resorption surface of the influence networks" (*Ecstasy*, 27).

So what valence does the simulated subject have? The self in simulation is a good or a bad thing, depending on one's wider perspective. Stone advocates a positive view, pointing to the playful possibilities within a completely malleable identity: "The technosocial space of virtual systems, with its irruptive ludic quality and its potential for experimentation and emergence, is a domain of nontraumatic multiplicity" (59–60). Observing a social tension between expectations that computers are primarily for play and expectations that they are for work (13–14), Stone locates virtual experiments with subjectivity in the domain of play, urging that we "view computers not only as tools but also as *arenas for social experience*" (15).

Several observers see possibilities for utopian, digital homes for simulated subjects, as in Howard Rheingold's contention that virtual communities stem from a "hunger for community" as "informal [real] public spaces disappear from our real lives" (68). He has great hopes for a restoration of true democracy among cybersubjects (74–75). Florian Roetzer sees utopian possibilities in the relocation of the subject to cyberspace. He says, "Now that modern utopias based upon the individual's fulfillment within society and its transformation have failed, or rather have been abandoned, it seems possible to satisfy the desire for communal structures in cyberspace" (128). This is seen as an entirely positive development, a new utopia, for "cyberspace is considered to be the solution to all problems in the real world, which one supposedly leaves behind by stepping over the technological threshold" (128). Kevin Robins likewise sees utopian possibilities for the subject's psyche in an escape from reality: "the technological realm offers precisely a form of psychic protection against the defeating stimulus of reality" (142). Gabler notes one way in which the self is playfully constructed in simulation, the use of fashion "not to signal one's status" but instead to signal "the personality one wanted to project" in the changing moment (206). The defining denial of the physical body that we noted earlier is key to the simulational subject is presented as utopian in Lupton's observation that "a central utopian discourse around computer technology is the potential offered by computers for humans to escape the body" (100).

A less positive view of the simulational subject is found in Boorstin's view of fame: "*The celebrity is a person who is known for his well-knowness. . . .* He is the human pseudo-event" (57). Note the simulational loop in the defining quality of "well-knowness." Note also that Boorstin's statement is a negative critique of what happens to a thoroughly simulational subject, the celebrity. This critique alleges a lack of substance in the simulated subject; there is no reality of actual achievement to ground the floating representations of such a fame.

Slouka thinks that the individualism that we found goes with real subjectivity begins to dissipate in simulation, and he sees such a trend regarding the centrality of the individual in Western culture (4–5). The simulational subject will be but part of a "digital hive" in Slouka's view (95–96). Margaret Wertheim argues that "the reality of psyche" is opposed by "contemporary scientific epistemology" as a consequence of the dominance of cyberspace (49). A challenge to a real psyche would also seem to merge the subject into Slouka's hive. Gergen also uses a language of loss of individuality in arguing that "as social saturation proceeds, we become pastiches, imitative assemblages of each other. . . . Each of us becomes the other, a representative, or a replacement" (*Saturated*, 71). If one represents another so as to be able to replace the other, one is a copy and thus simulational.

Paradoxically, one often encounters the charge that the simulational subject enrolled in the hive is less communicative, less responsive to society and the environment, than is the stand-alone real subject. One can think here of the model of *Star Trek*'s Borg, in which completely assimilated beings move robotically, unable to socialize with others or among themselves because they are *too* integrated with others. Baudrillard anticipates that vision in saying that "the mass media are anti-mediatory and intransitive. They fabricate non-communication . . . if one agrees to define communication as an exchange" (*For*, 169). The media "*are what always prevents response*, making all processes of exchange impossible (except in the various forms of response *simulation*)" which in his view is no response at all (*For*, 170). As an example, Baudrillard cites the isolating effect of television, which engrosses people in its simulations: "TV, by virtue of its mere presence, is a social control in itself . . . it is the *certainty that people are no longer speaking* to each other, that they are definitely isolated in the face of a speech without response" (*For*, 172).

Some complain that the simulational subject is removed from politics, as in Robins's remark that "techno-community is fundamentally an anti-political ideal" (151). This seems to be the dark side of the technological utopias, and it insists on the precession of reality. If technotopias can be configured so as to eliminate scarcity or conflict, then of course politics would disappear. That is a suspicious development only if one insists that politics is "really" there in some sense all the time, whether one likes it or not.

We have seen some distinct differences among the rhetorics of reality, representation, and simulation when it comes to subjectivity. What the self is, and how we see ourselves, varies according to whether we see it as real, as representation, or as a simulation. We have also seen how conceptions of the subject in each of the three cases also impact views on culture and context. We now turn to an examination of how the three key terms are used in understanding the role of aesthetics in personal experience.

AESTHETICS

Aesthetics is usually taken to refer to the appreciation of beauty, of sensory experience, of form and proportion, and perhaps most of all, of art. Key to the aesthetic experience is the dimension of pleasure or the satisfaction of desires. As Ronald Schenk observes, by the eighteenth century "beauty came to refer to the capacity of things to evoke the inner experience of pleasure" (101). Aesthetic experience is relevant to the question of pleasure in one way or another. The aesthetic is not always nice, or polite, but it always produces a subjective reaction on the dimension of pleasure and the desires that motivate people. Even if art is disturbing, the disturbance is relevant to the question of pleasure.

What are the connections between reality, representation, and simulation on the one hand, and aesthetic experience on the other? What kinds of aesthetic experiences do our key terms ground? What do people feel as they experience art, beauty, or sensation as if it were real, representation, or simulation? How does art itself change when considered as one or another of our key terms?

We will also consider how central the aesthetic is to each of our three key terms. Robins, for instance, declares that "artificial reality is designed and ordered in conformity with the dictates of pleasure and desire," which would seem to put the aesthetic at the very heart of simulation. Likewise, Heim contends that "to fascinate for the long haul, that is the task of art" (*Virtual*, 55)—using simulational language of fascination and engrossment. But how central is the aesthetic for reality and representation? These are among the many issues we will consider.

One useful, basic distinction that is widely used to discuss aesthetic experience is that between *form* and *content*. Content is the subject matter of art, what it is about. A portrait of a queen has the queen for its content. One might say that the content of *Romeo and Juliet* is conflict, bigotry, and love. Form is the technical manifestation of the art, including patterns and structures that order the materials used. The content of a queen's face may be rendered in many different artistic forms, as may the themes of conflict, bigotry, and love.

Reality. The aesthetics of reality is grounded in first hand, immediate lived experience. Real aesthetics is appreciation of a sunset, a woodland scene, or a peaceful desert. The aesthetics of reality thus has infinite complexity and richness, since (in this rhetoric) it is neither reduced nor represented. Stone expresses this idea ironically, using a technological metaphor, by saying that " 'reality' is wide-bandwidth" (93). A real aesthetic is not *art*-ificial, it is appreciated but not made.

A rhetoric of reality is somewhat suspicious of art and prefers to find aesthetics in the "real thing." This perspective may be traced at least to Plato in several of his writings. In the *Republic*, Plato expresses a preference for reality, which for him is ideal—a reality of ideas. Material experience is but a representation of those ideals, and artistic expression is but a representation of material experience—being two steps away from reality, it is highly suspicious (Vitanza, 2). It would not be inaccurate to say that for Plato, the dialectical discourse that leads to discovery of the ideal world of forms is an aesthetic experience of the real. The elegant structures of genus and species, category and division, that Plato constructs are his paintings, symphonies, and dance.

One could be a realist but not an idealist, in which case what is conventionally called art would still be suspect because it is a step removed from the real basis of aesthetics. Ernst Cassirer describes this position exactly in referring to

that naïve realism which regards the reality of objects as something directly and unequivocally given. . . . If reality is conceived in this manner, then of course everything which has not this solid sort of reality dissolves into mere fraud and illusion. . . . From this point of view all artistic creation becomes a mere imitation, which must always fall short of the original. (6)

Such a rhetoric locates the aesthetic in reality itself; it is contra-artistic but not contra—aesthetic. A rhetoric of reality simply tucks the aesthetic into an appreciative experience of the real. Expressed in terms of the distinction between form and content, then, real aesthetics does not represent: it is not *about* anything; it is nothing but *content*. Whatever form occurs in real aesthetics is immanent in the experience itself; form brought to the experience after the fact is not part of the original experience of the real.

Representation. When art is seen on the plain of representation, it is both content and form. Representational art is supposed to be about something in real experience (content), yet in representation form is of equal importance. How the content is represented to the aesthetic audience is of prime importance in the experience of representational aesthetics. As representation, aesthetics becomes *art*, a physical manifestation that stands for, or directs the attention toward, something other than itself. We see both form and content in Croce's view that "representation is distinguished as *form* from what is felt and suffered, from the flux or wave of sensation, or from psychic matter; and this form, this taking possession, is expression" (11). Here, the "what is felt" and so forth are the content, which is expressed within the form of representational aesthetics.

A view of the aesthetic as representational is deeply entrenched in human history. Renaissance development of perspective in art was an emphasis on representation, and John Adkins Richardson notes the importance of representation in some classical art forms, for "the Greeks seem to have been incapable of considering art from any angle other than minesis" (17), which is representational. Accurate imitation of a physical object, be it face or fruit bowl, is not the only standard of representation, of course. Art has also been expected to represent spiritual, cultural, or experiential truths. Art has been held to a standard of representing emotions. Those standards apply to differing degrees throughout the history of art around the world. Sometimes good art was what "looked like" the physical object that it represented, sometimes good art was what conveyed a spiritual truth to the viewer by way of icons that bore no clear resemblance to actual people. Susanne Langer argues that representation has been taken to be central to the task of art, and that it asserts its authority whether the artist wills it or not: "It is so easy to achieve organic unity in a design by making it represent something that even when we would experiment with pure form we are apt to find ourselves interpreting the results as human figures, faces, flowers, or other inanimate things" (*Philosophy*, 249). Elsewhere, Langer expresses a representational view of art in making form or pattern itself the thing represented: "Herein lies the chief and immediate virtue of representation in art. Not duplication of things which are already in existence, but the gathering and projection of their forms" (*Mind*, 166). She uses form here, not in the sense I have used it—as manifestation, to distinguish it from content—but in the sense of a pattern of feeling or experience. Langer argues that art represents not necessarily what is in the world but instead how we see what is in the world: "The laws of representation which govern image making are not laws of optics, but of visual interpretation, which begins with the act of looking" (94–95). So representational aesthetics holds art to the task of representing, even when the referent is something abstract such as form or pattern or internal such as feelings and perceptions.

Other observers echo Langer's expression of art as representational even when what it represents is abstract or internal. Norton argues that science fiction is representational of our inner hopes and fears: "Our speculative constructions of future world are acknowledged by those who make and those who enter them as representations of our desires" (19). Richardson notes that in the Renaissance, art was expected to represent ideal form rather than material reality (18)—and unlike art in Plato's perspective, art in the Renaissance view was expected to perform such a representational function.

At least in the past, a view of art as representational was taken to be the prime task of art. Langer sees an "ancient and almost ubiquitous practice of representation in painting and sculpture" in nearly every age but our own (*Mind*, 87). If a portrait was "very like" the one who sat for it, that was the standard for good art for a long time in western culture. Thomas Crow argues that painting and sculpture have seen "the nearly complete erosion of their old representational purposes by photographic and electronic media" in the last century and a half (18). Crow's point nevertheless illustrates the centrality that representation once played in all art in modern Western culture.

A representational view of aesthetics in many ways parallels a representational theory of language. Expectations of art come to parallel expectations for language. When we expect aesthetics to be representational, we expect a balance between form and content. The technical manifestation of art is important, as is the choice of wording in a representational view of language, for its ability to re-present content or the world. Clarifying representational aesthetics by contrasting it with simulational aesthetics, Hayles notes simulation's reduction of everything to sheer information. But as she says, "the price it pays for this universality is its divorce from representation. When information is made representational . . . it is conceptualized as an action rather than a thing. Verblike, it becomes a process that someone enacts, and thus it necessarily implies context and embodiment" (56). We can apply Hayles's comment to the aesthetic, noting that the verblike structure of representation links art's form with its content. Art is not merely a painting on the wall, in this representational view, it is a painting that is verblike, it is doing something, and what it is doing is representing some aspect of the world to the viewer.

We have also seen how a representational theory of language holds signs to a standard of truth, or accurate representation. So it is with representational aesthetics, in which works of the imagination may be understood, in Kendall Walton's terms, as either true or false (*Mimesis*, 13). If linguistic representation is held to be epistemic, so is aesthetic representation.

One way in which representational art is epistemic is in putting the individual into a relationship with the world. We saw above how simulational subjectivity deprives the subject of perspective that orients it in experience. Many observers have identified the providing of perspective as one of the key functions of representational art. Ronald Schenk compares medieval art, with a "transcendent" epistemology, to the dawn of highly representational art in the Renaissance, which developed "perspective" as "a method of representation" (90). Schenk sees the development of perspective as a key bulwark of Cartesian dualism: "Linear perspective in the Renaissance . . . transformed perception into the detached, passive registration of 'outer' information (object) by the 'inner' mind (subject)" (101). The centering of the subject through perspective is key to representational epistemology, in Schenk's view: "Truth becomes grounded, not in appearance, but in the self-certainty of the ego" (101).

John Adkins Richardson likewise notes that Renaissance perspectivism centers the subject by privileging the point of view of a particular observer, and validates the knowledge gained from that point of view (15). Walton argues that representational art requires the connection of a subject to the world, which is a kind of centering: "Appreciation of representational works of art is primarily a matter of participation. . . . [V]iewers and readers are reflexive props in these games" (*Mimesis*, 213). "Props" sounds a little passive here, but can be understood in the sense that a centered, viewing subject is required for the aesthetic experience to work at all.

Linguistic representations also have political impact; they purport to name the world as being one way or another. A representational view of art works in the same way. Murray Edelman notes, although not with approval, that "art that purports to be realistic is likely . . . to be blatantly ideological, because the seeming realism is always a construction of the dominant ideological currents influence the observer; it cannot be a mirror of an objective, universally recognized reality. That it seems to be such a mirror strengthens its potency as ideology" (62). Edelman's use of the mirror metaphor makes it clear that by "realistic" art he does not intend a rhetoric of reality but instead means an art that represents reality precisely. The claim that representational art makes to mirror the world is often not seen as an entirely positive thing. Nicholas Negroponte complains that "like a Hollywood film, multimedia narrative includes such specific representations that less and less is left to the mind's eye. By contrast, the written word sparks images and evokes metaphors that get much of their meaning from the reader's imagination and experiences" (8). Negroponte would seem to be distinguishing representation from evocation, and that may point to a distinction beween representational and simulational aesthetics as well, as we shall see in the next section. Negroponte resists the role of representation in saying that the world is one way or another.

Bell hooks has written extensively about the political role that art plays when it claims to be representational: "There is a direct and abiding connection between the maintenance of white supremacist patriarchy in this society and the institutionalization via mass media of specific images, representations of race" that claim to be accurate (2). Media institutions are an instrument whereby culture-wide racism is perpetuated by representations, for "the real world of image-making is political—that politics of domination inform the way the vast majority of images we consume are constructed and marketed" (5). We ignore the representational function of media images at our peril, given the political work that they do in that representation. In particular, the unavoidably representational function of popular art forms recruits oppressed people to participate in their own subordination: "forms of representation in white supremacist society that teach black folks to internalize racism are so ingrained in our collective consciousness that we can find pleasure in images of our death and destruction" (6–7).

When art is regarded as representation, it is held to many of the same expectations as language. Representational art is epistemic, it orients the individual in relation to the world, and it furthers power claims in depicting the world one way or another. With variations in what is represented, the representational ideal has been applied to art during different periods throughout history. A representational discourse of aesthetics balances form or technique with content, or that which is represented. As does language, representational art must say what it says so as to match up accurately with the world. What happens to aesthetics when the forms of art are no longer taken to be representational but instead become the very content of the aesthetic experience? That is the question addressed in our next section.

Simulation. A discourse of real aesthetics emphasizes content and a discourse of representative aesthetics emphasizes a balance between content and form. Simulational aesthetics tends not to go beyond form. It looks at the signs composing an aesthetic experience as a closed system, and thus the form, pattern, or structure integrating those signs is of paramount importance. A paradigm expression of this aesthetic would thus be cubism, which in Richardson's view "relied . . . upon the abandonment of content" (58). A simulational aesthetic is not experienced for its ability to represent or resemble anything in reality, and thus it is antimimetic, as in Croce's aesthetic (16–17), looking instead at the forms that underlie the expressions and the experience of the signs of art themselves. Such an aesthetic might fairly be described in Schenk's terms as "beauty as proportion" which "is based upon abstractions, that is, numerical properties, not what appears concretely to the senses" (83). A refusal of mimesis is a refusal of connection to the world, and it generates a simulational aesthetic, as in Nigel Clark's observation that "the shift away from the mimetic orientation of photography, film and early television to computer generated imagery constitutes the onset of an entirely new regime of visuality" in simulation (127).

The key to simulational art is that the aesthetic experience is not led beyond the representations themselves, which have no referents. Murray Edelman is very clear in arguing against a representational view of art: "works of art do not represent 'reality,' 'the real world,' or 'everyday life,' even if those terms are taken to carry a specific or meaningful reference. Rather, art *creates* realities and worlds. People perceive and conceive in the light of narrative, pictures, and images" (7). The simulational experience is no less moving than it is for representational art. When Jerrold Levinson raises the old question of how abstract art can arouse emotion, he is inviting us to think about the power of formal experience in and of itself (27). Langer argues throughout her work that art expresses feelings (*Philosophy*, 257). But by this she does not mean that a given sign in an aesthetic experience refers to a particular emotion; instead, art is a "projection" of a feeling or idea in the sense of being a continuous extension of it; it does not represent the feeling, it is part of it (*Mind*, 74–76). For Langer, art is "the making of forms which express the nature of feeling" (*Mind*, 64), it is "images of the forms of feeling" (*Mind*, xviii) and here I would emphasize the idea of forms, rather than content. Writing decades before the widespread appearance of digital cyberspace, Langer argued that the space created in art is virtual rather than representative:

> Those spatial properties . . . which are abstracted in the interest of artistic expressiveness are not essentially the geometric ones; they are noted and formulated chiefly with an eye to their dynamic, cohesive and other non-geometric aspects, because the space they are to organize is not actual space . . . but virtual space. All presentation of the artist's idea—his conception of human feeling—is made through the expressiveness he gives to that virtual space. (*Mind*, 97)

Langer is explicit in arguing that art does not represent but must instead be appreciated on the formal level alone: "The art image has an irresistible appearance of livingness and feeling, though it may not represent anything living. . . . It is this sort of vitality and feeling that constitutes the import of the work; it is conveyed entirely by artistic techniques, not by what is represented" (*Mind*, 96–97).

When Baudrillard says that "simulation is characterized by a *precession of the model*" he resonates with the formal nature of a model (*Simulations*, 32). Simulational aesthetics centers on the model, not what the model means in reality. An artist's model is not seen as this particular flesh and blood person with a history, hopes, and fears; the model is experienced as an abstract example of the human form. No one believes that Salvador Dali painted real melting watches and no one makes any attempt to find representation in Jackson Pollock's work. The shibboleth of "art for art's sake" was made for simulational art. That expression is echoed in Walton's claim that "imagining," which one would take to be foundational to the aesthetic, "is *essentially* self-referential" or only about itself (*Mimesis*, 28). In the tension between form and content, simulational art is thus largely or entirely formal. It is as Baudrillard termed it "plastic" in reducing everything to the common denominator of form (*Simulations*, 91–92, 109–10). Simulation's common denominator is pure information without content. Hayles describes the work of Claude Shannon, Norbert Wiener and others who defined information as pattern instead of meaning (53). Its content is the form and experience of the form.

Any aesthetic experience must be of some material substance or else the ear could not detect music, the eye could not follow the dance. But the material is experienced for the form it manifests, in simulational art. Hayles argues that "virtuality is the cultural perception that material objects are interpenetrated by information patterns" (13–14). Our era is one of increasing interest in form and pattern over material, she argues, observing "contemporary pressure toward dematerialization, understood as an epistemic shift toward pattern/randomness and away from presence/absence" (29). Schenk describes an aesthetic focused on form as one of "light":

The aesthetic eye perceives appearance in its particular presenting form. In the perceiving, an image is created, and in the image lies meaning. The power that allows for this process, beauty, is imagined as light—light that allows for the particularity of each thing and event to display its own perfection. At the same time the power of beauty allows for the unity of all being and, as such, is the ground for all experience. (44)

An aesthetic experience that unfies "all being" is necessarily formal, following simulation's general policy of reducing everything to one common denominator of information, form, or pattern.

Periods of history when representational art declined are often productive of simulational aesthetics. Richardson notes that "when Christianity became the dominant belief system of antiquity, realism would descend into oblivious abyss" because Christianity is not interested in the world (15). One might well argue that the icons of the early church were representative of spiritual realities, but the lack of interest in highly realistic art from classical times to the Renaissance may also be understood as an aesthetic with some simulational tendencies.

After centuries of a preoccupation with representational art, Western culture began a shift away from realistic art with clearly identifiable referents in the late nineteenth century. First the Impressionists and later the several schools of what became known as "abstract" or "modern" art (although it might better be called postmodern art) may be understood as the advance guard of a simulational culture. Painting had to give up its representational office with the arrival of photography (which can represent even better). As Yve-Alain Bois says, "Challenged by the mechanical apparatus of photography, and by the mass produced, painting had to redefine its status, to reclaim a specific doman" (31) which was increasingly simulational. Larry Day agrees in referring to the development of abstract art: "With the disappearance of God and with the taming and domestication of heroes, painting became a thing-in-itself, answerable only to its chosen conventions. It lacked a subject. It had nothing to point to" (45)—in other words, it became arepresentational. Norton likewise refers to "the preoccupation of abstract expressionists with surface and material, with color, form, and painterliness, [which] produced works with significance but without meaning" (27)—the idea of signs without meaning being completely simulational. Michael Heim describes modern art in similar arepresentational terms, appreciated not for what they mean or point to but for the self-contained experiences they create: "Modern art objects had aesthetic appeal when the viewer could stand apart from them to appreciate their sensory richness, their expressive emotion, or their provocative attitude" (*Virtual*, 51). Richardson offers this example of a clearly simulational aesthetic that developed earlier in the twentieth century: "Cubism is the first non-ornamental painting to portray nothing but itself, to assume that a painting is only a painting . . . and that a picture ought to look no more like a segment of real space than a house ought to resemble a baker's roll" (52).

Although we have taken abstract, arepresentational art as a paradigm of simulation, even representational art may be taken as simulational. Simulational art is also spoken of as an aesthetic experience available from materials that *seem* to be representational. Art may be experienced for the experience it gives within an arepresentational structure. As Walton notes, "Aestheticians rarely worry about whether there really is a Tom Sawyer or a Moby Dick" (*Mimesis*, 6). He means that although the novels include representations that might send the reader on a conceptual hunt for real referents, *Tom Sawyer* and *Moby-Dick* can be experienced as closed systems, the aesthetic experience arising from formal appreciation of how the language is used to make these systems. Richard Thieme says that "in the virtual world, the appearance of reality becomes reality" (53), and that may be a good explanation of how seemingly realistic art can become simulational if its signs are experienced for their own sake, on the surface of their appearance.

Kendall Walton has developed a theory of aesthetics in which representational art works as props in the act of imagining, an act he describes in simulational terms (*Mimesis*, 35–43). He describes these simulations as make-believe, claiming that "*representations* . . . are things possessing the social function of serving as props in games of make-believe" (*Mimesis*, 69). This view provides "a way of distinguishing *fiction* from *nonfiction*. Works of fiction are simply representations . . . whose function is to serve as props in games of make-believe" (*Mimesis*, 72). Note that a nonfictional representation might be expected to represent, to refer to something in reality, but he denies that function to fiction, which uses representations but only as props in simulational imaginings. Walton's argument explains how representational aesthetics may nevertheless be employed in simulation.

One way to understand simulational aesthetics is to focus on the idea of surface, to identify those aesthetic experiences that stay within the material, on the surface of the work, whether that work can claim to be representational or abstract. Baudrillard argues that "today the scene and the mirror [object and representation] have given way to a screen and a network. There is no longer any transcendence or depth, but only the immanent surface of operations unfolding, the smooth and functional surface of communication" (*Ecstasy*, 12). When Stone refers to "the triumph of the empty category on which the current empowerment of art depends," she describes a fascination with the arepresentational signs of which art is composed regardless of whether those signs could be referential or not (23). Baudrillard asserts that aesthetics in an age of simulation has moved entirely to the surface plain of signs and information: "Contemporary aesthetics, once the theory of the forms of beauty, has become the theory of a generalized compatibility of sign, of their internal coherence (signifier-signified) and of their syntax. . . . The aesthetic is thus no longer a value of style or of content; it no longer refers to anything but to communication and sign exchange" (*For*, 188). Yve-Alain Bois argues that art becomes pure surface especially under capitalism: "Art objects are absolute fetishes without a use value but also without an exchange value, fulfilling absolutely the collector's fantasy of a purely symbolic or ideal value, a supplement to his soul" (37).

One indication of simulation is infinite reproducibility, as we have seen. Such reproducibility is facilitated by an aesthetic of surface and form. Baudrillard argues that art in today's simulational world is doing precisely that as it becomes preoccupied with reproducing itself: "Very quickly the work turns back on itself as the manipulation of the signs of art: over-signification of art. . . . It is then that art enters into its indefinite reproduction: all that reduplicates itself, even if it be the everyday and banal reality, falls by the token under the sign of art, and becomes aesthetic" (*Simulations*, 150–51).

Baudrillard's point may be seen clearly especially in today's popular arts, with their heavy use of intertextuality, sampling, recycling and incorporation of older styles and images, and self-references. That kind of self-duplication is also referenced in Boorstin's complaint that we view reality as "plastic" and so our culture is quick to dissolve textal "forms," turning books into movies and so forth (118–80). The more "digital" or simulational we are, the more "the quality of one medium can be transposed to another," according to Negroponte (20).

Ronald Schenk has developed a theory of arepresentational art that can be employed to understand the simulational. Schenk's aesthetic features surface appearance over reference:

The aesthetic vision does not imply pure mirroring, because it entails the *joining* of two worlds, that of the seer and that of the seen, making or producing a third world in image. Gadamer understood beauty to be that which exists *between* idea and appearance. This in-between state of *methexis* or coparticipation is the image. The perception of image, then, is the presencing of idea in appearance. (56)

Schenk describes such art as aphroditic, and says that "Through Aphrodite, all ornamentation and surface detail is taken as being essence, the depth lying in the surface. Through Aphrodite's eye, meaning lies in appearance itself" (43) and in the material of appearance, rather than in representation. Schenk claims Immanuel Kant as a philosophic ancestor, for Kant separated beauty from cognition, making aesthetics unable to lead to knowledge, clearly an arepresentational stance for art (107–8). Schenk's aesthetic invites the viewer to live within the simulational world created by art and to disregard any disjunction between what things appear to be and what they are: "the recovery of beauty is important as a movement toward healing the wound in the modern psyche caused by the separation of appearance and being. . . . When meaning is seen in appearance at hand, then beauty provides a habitat for consciousness" (145).

Simulational aesthetics may be understood in terms of the standards for excellence we employ. One standard for representational art is how close it comes to resembling its referent, in other words, how accurate it is in reflecting the world. But Langer disallows *accuracy* as a standard for art, thus expressing a simulational criterion for art (*Philosophy*, 250). Instead, the standard for simulational art is technical expertise in manipulating its materials for purely formal effect. Hayles refers to the Turing Test for intelligence, which disembodies or is indifferent to the material nature of whatever is intelligent, and suggests that we apply it to art: "the erasure of embodiment is performed so that 'intelligence' becomes a property of the formal manipulation of symbols rather than enaction in the human life-world" (xi). The same can then be said for simulational aesthetics: manipulation of arepresentational symbols is the standard for its success. Schenk refers to this standard of art as "the paradigm of light" (because light is pure information) and claims that "beauty in the paradigm of light is the inherent perfection shining through each particular form" (133), not content. Langer denies the standard of truth attached to external reference for art, saying instead that a new self-contained experience is created in each aesthetic encounter: "To understand the 'idea' in a work of art is therefore more like *having a new experience* than like entertaining a new proposition; and to negotiate this knowledge by acquaintance the work may be adequate *in some degree*. There are no degrees of literal truth, but artistic truth . . . has degrees" (*Philosophy*, 263). Propositions are claims to represent something about the world, and have no place in the creation of an experience that is simulational.

Formal systems are commonly found, and the experience of them may well be understood as aesthetic. Anybody who has worked out mathematical problems "just for fun" is enjoying an experience with no referents, a highly formal exercise that produces pleasure—in other words, a simulational aesthetic. Richardson thus notes that "preoccupation with form over content is characteristic of a vast number of tendencies in philosophy, the physical sciences, and the arts" especially during certain historical periods; here he cites 1870–1914 (20). The propensity of a category of aesthetic experience to be reducible to form is thus one standard for its simulational capacity.

Music is often described in simulational terms as an art of form. Langer makes that argument in saying that "what music can actually reflect is only the morphology of feeling" or the forms of feeling (*Philosophy*, 238). Someone experiencing music is usually caught up in the experience itself, with little or no concern for what it represents. Music rarely points to some clear referent; it is nearly all form.

Cyberspace is of course a prime site for simulational aesthetics. Cyberspace is also formal; each new world within a Uniform Resource Locator (URL) is experienced on its own terms; to ask what it represents misses its raison d'etre. Hayles describes the experience of cyberspace as highly formal: "Existing in the nonmaterial space of computer simulation, cyberspace defines a regime of representation within which pattern is the essential reality, presence an optical illusion" (36).

It should not surprise us that many of the reservations that people have in regard to simulation generally also apply to simulational aesthetics. Some may even deny the status of art to that which is simulational. Note how Michael Heim does so in describing simulation as mere entertainment: "Art holds a mirror to our deeper selves, displaying our fears, hopes and doubts. Entertainment, by contrast, exploits a narrow range of excitement. The repeated simulation of entertainment shrinks us, while the contemplation of art expands our scope" ("Design," 66). If art is a mirror, it represents. In Heim's view, art that only engrosses is simulational.

The equation of simulation with entertainment is widespread. We have seen Gabler's many objections to simulation before. He finds that the location of the aesthetic in entertainment has become so pervasive that it merges with life: "It is not any ism but entertainment that is arguably the most pervasive, powerful and ineluctable force of our time—a force so overwhelming that it has finally metastasized into life" (9). If entertainment's aesthetic experience is inseparable from life then it has no reality outside itself to refer to, and is thus all form, all simulation. Simulational art is criticized by Gabler for the same reason that Heim poses above, that it draws one into oneself: "Art was said to provide *ekstasis*, which in Greek means 'letting us stand outside ourselves,' presumably to lend us perspective. But everyone knows from personal experience that entertainment usually provides just the opposite: *inter tenere*, pulling us into ourselves to deny us perspective" (18). This is entirely simulational language, with its bemoaning the loss of perspective and orientation that comes from simulation's closed loop. Baudrillard likewise sees media, the site of today's entertainment as well as of aesthetic experience for much of the world, as fundamentally simulational: "we must think of the media as if they were, in outer orbit, a sort of genetic code which controls the mutation of the real into the hyperreal" (*Simulations*, 55).

The sheer rhetorical attractiveness of entertaining simulation gives pause to many, as in Baudrillard's argument that "surface and appearance, that is the space of seduction. Seduction as a mastering of the reign of appearances opposes power as a mastering of the universe of meaning" (*Ecstasy*, 62)—the result is that "seduction is . . . ineluctable, and appearance always victorious" (73). Applied to aesthetics, Baudrillard's argument is that a shift of public consciousness from the "real" processes of power to a focus on style, surface, and appearance is powerfully motivating. But because it sees surface and not reality, it may miss what power is doing in reality.

A simulational aesthetic lives within its own closed world of form. It is an insulated experience, an imagining and a make-believe in which the technical manipulation of signs to create forms and patterns is of primary importance. Many of the expectations that people have for simulation in other dimensions of life such as subjectivity may be seen echoed in aesthetic simulation.

CONCLUSIONS AND TRANSITIONS

In the first four chapters we have come to an understanding of the complex discourses of reality, representation, and simulation. We have seen that these three key terms need to be understood as rhetorical claims rather than as facts or as objective realms of experience. We have traced the rhetorical implications of each term in studying what it means to say something is reality, representation, or simulation on the dimensions of *permanence and change, commodification, subjectivity*, and *aesthetics*.

Our examples have been drawn largely from philosophers and critics who make it their professional business to speak in our three key terms. In our last three chapters we will turn to rhetorical discourse found in popular culture, to show how some of the texts of our everyday lives depend heavily on rhetorics of reality, representation, and simulation. Chapter 5 studies the rhetoric of reality as exemplified by William Gibson's science fiction writing. We shall observe Gibson's strategies designed to make the emerging phenomenon of cyberspace seem real. Chapter 6 studies the rhetoric of representation found in an on-line news group, rec.motorcycles. Like any news group, rec.motorcycles is nothing but representations, pixels on a screen; its participants are often eager, therefore, to show how their postings represent real experience on motorcycles. Chapter 7 studies the rhetoric of reality expressed by the film *Groundhog Day*. This film examines the experience of being trapped in a simulational loop, with the same day repeating itself constantly and with no external consequences for any actions taken with that loop. In such a world, the film asks, how shall we live? In this final trio of chapters, we trace the rhetorics of reality, representation, and simulation in everyday usage.

Chapter 5

A Rhetoric of Reality in the Novels of William Gibson

In 1984 (fittingly), William Gibson burst upon the science fiction and wider cultural scene with the publication of his novel *Neuromancer*. That book imagined a world in the near future obsessed with crime, overrun by pollution, and dominated by technology and the corporations that control it. Most of all, *Neuromancer* envisioned a new world of cyberspace in which the disembodied minds of computer whizzes fly through a multicolored cityscape of information to invade, ransack, violate databases, and do other electromischief. *Neuromancer* was the first in a string of novels that share themes and characters, but with two more novels forms a tightly knit trilogy: *Count Zero* published in 1986 and *Mona Lisa Overdrive* published in 1988.

This trilogy of novels was certainly not written at the "dawn" of the computer age, whenever one might calculate that to be, but it was written during a period of rapid expansion of personal ownership of computers as well as rapidly increasing commercial use, application, and power of computers. More and more people went home clutching their 256K dual floppies, or dreamed of owning one of the new hard drive computers just on the horizon of home applications. The Internet and the World Wide Web had hatched from Bitnet and were welcoming more and more tourists to their domains. During that time, the culture and its observers struggled to understand the effects of computers, and the idea of a digital realm that would first be called *cyberspace* in *Neuromancer* was gaining increasing currency.

The temptation is strong to fear or to dismiss anything new, especially new technology. Video games and Web sites of increasing sophistication were nevertheless regarded with suspicion as not real, serious, or important. The power of the new technologies and the cyberworlds they created was only dimly understood by a few visionaries such as Gibson. Rhetorics of simulation were not yet strong enough to challenge dominant rhetorics of reality and representation, to give cyberspace its proper place in the culture.

In such a context Gibson came with clear rhetorical purpose and great persuasive effect. The main argument of his books, shown in this chapter, is that cyberspace is real and continuous with the reality of material experience. Gibson writes to gain some respect for cyberspace as it struggled to gain a footing in the cultural landscape. Perversely, this most simulational of spaces was presented as but stark reality in his trilogy. Although his works grudgingly state from time to time that cyberspace is but representations on a screen and thus not real, nevertheless the bulk of his discourse most vigorously applies a rhetoric of reality to the matrix. This chapter uses the four categories of permanence and change, commodification, subjectivity, and aesthetics as ways to present Gibson's rhetoric of reality. We will see that in many ways his novels display the characteristics of such a rhetoric discussed in chapters 3 and 4. First, we begin with synopses of the novels.

SYNOPSIS: *NEUROMANCER*

Neuromancer centers on Case, a "console cowboy" or cyberspace expert. Case double-crossed a former employer who, in retaliation, rendered his brain incapable of moving through cyberspace. In despair, he hutsles on the black market and scores small-time swindles in a seedy district of Tokyo, sliding closer to ruin through drugs or violence. There he is found by Molly, a "razorgirl" with scalpels implanted under her fingernails, mirrorshades with enhanced optics implanted over her eyes, and reflex-enhancing electronics implanted in her nervous system. She recruits him for a team led by the shadowy, mysterious man Armitage, a team that is to go on an equally mysterious mission.

Armitage pays for Case's brain injuries to be repaired, a seemingly impossible task that bespeaks vast financial and technological resources. The repair comes with a catch, Case learns: toxin sacs have been implanted in his arteries, which will burst at some date in the future. Only Armitage knows how to remove them, thus guaranteeing Case's loyalty to Armitage.

Armitage's team first steals a "construct" from a large corporation, a construct which is the digitally recorded personality, skills, and memories of a dead legendary console cowboy, McCoy Pauley, the "Dixie Flatline." They also acquire a cutting edge Chinese military "icebreaker" software program guaranteed to penetrate any "ice" or security systems for data. With these tools, the team voyages to Freeside, an orbiting vacation resort that also contains at one end the Villa Straylight, home of the legendary Tessier-Ashpool industrial family.

The real purpose of their mission and the forces behind it are gradually becoming clearer. The team is to break into the Villa Straylight both physically and through cyberspace. They must find a key computer terminal in the Villa, discover its password, and speak the password to the computer. This action will free an artificial intelligence (AI), Wintermute, who has been the real instigator of events. AI's are carefully monitored by the Turing Police, in fear that they would become "demons" were they to grow unchecked. But that is precisely Wintermute's plan: it wants to break free from its bonds so that it may merge with another AI, Neuromancer. Both AI's are owned by the Tessier-Ashpools. Wintermute needs the assistance of humans to do this, for it cannot electronically find and speak the password to the computer terminal in the Villa.

After many battles in physical space and in cyberspace, run-ins with the police, assistance from an orbiting colony of Rastafarians, incredible physical violence, murder, and sex, Case and Molly accomplish their mission. Wintermute and Neuromancer are set free but they also mysteriously disappear into the matrix of cyberspace, leaving news that they are communicating with beings of their own kind in other star systems. Case and Molly go their separate ways.

SYNOPSIS: *COUNT ZERO*

This complex novel follows three story lines, pulling them together in a violent climax at the end. The book begins with Turner, a mercenary assassin and strong-arm specialist, being nearly blown to pieces in retaliation for one of his own bombings. Put back together through the miracles of medicine, Turner is recruited for another assignment: Christopher Mitchell, top scientist at Maas-Biotech, is defecting to work for Hosaka, a competing company. Mitchell has developed a new, revolutionary hardware that combines biology with technology in biochips, promising unheard-of advances in computing power. Mitchell is to escape somehow to a deserted shopping center in Arizona, where Turner is to facilitate his escape before Maas can destroy the site in retaliation. Turner hussles the person who glides in on an ultralight aircraft into a jet and escapes just before the center is destroyed—by Hosaka, as it turns out, attempting to destroy evidence of their complicity in the defection. Landing the aircraft miles away, Turner discovers that he has rescued Angie Mitchell, Christopher's daughter. Christopher planned all along for her to escape, and he has died in the attempt. While scanning Angie for deadly implants that might harm him, Turner makes the astonishing discovery that her nervous system is full of electronic implants. Furthermore, from time to time she appears to be channeling "loa," which are vodun or so-called voodoo gods. Turner and Angie set out for New York City where he hopes to find sanctuary for Angie and financial reward for himself. He is hotly pursued by agents from Maas and Hosaka, both of which want Angie and her mysterious powers.

Meanwhile, teen-ager and aspiring console cowboy Bobby Newmark, whose cyberspace handle is "Count Zero," is almost killed in a lower-class industrial suburb in New Jersey when some software he is testing for a friend draws the attention of a powerful force in cyberspace that attacks him through his nervous system. He is saved at the last minute by the cyberspace apparition of a young woman who intervenes and sets him free. Going in search of the friend who gave him the software, he is attacked and robbed of the software and left for dead by his assailants, and, as he learns later, his apartment is destroyed by a bomb.

Bobby is found and healed by a wealthy, powerful group of African Americans who practice voodoo (the term used in the book). They have become convinced that voodoo gods, or "loa," live in cyberspace. Two women among them regularly become the "horses" of these gods; that is to say, they channel them or are over-taken by them and speak for them. One of these gods is The Virgin; they were monitoring cyberspace when Bobby was nearly killed, and are convinced that it was The Virgin who intervened to save him. Thus, they want to know what his connection is to these forces.

It turns out that the software Bobby was trying was based on Maas's new biochips and was stolen from their labs. Thus, Maas is now trying to find him and either kill him or retrieve its stolen software. Gradually the voodoo priests come to believe in Bobby's innocence, but his connection to The Virgin intrigues them. They, too, travel to New York to exploit certain connections that they believe will reveal to them more of the truth about the loa in cyberspace, taking Bobby with them.

To a readership familiar with *Neuromancer*, it is strongly hinted in this text that these loa are the emancipated parts of the enormous cyberspace intelligence that was formed in the first novel when Wintermute and Neuromancer merged. The original super-AI has spread itself throughout the Internet, and one way it escapes detection by the Turing Police is through fragmentation into these loa. It is also strongly hinted to the reader that Angie Mitchell herself is The Virgin, and because of the technology in her head, based on her father's development of the biochip, she is able to access cyberspace without any other sort of technology or link.

Yet a third story line has been developing all along, to tax the powers of the at-tentive reader. Marly Krushkova is a failed and desperate former art curator who unexpectedly is offered a job by the world's wealthiest man, Josef Virek. Virek wants Marly to find the artist who makes a series of exquisite boxes containing in-teresting objects in unusual arrangements. Virek himself appears to Marly only in virtual or holographic form. The horrible truth is that his body is so riddled with cancer that it occupies three truck trailers in Stockholm. Doctors struggle to keep him alive despite the grotesquely expanding cancers that run throughout what was his body. Virek has a hidden agenda in hiring Marly, for he has discovered that Christopher Mitchell did *not* invent the biochip but was instead fed the information needed to do so, and that whoever is making the boxes also has a connection with the source of the biochip information; it may be one and the same entity. Virek hopes he can use his wealth to buy an ability to turn himself digital, encoded in biochips, and thus escape his gargantuan, diseased body.

Marly uses her own resources and connections, fueled by Virek's incredible wealth, to pursue the maker of the boxes. Eventually she comes not to trust Virek and ends up on the run, Virek's agents in hot pursuit. She locates the maker of the boxes in what was (in *Neuromancer*) the Villa Straylight, now cut off from Freeside and floating free in orbit. The maker is a robot, fashioning the boxes from the encoded memories of the Tessier-Ashpool family. But behind the robot is the powerful AI created from Wintermute and Neuromancer, and it is indeed the source of knowledge of how to make biochips. Virek's agents pursue Marly to this abandoned hull in space and threaten to kill her in claiming the robot for their own—but at that moment the AI interferes, pulls the plug electronically on Virek, and undoes all his plots. Marly is allowed to escape and return to a peaceful life.

Meanwhile, Turner and Angie, Bobby and his voodoo friends, all come together in a nightclub in New York where they are laid siege to by agents of Hosaka who want Angie and her ability to access cyberspace through her thoughts. Another bloody battle ensues in physical space and in cyberspace. Eventually, aided by friends with grudges against Hosaka and by the AI, the protagonists defeat their enemies. The voodoo priests take Bobby and Angie under their protection and Turner gives up his career of violence.

SYNOPSIS: *MONA LISA OVERDRIVE*

Having gone from one story line in *Neuromancer* to three lines in *Count Zero*, Gibson essays four intertwined plots in *Mona Lisa Overdrive*. The gentle reader is asked to have patience as we review them.

Teen-aged Kumiko Kanaka is being sent by her father, a powerful overlord in a Japanese business empire, to stay with his friend Roger Swain in London during a power struggle that might prove to be dangerous. With her she has a hand-held holographic generator that creates the apparition of Colin, a young Englishman who is a source of guidance and information for her. Arriving in London she finds Sally Shears, recognized by the reader as none other than Molly from *Neuromancer*. Sally/Molly is being blackmailed by Swain, who has information about her criminal past, to use her violent talents in his employ. Sally takes Kumiko on various excursions in an attempt to discover and disarm Swain's information source that gives him his power over her.

Meanwhile, Slick, Bird, and Gentry are eking out an existence in the industrial wastelands of New Jersey, living in an abandoned factory. Slick cobbles together giant fighting robots, while Gentry dreams of the "shape" of cyberspace and longs to understand it. To this postindustrial barrens comes Kid Afrika, to whom Slick owes a favor. The debt is to be paid by hiding Count Zero, also known as Bobby Newmark, who is lying catheterized on a stretcher, hooked up to an "aleph," some sort of electronic device; he has been lying unconscious for months. Now it appears as if sinister agents are looking for him, and the Kid wants no part of it.

Gentry recognizes that Bobby is living in cyberspace, a copy of which he believes to be inside the aleph. Eager to learn its true nature for himself, Gentry taps into the world Bobby inhabits, accompanied by Slick. Bobby is spending an extended period of time in cyberspace courtesy of the new biochip-based technology he has with him on the stretcher, and it is this technology that agents from Maas are trying to recover.

On the west coast of the United States we find Angie Mitchell, some years older than we saw her in *Count Zero*, recovering from serious drug addiction. Angie has become not merely a star but *the* star of world-wide popular culture, loved and adored by billions. Her ability to access cyberspace without the help of any technology but that in her own head has faded; but suddenly a new, unfamiliar loa,

Grande Brigitte, comes to her and warns her of plots and violence against her. Angie, intrigued and on guard, returns to the world of celebrity so as to discover what threatens her. There she discovers that several of her associates have sinister connections to the old Tessier-Ashpool family conglomerate from *Neuromancer*, and she begins to investigate. All the while, she wonders whatever became of Bobby Newmark, with whom she had a relationship after their escape in *Count Zero*.

In a trailer park in Florida, Mona Lisa suffers in an abusive relationship with her boyfriend Eddy while fantasizing about her idol, Angie Mitchell. One day Eddy turns up with a business associate who lures them to New York with the promise of a career for Mona in entertainment. Once in the big city, Eddy is killed and Mona forced to undergo plastic surgery that turns her into a look-alike for Angie Mitchell.

Eventually, Sally discovers the sources of Swain's power over her. She goes to New York to free herself from this power and there learns that the task Swain wants her to perform is the assassination of Angie Mitchell, a death that would allow the corporation for which she works to control her image in ways that they fear are otherwise impossible given her technological powers. Mona Lisa has been surgically altered to replace Angie so that the corporation can continue to profit from her. Meanwhile, Kumiko has discovered that Sally is to be disposed of herself once she kills Angie, and so she escapes from Swain and takes this news to an ally of Sally's in London, on the run from Swain's agents.

Sally manages to free both Angie and Mona from their corporate captors, thus foiling the plot to assassinate Angie. She takes them to the abandoned factory where Gentry and Slick are holding the increasingly frail Bobby. On the way, the loa informs Angie that an AI used by her employer has been the instigator of developments all along, and that it, too, is a fragmented part of the super AI created by Wintermute and Neuromancer. They arrive as Gentry and Slick use the giant robots to fight off the corporate agents who are attempting to retrieve the aleph and Bobby. By the time Sally and company arrive, Bobby has died physically. A grieving Angie hooks herself into the aleph, and it is learned that the aleph is an enormously complex block of biosoft, or biochip technology, that contains a model of the entire matrix of cyberspace within. Angie's personality flees into this universe and she dies physically as well. The reader learns that back in London, Kumiko has been reunited and reconciled with her father following Swain's death, that Sally/Molly has erased the data that allowed her to be blackmailed, and of most importance, that Bobby, Angie, the hologram Colin, and another personality construct of their acquaintance, the Finn, are all living happily in the universe contained within the aleph.

In these three novels, cyberspace looms as hard and stark, as real as the gritty world outside the computer room. Most of the action of each novel does not take place in cyberspace, of course. Each novel is dominated by scenes of a tough, violent world ruled by commercial pragmatism. But cyberspace is shown to be *continuous* with those realities. The key turn in Gibson's rhetoric of cyberspace reality is to make it part and parcel of an unmistakably real world. The hard-boiled pragmatists of Gibson's mean streets see those streets as one and the same as the streets of light above which they fly once wired into their computers. What happens in one place happens in another; violent conflict in cyberspace spills out of the machines and into the world. The world appears in cyberspace just as it does "in person." A rhetoric of reality pervades all experiences in the novels so as to say that there is no difference between the streets and the matrix: it's *all real*.

To demonstrate how Gibson uses a rhetoric of reality, let us look at how all three novels use the dimensions of permanence and change, commodification, subjectivity, and aesthetics. The titles of Gibson's novels are abbreviated in the in-text references in this chapter as N for *Neuromancer*, C for *Count Zero*, and M for *Mona Lisa Overdrive*.

PERMANENCE AND CHANGE

Cyberspace is as real as the material world in Gibson's trilogy. People exist in either and both as if in realms of continuous, connected space. The matrix is described in material terms indicative of empirical permanence. Cruising cyberspace in the company of an artificial intelligence, Case is told, "To live here is to live, there is no difference" from the physical world (N, 258). Angie, Mona's Doppelganger, experiences "dreams" that are in fact in cyberspace; yet "the dreams are real," she is told, thus making cyberspace real (M, 22). Later, in *Count Zero*, Angie is assured again that "those dreams of yours are real" (C, 240).

One way to grant cyberspace solidity and permanence is to call it a world or a universe. Count Zero, comatose and lost in the cyberspace aleph to which he is electronically attached, " 'could have anything in there,' Gentry said, pausing to look down at the unconscious face. He spun on his heel and began his pacing again. 'A world. Worlds' " (M, 154). Slick enters the matrix of the aleph and discovers "a whole world. There's this house, like a castle or something, and he's there" (M, 207), to which Gentry replies, "He's got a lot more than that. He's got a universe more than that" (M, 210). Viewing a growing artificial intelligence in cyberspace, Tick observes that it "could have a bloody world in there" (M, 265). Mona Lisa's world of soap opera simulations is likewise inseparable from physical space, and no less real for being digital: "Mona's universe consisted in large part of things and places she knew but had never physically seen or visited" (M, 85). Angie is in the business of making commercial simulation programs, yet these are experienced as real worlds, as a player "slid into the Angie-world, pure as any drug" (M, 143). In the end, Angie and Bobby both go off into their own world of cyberspace, leaving behind their physical bodies which are unneeded because the matrix is as real as is material reality (M, 284–87).

In *Count Zero*, Turner, recovering from a horrific explosion, "spent . . . three months in a ROM-generated simstim [total simulational environment] construct of an idealized New England boyhood of the previous century" in which his surgeons "visit" him to report on his physical progress; the experience may technically be a simulation, but it is described in real terms as a stable, material environment (C, 1). The characters in the book identify the matrix at one level as "a tailored hallucination," but their experiences there are of a reality: "anybody who jacks in knows, fucking *knows* it's a whole universe" (C, 119).

If cyberspace is a universe, *the* universe, then surely a guarantor of the reality of cyberspace would be the presence of God in the matrix. God rears His majestic head to some extent in *Neuromancer* in the form of a Rastafarian colony orbiting earth, Case's allies in assaulting the Tessier-Ashpool computer. These believers invoke the Almighty, but not to the extent that is observed in the later books. Once the artificial intelligences of *Neuromancer* are set free, they metastasize throughout the matrix (C, 159). Of all the identities that they might assume, they take the forms of vodun (voodoo) *gods*, or *loa* (C, 169). These cybergods then come to those who venture into the matrix as Papa Legba, or Grand Brigitte—and we are to discover in *Count Zero* that Angie Mitchell, unwittingly able to enter cyberspace without technological prostheses, is Vyej Mirak, Ezili Freda, the Virgin of Miracles (C, 58). These cybergods *act* like gods, intervening in everyday life no less than the Old Testament Jehovah ever did. Bobby is introduced to " 'Jackie [who] is a mambo, a priestess, the horse of Danbala. . . . Danbala rides her, Danbala Wedo, the snake. Other times, she is the horse of Aida Wedo, his wife.' Bobby decided not to pursue it" (C, 84). Journeying with Jackie in the matrix, Bobby confronts these gods directly, as they overcome Jackie:

"*Danbala ap monte I*," the voice said, harsh in his head, and in his mouth a taste like blood. "Danbala is riding her." . . . "Legba," she said, "Legba and Ougou Feray, god of war. Papa Ougou! St. Jacques Majeur! Viv la Vyej!" Iron laughter filled the matrix, sawing through Bobby's head. "*Map kite tout mize ak tout giyon*" said another voice, fluid and quicksilver and cold. "See, Papa, she has come here to throw away her bad luck!" "And then that one laughed as well, and Bobby fought down a wave of sheer hysteria as the silver laughter rose through him like bubbles." (C, 166–67)

The gods also ride Angie Mitchell, crossing from cyberspace into physical space at will, to show their reality. Turner is fleeing with Angie from hostile pursuers when he hears her say:

"There is a sick child in my house." The hover nearly left the pavement, when he heard the voice come from her mouth, deep and slow and weirdly glutinous. "I hear the dice being tossed, for her bloody dress. Many are the hands who dig her grave tonight, and yours as well. Enemies pray for your death, hired man. They pray until they sweat. Their prayers are a river of fever." And then a sort of croaking that might have been laughter. Turner risked a glance, saw a silver thread of drool descend from her rigid lips. The deep muscles of her face had contorted into a mask he didn't know. "Who are you?" "I am the Lord of Roads." (C, 184)

Later, Angie is overcome by another god: "She groaned, stiffened, rocked back. 'Hired man,' the voice said. . . . He lowered the gun, 'You're back.' 'No. Legba spoke to you. I am Samedi.' 'Saturday?' 'Baron Saturday, hired man. You met me once on a hillside. The blood lay on you like dew. I drank of your full heart that day' " (C, 200). Samedi returns later to slay, in cyberspace but also in reality, the voracious Virek; it does so by entering Bobby: " 'My name,' a voice said, and Bobby wanted to scream when he realized that it came from his own mouth, 'is Samedi, and you have slain my cousin's horse' " (C, 233). Those who are over-taken by these gods are referred to as speaking in tongues, as do Christian charismatics filled with the Holy Spirit (C, 135).

"The Wig," a visionary living in the orbiting wreck of the Tessier-Ashpool space station, believed "that God lived in cyberspace, or perhaps that cyberspace *was* God, or some new manifestation of same," and the book does not deny the claim (C, 121). Marly enters that space station and is warned away by the priests of that god who is living there: " 'You have no right to disturb us here,' a man's voice said. 'Our work is the work of God, and we alone have seen His true face!' " (C, 194). The artistic boxes that Marly is to track down originated here, and they are indeed relics, tokens of the Holy, for they were made by a giant robot on board the station, the mechanical hand of an artificial intelligence. "The Wig" himself is there, and he tells Marly: " 'The boxes!' Little balls of spittle curled off his lips, obeying the elegant laws of Newtonian physics. 'You whore! They're of the hand of God!' " (C, 196).

The gods are still showing their reality, and the matrix's precession, by over-coming people in the material reality of *Mona Lisa Overdrive*; "And they are there, the Horsemen, the loa: Pappa Legba bright and fluid as mercury, Ezili Freda, who is mother and queen; Samedi, the Baron Cimetiere . . . Similor; Madame Travaux; many others" (M, 255–56). Angie Mitchell reappears in this book, and is over-come on a beach: "The one who came was named Mamman Brigitte, or Grande Brigitte, and while some think her the wife of Baron Samedi, others name her 'most ancient of the dead' " (M, 20). In the time elapsed since *Count Zero*, the gods have come often to Angie: "She was ridden by gods, in New Jersey. She learned to abandon herself to the Horsemen. She saw the loa Linglessou enter Beauvoir in the oumphor, saw his feet scatter the diagrams outlined in white flour. She knew the gods, in New Jersey, and love" (M, 22). Angie knows well "Legba, Mamman Brigitte, the thousand candles" (M, 102). When Bobby questions the reality of these gods, Angie insists upon it: " 'But they come to me,' she'd argued. 'I don't need a deck' " (M, 126). Seeking the truth, Angie asks "Continuity," a cyberspace construct that is a sort of personal assistant to her, whether "the matrix is God," to which it replies, "In a manner of speaking, although it would be more accurate, in terms of the mythform, to say that the matrix *has* a God" (M, 129)—and who should know better but an entity of that very matrix?

Compared to the reality of the cyberspace gods, the old-fashioned Christian gods Angie passes by on the street are rather tatty:

A soapbox evangelist spread his arms high, a pale fuzzy Jesus copying the gesture in the air above him. The projection rig was in the box he stood on, but he wore a battered nylon pack with two speakers sticking over each shoulder like blank chrome heads. The evangelist frowned up at Jesus and adjusted something on the belt at his waist. Jesus strobed, turned green, and vanished. (M, 59)

Note that this holographic god originated in the evangelist's material reality, was put into the cybernetic hologram by the preacher, and it is a pathetic job compared to the power of the gods that come from cyberspace into material reality.

Cyberspace is made real through equation with the indubitably real physical world. There are several strategies through which Gibson makes those links. A major strategy of presenting cyberspace as real is to describe it in tangible physical terms. It is remarkable that in all three books, very few data are sought or obtained as such. Rarely will someone go to the computer to look something up, to obtain information or a specific datum. Instead, cyberspace is a place to enter, in which to act. It is spoken of as if it were a physical context. The character "Gentry was convinced that cyberspace had a Shape, an overall total form" (M, 76), which would be characteristic of real entities. When Case is able to reenter cyberspace after corrective surgery, he is going "home" to a real space existing objectively and independently. This space "flowed, flowered for him, fluid neon origami trick, the unfolding of his distanceless home, his country, transparent 3D chessboard extending to infinity. Inner eye opening to the stepped scarlet pyramid of the Eastern Seabord Fission Authority burning beyond the green cubes of Mitsubishi Bank of America, and high and very far away he saw the spiral arms of military systems, forever beyond his reach. And somewhere he was laughing, in a white-painted loft, distant fingers caressing the deck, tears of release streaking his face" (N, 52). Note that Case's physical body is "distant" but continuous with the experience being described in cyberspace. Later Case will launch his attack on Sense/Net from "a 'pirate's paradise,' on the jumbled border of a low-security academic grid" (N, 81)—note the description of cyberspace in physical terms.

What is real is physical and solid. The universe is material. The data sets that make up cyberspace are on the one hand understood to be represented as geometric shapes. Mention is occasionally made that the objects "seen" in cyberspace are representations of data. But on the other hand, these representations are described in nearly all of the books' discourse as if they are material; those shapes are never experienced as data but instead as physical entities such as "red solid, a massive rectangle" (N, 101), or "that little pink box, four jumps left" (N, 168). Movement in the matrix is spoken of as movement among physical masses. The "Eastern Seabord Fission Authority" is a "plateau," and movement from one data base to another in reaching the plateau is physical movement: "They ascended lattices of light, levels strobing, a blue flicker" (N, 115). The artificial intelligence Wintermute initially appears as "a simple cube of white light" (N, 115). A virus that Case introduces "was unfolding around them. Polychrome shadow, countless translucent layers shifting and recombining. Protean, enormous, it towered above them, blotting out the void" (N, 168). The data of cyberspace are physically stable and oriented in terms of left and right, up or down: " 'That's it, huh? Big green rectangle off left?' 'You got it. Corporate core data for Tessier-Ashpool S.A.' " (N, 167).

Count Zero likewise makes the matrix seem real through the appearance of "complex geometric forms" such as a "blue pyramid" or "cluster of orange rectangles" (C, 82). Travelers in cyberspace negotiate "liquid flowers of milky white" or "thousands of tiny spheres or bubbles" (C, 83). Movement through the matrix is described in entirely physical, kinesiological terms:

Now and ever was, fast forward, Jammer's deck jacked up so high above the neon hotcores, a topography of data he didn't know. Big stuff, mountain-high, sharp and corporate in the nonplace that was cyberspace. . . . He took a right-angle left at random, pivoting smoothly at the grid intersection, testing the deck for response. It was amazing. (C, 165–66)

The "nonplace" is in fact so real, so physical, that only these terms of physical movement can describe it.

Cyberspace is experienced as physical forms in *Mona Lisa Overdrive* as well. "The Fission Authority had always looked like a big red Aztec pyramid" (M, 76). Kumiko, fleeing Roger Swain, realizes she cannot use her credit card in real space because it will be seen as a "flare like magnesium on the grid of cyberspace" (M, 218). Kumiko takes refuge with Tick, who tells her that big changes are happening in the matrix. But, as is true for so many changes in real things, Tick explains that it is "easier to show you than try to explain it" (M, 245), as if it were a physical object to be seen. And cyberspace does become a real thing in the form of a hologram of the geometric shapes that is the matrix (M, 247). Although the characters understand that the Fission Authority "didn't have to" look that way (which is representational language), its manifestation as a red pyramid is not manipulable by those who encounter it. It cannot be "spoken" in a different way. Its solidity is a permanence obtaining to reality alone.

One strategy in pursuit of that equation of reality and cyberspace is to use a narrative that makes the material coextensive with the digital. What happens in cyberspace is manifested in the material world, thus making them continuous. The equation of reality and cyberspace can be seen in the ways in which scenes and images from both continuously alternate in Case and Molly's attack upon Sense/Net (N, 61–69). Molly is described as punching a security guard in person in exactly the same terms that are used to describe Case "punching his way into the sphere" of data in the matrix (N, 63). The narrative shifts from cyberspace to material space so seamlessly that it merges them.

There is no difference between what happens to the physical body and what happens to the agent in cyberspace; one leaves the body for an equally real immersion in the matrix. As Case says, "I jack in and I'm not here. It's all the same" (N, 105). Cyberspace and material experienced are equated as real through their pragmatic effects. If both the real and cyberspace behave the same way, they are essentially the same. Events in cyberspace can affect the material body as if cyberspace were continuous with reality. Attacking Wintermute in *Neuromancer*, Case feels "a steady pulse of pain, midway down his spine" which suddenly knocks him unconscious (N, 116). Case awakens feeling physical pain and thinking he has returned to physical reality, but he is in cyberspace; it is coextensive with the material world. Eventually the truth dawns on him as he realizes, "This is the matrix" rather than the streets of Tokyo from which they are indistinguishable (N, 119). Later, Molly asks Case about the experience: "And it was real?" to which he replies, gesturing to the café in which they sit, "Real as this" (N, 128). Molly does not ask if it seemed as if it were real, she asks if it was in fact real; and Case's response "real as this" refers not to some dubious simulation but to the material world in which they sit. In *Mona Lisa Overdrive*, launching quickly into cyberspace, Kumiko experiences "vertigo" as if she were really in a high place (M, 262).

In *Count Zero*, cyberspace is equated with reality by making them continuous and coextensive. Physical distance is measured in "klicks" (C, 40), while movement in cyberspace is effected by "clicking" on a mouse: " 'When you punch out past the Basketball,' Jammer said to Bobby, 'you wanna dive right three clicks and go for the floor' " (C, 210). Marly's transition from material space to cyberspace as she enters a room in Virek's offices is likewise seamless, equating the matrix with the real: "As her fingers closed around the cool brass knob, it seemed to squirm, sliding along a touch spectrum of texture and temperature in the first second of contact. Then it became metal again, green-painted iron, sweeping out and down, along a line of perspective, an old railing she grasped now in wonder. A few drops of rain blew into her face" (C, 12–13) and she is into a cyberspace that is as real as the material world she has just left. Later, having received a lucrative and unexpected job offer from Virek, she returns to material reality but finds it less real than the matrix: " 'I'm in shock,' she said to the bags on the bed. 'I must take care. Nothing seems real now' " (C, 25). Angie, in *Count Zero*, likewise cannot tell the difference between where cyberspace and the material divide, because of her ability to enter cyberspace with no technological apparatus: " 'Sometimes when I'm awake. It's like I'm jacked into a deck, only I'm free of the grid, flying' " (C, 158). Later, Jaylene Slide speaks to Bobby in cyberspace but explicitly equates it with Los Angeles, the material city: "This is my space, my construct. This is L.A., boy. People here don't do *anything* without jacking" (C, 212).

A major strategy in which the physical world is equated to cyberspace is through the violence that connects material and cyber reality. In *Mona Lisa Overdrive*, Kumiko sitting in a material room watches Tick's face bruise as he experiences violence in cyberspace, making it as real as if someone had hit him with a material fist (M, 288). Cyberspace is thus presented as a reality of no shakier foundation than is material experience. Cruising cyberspace in *Count Zero*, Bobby loses his companion: " 'Where's Jackie?' 'Sittin' cold-cocked in cyberspace while you answer my questions' "—and then his interlocutor appears to threaten him with physical violence in cyberspace: " 'I'm Slide,' the figure said, hands on its hips, 'Jaylene. You don't fuck with me. Nobody in L.A . . . fucks with me' " despite the fact that they are in the matrix—which is as real and as violent as Los Angeles (C, 211).

Even violence occurring in the material world is so interconnected with technology that it makes cyberspace real—really violent. The discovery of violence everywhere makes one realm connected to the other. At the start of *Count Zero*, Turner is tracked down by "a slamhound" which has been programmed to search for his pheromones—it explodes and nearly kills him in New Delhi (C, 1). It is a fitting culmination to a career of violence for Turner, who once drove an exploding bus into a hotel lobby (C, 20). Violence dogs Turner everywhere; as he waits for the defector Mitchell to arrive in Arizona, it becomes clear that all members of the Hosaka team are prepared to kill one another if need be (C, 42, 44, 64). When he escapes from an explosion that kills everyone but him and Angie Mitchell, he seeks refuge at his brother's compound, where violence is offered to intruders by "augmented hounds" that merge reality and cyberspace in their heavily prostheticized bodies (C, 130). Bobby, in *Count Zero*, lives near the Big Playground which is "a dicey place" in which one can get "chopped" by "predatory loonies" such as the "Penis Collector" (C, 31). This Eden is no more real in terms of violence than is cyberspace, however, for Bobby barely escapes death while in the matrix and his enemies there later bomb his apartment: " 'There's somebody doesn't mess around' " in this world (C, 39).

Violence bridges cyberspace and the material, making the former real, in *Mona Lisa Overdrive* as well. Angie is told by "Grande Brigitte" in cyberspace that she should "fear poison," and sure enough Angie's experience in the matrix causes her nose to bleed (M, 23). Tick is assaulted in cyberspace, which results in real physical violence and pain: "Tick had gotten to his feet and was gingerly massaging his arm. 'Christ,' he said, 'I was sure she'd dislocated it for me' " (M, 268). Violence originating in material reality seems not as real as that beginning in cyberspace; when Sally attacks someone assailing Kumiko, "the sudden, casual violence might have been a dream" (M, 134).

We have seen that one sign of the permanence of reality is its complexity; that which is real is many-layered and thus not entirely knowable or predictable. Cyberspace is likewise described as possessing "unthinkable complexity" (N, 51). The artificial intelligence Wintermute has "extreme complexity" (N, 115). Data appear visually as physical entities precisely because of this complexity: "People jacked in so they could hustle. Put the trodes on and they were out there, all the data in the world stacked up like one big neon city, so you could cruise around and have a kind of grip on it, visually anyway, because if you didn't, it was too complicated" (M, 16). Sheer size seems to be the only difference between cyberspace and material reality, as the Dixie Flatline construct, living in the small world of cyberspace, asks Case, "You havin' fun in the big world outside?" (N, 217). The idea of relative size but comparable complexity is also reflected in *Mona Lisa Overdrive* as the characters examine a model of cyberspace. "Now Gentry went to the big display unit, the projection table. 'There are worlds within worlds,' he said. 'Macrocosm, microcosm. We carried an entire universe across a bridge tonight, and that which is above is like that below' " (M, 108).

Cyberspace can certainly be seen as representations of data, it can be seen as sheer simulation. Gibson is aware of these possibilities, and mentions them from time to time. But the pains he takes to depict the matrix as permanent, as continuous with material reality, as independent worlds and universes, as sources of violent power that can affect material reality, as the home of gods, certainly argue for the reality of cyberspace. Let us turn now to Gibson's discourse of commodification, which likewise urges his audience to see the matrix as real.

COMMODIFICATION

We saw above that although Gibson acknowledges the representational nature of some aspects of cyberspace, he treats them as entirely real. A similar paradox is found when it comes to the dimension of commodification in his novels. The pursuit of business and its financial rewards seems to be the dominant, perhaps the only, value expressed in Gibson's world. People are preoccupied with products, shopping, and acquisition. Yet there is very little depiction of the accumulation of wealth or capital by most people, of the amassing of products, or of living large. Most of Gibson's characters live on the economic edge. Beyond a few very wealthy characters, there is little excess in Gibson's world, despite a frantic pursuit of getting and spending. How can people pursue money so assiduously, spend it constantly, and have so little to show for it? The answer, we will see, is that real commodities matter the most in Gibson's world; the amassing of capital and other financial representations seems not to matter for most people. Money is acquired as an end in itself, and commodities are celebrated for their use value throughout the novels. Gibson's universe is a world of goods, which is an argument in the rhetoric of reality.

A key term in Gibson's novels is *biz*, slang for business (N, 5; C, 113): "Here he was with a major operator, up to his neck in some amazing kind of biz" (C, 115). At one level, biz means getting and spending, the acquisition of money so as to buy goods. The centrality of financial reward in the novels is clear. Anything that is done is done with some justification of gain, however far removed from the immediate circumstance. The bottom line seems always to be in everyone's mind. More commonly, biz simply means hustling for the love of hustling. Financial rewards come attached to what the characters do, but hustle is its own reward.

Biz bespeaks a preoccupation with commercialization that runs throughout Gibson's novels. Business reigns supreme. Governments are nearly absent from all the novels. Despairing of finding a counter to Swain's power, Tick in *Mona Lisa Overdrive* exclaims, "Christ, we've still got a *government* here. Not run by big companies. Well, not directly" (M, 261). Corporations drive the action, and people move within their hegemony absorbed with commerce: "Power, in Case's world, meant corporate power" (N, 203). Part Two of *Neuromancer* is called "The Shopping Expedition" (N, 41), and that is precisely what Case and Molly do as soon as they leave Japan in Armitage's employ:

He stood, pulling on a wrinkled pair of new black jeans that lay at his feet, and knelt beside the bags. The first one he opened was Molly's: neatly folded clothing and small expensive-looking gadgets. The second was stuffed with things he didn't remember buying: books, tapes, a simstim deck, clothing with French and Italian labels. Beneath a green t-shirt, he discovered a flat, origami-wrapped package, recycled Japanese paper. (N, 44)

Commercialization consumes social relations. The Tessier-Ashpool family is in fact "a very quiet, very eccentric first-generation high-orbit family, run like a corporation" (N, 75). Their artificial intelligence says that this corporate family uses money as a use-value wall: "We have sealed ourselves away behind our money, growing inward, generating a seamless universe of self" (N, 173). Even identity, or lack thereof, can be bought. Hiring a street gang, "Armitage crossed stiffly to the table and took three fat bundles of New Yen from the pockets of his trenchcoat. 'You want to count it?' he asked Yonderboy. 'No,' the Panther Modern said, 'You'll pay. You're a Mr. Who. You pay to stay one. Not a Mr. Name.' 'I hope that's not a threat,' Armitage said. 'That's business,' said Yonderboy" (N, 68).

It is no accident that Chase is chased through the streets of Tokyo by an assassin named *Wage*. Chase himself chases wages, and little else (N, 9–10). His environment is a hypercommercialized Tokyo, where one may find "a dozen distinct species of hustler, all swarming the street in an intricate dance of desire and commerce" (N, 10–11). Life and death and everything are reduced to the terms of commerce. Case cruises the Internet hoping to enrich himself by stealing from the "rich fields of data" (N, 5). Case and a contact of his, Julius Deane, discuss the assassins pursuing him in the calm, objective language of commerce: "They might have been discussing the price of ginger" (N, 13). Deane sees everything as a market, including violent conflict: " 'Wonderful what a war can do for one's markets,' " he says (N, 35). We know who won at the end of *Neuromancer* by who gets paid in what way; this book's happily ever after is that "the passports Armitage had provided were valid, and they were both credited with large amounts in numbered Geneva accounts. *Marcus Garvey* would be returned eventually, and Maelcum and Aerol given money through the Bahamian bank that dealt with Zion cluster" (N, 268).

As with Case and Molly upon being hired by Armitage, Marly Krushkhova's first act after being hired by Virek is to shop until she grew "tired of shopping" and picked the first expensive hotel she could find in which to rest (C, 27). In *Count Zero*, everybody seems to be like Turner, "a mercenary, his employers vast corporations warring covertly for the control of entire economies" (C, 4). His allies in Christopher Mitchell's defection likewise call him "mercenary," as if that were his name (C, 69). Angie is astonished that Turner works for no one company, as did her father: " 'No company,' she said, to the window. 'How's that?' 'You don't have a company, do you? I mean, you work for whoever hires you.' 'That's right.' 'Don't you get scared?' " (C, 158).

Commodities and their acquisition seem to be everyone's only motive—the final climactic confrontation of the book takes place in a multistory mall appropriately called Hypermart (C, 146). Jammer even sees the gods of cyberspace who ride Angie Mitchell as ultimately commercial: "those Goddamn things know how to make *deals*!" (C, 168). After spending idyllic weeks with a beautiful woman who helps him to heal emotionally from a devastating injury, Turner discovers her true motive for being with him: " 'She's a field psychologist, on retainer to Hosaka' " (C, 9). Turner specializes in shopping for defecting corporate scientists: " 'You took Chauvet from IBM for Mitsu,' he said, 'and they say you took Semenov out of Tomsk' " (C, 43).

Young Bobby fantasizes about the databases he will crack and the deals he will cut, but only " '*If* you got the money' " (C, 170). Commodification is so ubiquitous that people regard each other through that lens: "The Gothick girl regarded Bobby with mild interest but no flash of human recognition whatever, as though she were seeing an ad for a product she'd heard of but had no intention of buying" (C, 36). Commerce defines identity for Bobby as for others; although he is quite hungry, he realizes he cannot buy food because "they'd have his chip number by now; using it would spotlight him for anyone tracking him in cyberspace" (C, 37) since money use equals identity. Money generates identity for the more wealthy as well; the Tessier-Ashpools' liberated artificial intelligence entity refers to "the family that funded my birth," genesis expressed in terms of commerce (C, 226).

Wealth is present in Gibson's books as an entity in its own right, almost as a character. As Virek explains to Marly, "Aspects of my wealth have become autonomous" (C, 13). Marly observes of Virek, "His money has a life of its own. Perhaps a will of its own" and in that sense it has become real (C, 74). His wealth takes on physical, real characterstics, as when Virek describes it as " 'a sort of black hole. The unnatural density of my wealth drags irresistibly at the rarest works of the human spirit' " (C, 14). All his actions are "lubricated by a film of money" (C, 177)—a physical, oily metaphor. Yet Virek continues to pursue gain. Marly's friend Andrea raises the question of whether his money has overwhelmed his identity: " 'he's the single wealthiest individual, period . . . but there's the catch, really: *is* he an individual?' " (C, 100). Virek's virtual assistant, Paco, agrees: "He is wealth itself" (C, 103).

In *Mona Lisa Overdrive*, preoccupation with commerce continues. Seeking a way to escape from Swain's house, Kumiko hits upon the perfect justification that will trump all objections to her going out: " 'I'll tell them,' she said, 'that I need to go shopping' " (M, 200). It is clear that cyberspace itself is a site of pursuing commodities. Slick believes that "people jacked in so they could hustle" by finding or stealing data to sell (M, 16). The Tessier-Ashpools, whose fortune haunts the entire trilogy, began as a family based upon gain: "It was marriage as merger" (M, 124).

Wealth is commodified as if it were a real thing in this book as well. Everything is commodified in Japan, including history: "History there had become a quantity, a rare thing, parceled out by government and preserved by law and corporate funding" (M, 5). Mona recalls learning as a girl how to kill catfish by putting a wire to their skulls, and "you just slip it in"—by comparison, she sees money as a weapon: "It's called money. You just slip it in" as if it were a physical knife (M, 147).

Everybody in Gibson's world hustles frantically for lucrative contracts, huge payoffs, for biz—but paradoxically, very few seem to be rich. Biz seems not to create much of anything with exchange value. The reader is given hints of huge corporations and wealthy people at their summits. We see minor characters such as Roger Swain or Julius Deane who are reported to be wealthy. But that wealth is not manifested in commensurably lavish lifestyles. The occasionally unambiguously wealthy person such as Josef Virek appears. But most of the characters have not amassed wealth from their hustling; what they have remains at the level of real goods, as befits a rhetoric of reality.

Most of the ordinary citizens of *Neuromancer* are "working all your life for one" company: "Company housing, company hymn, company funeral" (N, 37). Their lives are so barren that they flock to the bloodsports carried out in arenas where combatants fight each other to the death (N, 36–39). Christopher Mitchell is a top scientist for Maas, but must live in an isolated mesa that is "prison and fortress" (C, 88). The wealthy Julius Deane can find nothing to spend his money on but DNA and hormonal treatments to extend his life, clothing he never wears in public, and candied ginger (C, 12–13). Josef Virek is also wealthy, but his actual body has "been confined for over a decade to a vat. In some hideous industrial suburb" (C, 13); as real as his life in cyberspace may be, he cannot buy himself physical mobility. Case is much like Sally/Molly of the first and third books, and Turner of *Count Zero*, all of them "mercenaries" who live from hotel to hotel, scoring huge fees by "earning danger money" (C, 63) but never benefiting from them materially. Turner has so little freedom from his earnings that it appears as if he is forced to return to work when his boss Conroy comes to pluck him from his idyllic beach existence (C, 7–9). The money he has seems useless; he sent his brother large sums to take their sick mother to the best clinics, but she died regardless, for as his brother tells him, " 'What she mainly wanted was to see you' " (C, 156). Sally introduces herself in *Mona Lisa Overdrive* as "a businesswoman," but her business dealings do not keep her from a life of violence and constant danger (M, 68).

The answer to the paradox posed by constant pursuit of money that seems to benefit nobody is that money counts for so little because things count for so much. Gibson's rhetoric of reality features material goods with use value, real stuff, as the ultimate value. One striking evidence of the value of commodities in their own right is the constant, ongoing use of brand name references.

In Gibson's trilogy, people rarely just get into a car, turn on a computer, or drink a beer. The brand name of the product is quite often attached to the car, computer, or beer. Things in Gibson's world are not merely objects, they are commodities. We are reminded that his world has been bought and sold. But in the balance between objects with use value and exchange value, use value reigns supreme.

Examples of the commodification of real objects through brand names may be found on nearly every page, but let us examine some representative examples. The first page of the first book shows Case drinking a Kirin beer (N, 3). Julius Deane's bookcases are "Neo-Aztec," his lamp is "Disney," his coffee table is "Kandinsky-inspired" and his clock is "Dali" (N, 12). Case buys a pistol that is a copy of a Walther PPK (N, 19), and he will later be arrested by the Turing police wielding "a smooth black Walther" (N, 163). His hotel room contains a Hitachi computer (N, 20). He smokes Yeheyuan cigarettes (N, 30) and drinks Tsingtao beer (N, 22) when he isn't downing Tuborg (N, 92). Case's personal high-end computer is "an Ono-Sendai Cyberspace 7," but his loft also contains another "Hosaka computer; a Sony monitor . . . a Braun coffeemaker" (N, 46). In space he links the Ono-Sendai to a Cray monitor (N, 114). His ally Molly takes her drugs from an "Akai transdermal unit" (N, 78). Even in an orbiting space station, Case encounters brands geared to proprietary "expensive shops: Gucci, Tsuyako, Hermes, Liberty" (N, 142). One brand name that never appears in the trilogy is Microsoft; we simply do not know where that company has gone. Its memory is preserved in the "angular fragments of colored silicon," or "microsofts," that people can insert into ports implanted in their heads that give them extra memory or data capability (N, 57).

Count Zero is awash in brand name commodities, reiterating the message that use value commodities are of chief value in this world. Turner lives life on the move: "Home was the next airport Hyatt" (C, 2). He wears a Rolex watch (C, 3). He admires the firearms carried by others, such as a passing soldier's "carbine-format Steiner-Optic laser with Fabrique Nationale sights" (C, 4). He drinks Carta Blanca on the beach (C, 7). Turner is ferried about in a "black Honda" helicopter (C, 19). One of his associates at the site of Mitchell's defection chews "Copenhagen snuff" (C, 71).

Marly Krushkhova moves in a world of brand names as well, including a brand name of the future, "her good jacket—a Sally Stanley" (C, 10, 56). Her erstwhile boyfriend Alain smokes "Gauloise nonfilters" (C, 60). Her friend Andrea lives in an old apartment building lit by "Fuji Electric's biofluorescent strips" (C, 48). Marly shows her a hologram of Virek's boxes on a "Braun" generator (C, 49). Bobby Newmark, being poor, can afford only "the little Ono-Sendai" computer (C, 17) and "a six-year-old Hitachi entertainment module" (C, 18).

Commodities abound in *Mona Lisa Overdrive*, where products sport "the ubiquitous Maas-Neotek logo" (M, 1). The desperately poor residents of the Dog Solitude drive a "vintage Dodge" (M, 10). Mona, also poor, has a Lufthansa bag for luggage (M, 62). Her sad life has led her to prostitution in a Holiday Inn (M, 84). Angie Mitchell's more privileged life allows her to go about in a Lear jet (M, 19), and her every move is monitored by a hovering "tiny Dornier helicopter" (M, 17). Kumiko is nearly run over in London by "a fat black Honda taxi" (M, 34) as she enters a pub with Bass ashtrays on the table (M, 35).

If brand names anchor a sense of goods as commodities, naming the national origin of commodities grounds them in real processes of production. Throughout the trilogy, goods are identified consistently as to their national origin. The bartender Ratz in *Neuromancer* has a teeth full of specifically "East European steel" (N, 3), while his prosthetic arm is Russian (N, 4). The drugs that Case takes are Brazilian (N, 7). His cigarette lighter is made of "German steel" (N, 30). Molly makes him coffee on a "German stove" (N, 45). In *Count Zero*, Marly has an account in a Dutch bank, and draws her bath water through a Japanese filtration device (C, 25). She uses her wealth to buy a haircut "by a Burmese girl with a West German laser" and a shirt in "Flemish flannel" for her friend, Andrea (C, 49). She herself wears "the leather coat she'd bought in Brussels" (C, 59). Bobby Newmark has a Japanese knife in his apartment (C, 29).

Money is everywhere in Gibson's novels, but real commodities are what matters. A few wealthy individuals amass great fortunes, but we do not see a commensurate amassing of goods beyond what is immediately of use value. Close to the financial edge, Gibson's characters are grounded in a world of real goods. Even wealth itself is commodified, and finds form in metaphors of real objects. Having seen Gibson's rhetoric of reality in permanence and change and in commodification, let us turn to subjectivity.

SUBJECTIVITY

Grounded, centered subjects typical of a rhetoric of reality abound in Gibson's novels. His people live gritty lives on the streets, struggling for survival. But despite danger, divided allegiance, and often no place to call home, his characters maintain strong central subjectivities. Postmodern characters with fragmented identities are eventually destroyed. Gibson's main characters are entirely centered. Molly observes, " 'Anybody any good at what they do, that's what they *are*, right? You gotta jack, I gotta tussle' " (N, 50)—and elsewhere we read, "Her being, like his, was the thing she did to make a living" (N, 56)—"This was what he was, who he was, his being" (N, 59). These are affirmations of centeredness, of no conflict or separation between job and identity, of the subject grounded in the work of daily existence.

We have seen that Gibson argues for the reality of cyberspace. On the dimension of subjectivity, he likewise argues for the reality of cyberagents. Personhood is continuous across the material/cyber divide. By arguing for the reality of these cyberagents, Gibson argues for the reality of cyberspace in general.

If initiative, motive, and genesis of action are indications of real subjectivity, it is clear that cyberagents are real. It is the technology of the matrix that has made the reality of cyberagents possible; Case is told by the Turing police, "For thousands of years men dreamed of pacts with demons. Only now are such things possible" (N, 163). Artificial intelligences are clearly the originators of most of the action across all three novels, Wintermute and to some extent Neuromancer in the first book, and the many "gods" who split off from their merger in the later books. Lesser cyberagents are equally real. Artificial intelligences have such a large capacity for independent thinking that they must be controlled: "the minute, I mean the nanosecond, that one starts figuring out ways to make itself smarter, Turing'll wipe it. . . . Every AI ever built has an electromagnetic shotgun wired to its forehead" (N, 132).

Case has the Dixie Flatline to assist him in cruising cyberspace. The Flatline perfectly illustrates the continuity between subjectivity in material reality and subjectivity in cyberspace, because he used to be alive: " 'How you doing, Dixie?' 'I'm dead, Case. Got enough time in on this Hosaka to figure that one' " (N, 105). Dixie is an even better hacker now than he was before: " 'Hey, boy, I was that good when I was alive. You ain't seen nothin'. No hands!' " (N, 167). Gibson problematizes the difference between cyberagents and flesh and blood when the Flatline tells Case, " 'I'm not human either, but I *respond* like one. See?' 'Wait a sec,' Case said. 'Are you sentient, or not?' 'Well, it *feels* like I am, kid, but I'm really just a bunch of ROM. It's one of them, ah, philosophical questions, I guess' " (N, 131). Which of us could say more about our own identities? Subjectivity is so strong in Gibson's world that as long as one is not dead too long, one can die physically, stay alive in cyberspace, and return, as does Case: " 'You were braindead again, five seconds' " the Dixie Flatline tells him (N, 175), and later, the Rastafarian Maelcum says, " 'You dead awhile there, mon.' 'It happens,' he said. 'I'm getting used to it' " (N, 181).

Count Zero continues the theme of cyberagents who are depicted as real, with subjectivity crossing the material/matrix boundary. Josef Virek lives mainly in cyberspace; certainly his subjectivity does, although his material body resides in a vat in Stockholm. It is not clear where the grounding of his subjectivity is strongest, but clearly the implication is that subjectivities in cyberspace can be as real as any other. Bobby Newmark enters cyberspace but while there is nearly killed by enemies he encounters there—"Bobby was alone now, his autonomic nervous system overridden by the defenses of a database three thousand kilometers" away (C, 17). But he is saved by another equally real, equally digital entity: "And something *leaned in*, vastness unutterable, from beyond the most distant edge of anything he'd ever known or imagined, and touched him" (C, 18). If an entity of cyberspace can act in material space, it must be real. Bobby's mother is returning from Boston with a "new hole in her head," a socket for microsofts that allow her to access soap operas (C, 33). The mother's entire social interaction seems to be with cyberagents, who are real to her.

Artificial intelligences in this book are originators of motives, sites of decision and thus real subjects: Beauvoir tells Bobby, " 'Maybe an AI somewhere wants to augment its private cash flow. Some AI's have citizenship, right?' " (C, 79). Cybersubjects are so real they can negotiate with humans: " 'The last seven, eight years, there's been funny stuff out there, out on the console cowboy circuit. The new jockeys, *they make deal with things*, don't they, Lucas?' " (C, 118). The airplane Turner and Angie escape in is almost a subject: "The plane was smart, smart as any dog" (C, 125). Cyberagents are so real that they are sometimes depicted as real subjects while flesh and blood people are their technical instruments. Jackie is how the loa of cyberspace enter material reality. Thus, Lucas tells Bobby, " 'Think of Jackie as a deck, Bobby, a cyberspace deck, a very pretty one with nice ankles' " (C, 114).

Independent subjects emerge from cyberspace into the material world in *Mona Lisa Overdrive* as well. Kumiko, fleeing Japan to seek refuge with Roger Swain in England, has been given a device that generates a holographic companion, Colin, who is as real as any real subject. Angie Mitchell is a kind of flesh-and-blood cyberagent, able to access the matrix without a deck: "she'd dreamed cyberspace, as though the neon gridlines of the matrix waited for her behind her eyelids" (M, 48). She will discover later that her life and actions are largely controlled by the cybersubject Continuity, which she had thought was merely a digitized personal assistant (M, 258). Gentry is perceived by Slick to be a real embodiment of the matrix as well: "it seemed to Slick that the Shape must be right there, blazing through Gentry's forehead" (M, 83). Sally and Kumiko find that the physically deceased Finn has been re-embodied as a construct and speaks to people as an "oracle" from a shrine in an alley wall: " 'Finn,' Sally said . . . 'you gotta be crazy' . . . 'I should be so lucky. A rig like this, I'm pushing it to have a little imagination, let alone crazy.' Kumiko moved closer, then squatted beside Sally. 'It's a construct, a personality job?' . . . 'Sure. You seen 'em before. Real-time memory if I wanna, wired into c-space if I wanna. Got this oracle gig to keep my hand in, you know?' " (M, 164). Kumiko has been told that such digitized constructs are not real agents, but she has her doubts: "But did it wake, Kumiko wondered, when the alley was empty? Did its laser vision scan the silent fall of midnight snow?" (M, 166). An important way in which cyberagents are real in this novel is Gibson's introduction of the biochip. Since "silicon approaches certain functional limits . . . the biochip was necessary" (M, 256–57). A biochip merges the technological and the living, thus making cybersubjects real on a physical level.

Gibson emphasizes the reality of cybersubjects by treating the physical person, the body, as if it were fundamentally code, a cyberagent. Lisa Lee, an addicted friend of Case, is seen as computer code: "her face bathed in restless laser light, features reduced to a code" (N, 8). The personalities of those who were once physically real, such as the Finn or the Dixie Flatline, seem to be commensurate with code, since they come back to life as personality constructs in cyberspace (N 49–50, 76–77). Molly's "sensorium" is reduced to a digital signal that Case is able to read as they assault Sense/Net, he in cyberspace and she in person (N, 53). As Case goes into cyberspace it is not a move from the real to the not real but instead merely a transition from one reality to another, an "abrupt jolt into other flesh" (N, 56).

Gibson also emphasizes the reality of cybersubjects by questioning the agency, the personhood, of the flesh and blood. The term "meat" figures prominently, especially in *Neuromancer*, as a belittling reference to material people: "the meat, the flesh the [console] cowboys mocked" (N, 239). To be physically real is not as good as becoming a cybersubject: "In the bars he'd frequented as a cowboy hotshot, the elite stance involved a certain relaxed contempt for the flesh. The body was meat. Case fell into the prison of his own flesh" (N, 6). Cyberagents disdain experience that is largely oriented towards the physical body: "Travel was a meat thing" (N, 77), since it involved moving the body, not the cybersubject. Case's realization that he might live to escape his enemies in Japan is expressed as, "He was still here, still meat" (N, 37). Troubled by his emotional reaction to the ongoing violence of his life, he dismisses it as the weakness of the flesh: "*Meat*, some part of him said. *It's the meat talking, ignore it*" (N, 152). Experiences in cyberspace can be dismissed if they are good only for the pleasure of the flesh: "Cowboys didn't get into simstim, he thought, because it was basically a meat toy" (N, 55).

Physical being alone can be distasteful. Case can "smell his own stale sweat" in his reduced circumstances at the start of the novel (N, 5). He feels "simple animal fear" as he escapes assassins (N, 18). Lisa Lee, an addicted friend of his, has the "eyes of some animal pinned in the headlights of an oncoming vehicle" (N, 8). Gibson's strategy in this denigrating of the body is not so much to deny reality to the physical as to boost the reality, the value, the centeredness of the subjectivity in cyberspace.

We have seen that a major fact distinguishing simulation from reality is that there are few consequences for action in simulation, enduring and serious consequences in reality. An important dimension of Gibson's rhetoric of reality is the prevalence of serious and permanent issues of life and death of the subject, of people. The trilogy is, as we have noted, extremely violent. We know that these books do not describe a simulation because death is real. Death comes quickly in each novel: Case is being hunted by assassins, who are themselves destroyed by Molly, in the opening scenes of *Neuromancer*. Turner is blown apart, literally, on the first page of *Count Zero* and must be surgically reconstructed. Bobby Newmark's apartment is blown up, probably killing his mother, in *Mona Lisa Overdrive*. Real death coming to real people marks the rhetoric of reality in all three books.

Some characters such as the Dixie Flatline in *Neuromancer* or the Finn in *Mona Lisa Overdrive* were physical at one point, have died, and have returned in cyberspace as constructs. Count Zero and Angie physically die so as to move in together in cyberspace in *Mona Lisa Overdrive*. But the movement from physicality to cyberspace is not reversible, it is permanent and enduring. There is no reset button that will restore Angie to her body. Talk of ghosts, those who have irrevocably left the body, abounds in the novels. Bobby in *Count Zero* hears "ghost stories" from some matrix navigators (C, 38). Ghosts haunt Kumiko as well, the ghost of her mother, "ghosts beyond the window, too, ghosts in the stratosphere of Europe's winter" (M, 1). Sally talks to the dead Finn, who has become a computer construct: " 'I wanna talk to him,' she said, her voice hard and careful. 'He's dead.' 'I know that' " (M, 163). In *Neuromancer*, the patriarch of the Tessier-Ashpool clan commits suicide as Case and Molly arrive on board his space station; his despair is matched by that of the computer construct the Dixie Flatline, who makes but one request of Case: he wants to be erased when the adventure is over. Later, Neuromancer will exclaim, "I am the dead," insofar as he is the sum of the dead Tessier—Ashpool personalities (N, 244). Both the artificial intelligences, Neuromancer and Wintermute, are thus described as ghosts (N, 229, 250).

Gibson's world is one of startling medical advancements. Most parts of the body can be replaced by technological or biological prostheses. Organs and limbs are widely available and can be purchased on the open market. One can cycle one's parts over and over as needed, depending upon funds, of course. But the core subject remains, despite sometimes massive overhauling of parts. With the exception of Armitage, who destroys himself (N, 191–94), Gibson's subjects are fully centered. We see Molly reappear as Sally Shears, for instance, but it is clear that it is the same centered subject behind the trivial change in name. The reality of the subject persists despite physical replacement. In this sense also, the physical body is more durable, more enduring, in Gibson's books than it is in our world. Especially if a replacement is technological, of steel and plastic, the material self that grounds the real subject has a measure of permanence.

Prostheses are common throughout the trilogy. It is "an age of affordable beauty," however one defines that (N, 4). On the first page of *Neuromancer* we meet the bartender Ratz, "his prosthetic arm jerking monotonously as he filled a tray of glasses" (N, 3). In this bar a drunken argument breaks out among the patrons, not about sports or politics, but about who does the best "nerve-splicing" (N, 4). The Dixie Flatline, now a computer construct, died because of his "surplus Russian heart, implanted in a POW camp during the war," which he refused to replace (N, 78). Julius Deane, Case's business contact, has reached the age of one hundred and thirty-five technologically, from "a weekly fortune in serums and hormones" and a yearly trip "to Tokyo, where genetic surgeons re-set the code of his DNA" (N, 12). Confronting his nemesis Wage, Case notes that his "eyes were vatgrown sea-green Nikon transplants" (N, 12).

Molly herself is a marvel of prostheses: Her "glasses were surgically inset, sealing her sockets" (N, 24), which means that " 'I can see in the dark, Case. Microchannel image-amps in my glasses' " (N, 32). She has other, more deadly prostheses: "She held out her hands, palms up, the white fingers slightly spread, and with a barely audible click, ten doubled-edged, four-centimeter scalpel blades slid from their housings beneath the burgundy nails" (N, 25). The Finn scans Molly and detects "something new in your head, yeah. Silicon, coat of pyrolitic carbons. A clock, right?" (N, 49). Molly refers to a former boyfriend, Johnny (who must be Johnny Mnemonic of the eponymous film and the story in Gibson's collection, *Burning Chrome*), who had "chips in his head and people paid to hide data there" (N, 176).

Molly's associates, the Panther Modern gang, likewise favor prostheses: "His face was a simple graft grown on collagen and shark-cartilage polysaccharides, smooth and hideous. It was one of the nastiest pieces of elective surgery Case had ever seen. When Angelo smiled, revealing the razor-sharp canines of some large animal, Case was actually relieved. Toothbud transplants. He'd seen that before" (N, 59). Case himself has been surgically altered so that he can return to cyberspace, with new spinal fluid, blood, and pancreas (N, 32). Some prostheses even put one at risk of being robbed of them, for "employees above a certain level were implanted with advanced microprocessors that monitored mutagen levels in the bloodstream. Gear like that would get you rolled in Night City" (N, 10). These prostheses are not only more durable, and in that sense more real, than their originals, but no matter how many prostheses intrude into the subject, it remains centered and whole.

In *Count Zero*, Turner has been reconstructed with prostheses after being attacked. "They cloned a square meter of skin for him, grew it on slabs of collagen and shark-cartilage polysaccharides. They bought eyes and genitals on the open market" (C, 1). The ubiquitous "microsofts" across all three books are also prostheses, memory programs that people can insert into sockets in their heads (e.g., C, 3). Josef Virek has heavy "reliance on technology," as his actual body is so bloated with cancer that it is being kept alive in a vat (C, 13): " 'When I last requested a remote visual of the vat I inhabit in Stockholm, I was shown a thing like three truck trailers, lashed in a dripping net of support lines' " (C, 175). Angie Mitchell has had prostheses installed in her brain that enable her to access cyberspace without use of a computer: " 'It's all through her head,' Rudy said. 'Like long chains of it' " (C, 133).

Prostheses are common in *Mona Lisa Overdrive* as well. "Little Bird" sports not just a microsoft but "the green mech-5 microsoft" (M, 11). Mona is kidnapped and given prostheses that make her identical to Angie Mitchell, whom she is to replace (M, 172–73). It would appear as if any sort of physical change is possible through technology; Angie's assistant Porphyre has, for instance, changed race (M, 188).

The subject in Gibson's novels is centered and whole. Cybersubjects are no less real, and may be more real, than are physical people. Gibson's subjects are often made up of durable prostheses, yet a core subjectivity argues for the reality of the subject in his new electronic world.

AESTHETICS

Aesthetic experience in Gibson's novels is consistent with a rhetoric of reality. It is immediate, physical, grounded in the lived experience of the subject. Art is connected to use value. Josef Virek sends Marly to find the maker of the artistic boxes not only for their artistic value: " 'You should know, I think, that my search for our boxmaker involves more than art, Marly. . . . I have reason to believe that the maker of these artifacts is in some position to offer me freedom' " (C, 175).

There is immediate physical pleasure in entering cyberspace. Armitage gives case the magnetic key to his new deck saying, " 'You'll enjoy this, Case. Like Christmas morning' " (N, 46). It's more than that; Molly teases Case, " 'I saw you stroking that Sendai; man, it was pornographic' " (N, 47). His actual return to cyberspace after a long enforced absence is indeed described in nearly sexual terms:

He closed his eyes. Found the ridged face of the power stud. And in the bloodlit dark behind his eyes, silver phosphenes boiling in from the edge of space, hypnagogic images jerking past like film compiled from random frames. Symbols, figures, faces, a blurred, fragmented mandala of visual information. Please, he prayed, *now*—A gray disk, the color of Chiba sky. Now—Disk beginning to rotate, faster, becoming a sphere of paler gray. Expanding—And flowed, flowered for him, fluid neon origami trick, the unfolding of his distanceless home, his country, transparent 3D chessboard extending to infinity. . . . And somewhere he was laughing, in a white-painted loft, distant fingers caressing the deck, tears of release streaking his face. (N, 52)

At other times, Case similarly feels "the bodiless exultation of cyberspace" (N, 6), "a wave of exhilaration" (N, 115) cruising the matrix. In *Count Zero*, Marly likewise experiences cyberspace in nearly sexual terms as she takes on the simstim role of Tally Isham: "Now Marly found herself locked into Tally's tanned, lithe, tremendously *comfortable* sensorium. Tally Isham glowed, breathed deeply and easily, her elegant bones riding in the embrace of a musculature that seemed never to have known tension. Accessing her stim recordings was like falling into a bath of perfect health, feeling the spring in the star's high arches and the jut of her breasts against the silky white Egyptian cotton of her simple blouse" (C, 172–73).

The aesthetics of being in cyberspace are immediate and physical. The Dixie Flatline takes Case on "an intricate series of jumps with a speed and accuracy that made Case wince with envy" (N, 167). Case sees that the Chinese virus they have introduced to attack the Tessier-Ashpool core is beautiful:

Something dark was forming at the core of the Chinese program. The density of information overwhelmed the fabric of the matrix, triggering hypnagogic images. Faint kaleidoscopic angles centered in to a silver-black focal point. Case watched childhood symbols of evil and bad luck tumble out along translucent planes: swastikas, skulls and crossbones, dice flashing snake eyes. If he looked directly at that null point, no outline would form. It took a dozen quick, peripheral takes before he had it, a shark thing, gleaming like obsidian, the black mirrors of its flanks reflecting faint distant lights that bore no relationship to the matrix around it. (N, 180–81)

Later, Case notes that "the Chinese program was face to face with the target ice, rainbow tints gradually dominated by the green of the rectangle representing the T-A cores. Arches of emerald across the colorless void" (N, 204). Case and the Flatline move "straight up, above them the distanceless bowl of jade-green ice" (N, 257). Wintermute takes Case on a "fast-forward" virtual tour of the Tessier-Ashpool stronghold, and it is an immediate aesthetic experience: "The walls blurred. Dizzying sensation of headlong movement, colors, whipping around corners and through narrow corridors. They seemed at one point to pass through several meters of solid wall, a flash of pitch darkness" (N, 172).

Angie Mitchell uses a deck to jack in to the matrix and experiences this aesthetic reaction: "her finger found a random second stud and she was catapulted through the static wall, into cluttered vastness, the notional void of cyberspace, the bright grid of the matrix ranged around her like an infinite cage" (M, 49). As Kumiko and Tick enter cyberspace together, they see that "Tick's room was gone, its walls a flutter of cards, tumbling and receding, against the bright grid, the towering forms of data" (M, 262). Tick generates a "blue boat" to carry them along a "yellow plain" of data (M, 264).

Not every experience in frolicking through cyberspace is pleasant, but they are aesthetic nevertheless, and felt as primary physical experiences. Jacking into a computer program that will show him everything about Christopher Mitchell in a brief span of time, Turner complains that

Machine dreams hold a special vertigo. . . . It came on, again, gradually, a flickering, non-linear flood of fact and sensory data, a kind of narrative conveyed in surreal jump cuts and juxtapositions. It was vaguely like riding a coller coaster that phased in and out of existence at random, impossibly rapid intervals, changing altitude, attack, and direction with each pulse of nothingness. (C, 23)

We have noted the possibility of receiving real pain at the hands of cybersubjects. Case gets too close to some sensitive data in cyberspace and "The dark came down like a hammer. Cold steel odor and ice caressed his spine. . . . A steady pulse of pain, midway down his spine" (N, 116). Case complains to the Dixie Flatline that " 'that laugh of yours sort of gets me in the spine' " (N, 169), and later the laugh "scraped Case's nerves like a dull blade" (N, 201). Tuning into Molly's sensorium electronically, Case can feel that she has been injured: "Into her darkness, a churning synaesthesia, where her pain was the taste of old iron, scent of melon, wings of a moth brushing her cheek" (N, 221).

CONCLUSION

We have taken cyberspace to be a model for simulation, so it is entirely perverse to think of it as a paradigm of reality. But William Gibson is eager to do just that in his novels. He wants his reader to think of cyberspace as real, and thus invokes the categories of a rhetoric of reality that we have seen expressed through permanence and change, commodification, subjectivity, and aesthetics.

In describing cyberspace through a rhetoric of reality, Gibson borrows the pre-cession and *gravitas* of reality for a technological world that was just being intro-duced widely to public consciousness in the middle 1980s. His rhetorical strategies are then a backhanded way of saying that simulation is not a good thing, not some-thing that can be taken on its own terms or taken seriously. Reality is the default position for life, in Gibson's work, the standard by which other experiences are judged. He attempts to slip cyberspace into the mansion of reality.

Chapter 6

A Rhetoric of Representation in Rec.motorcycles

There are those, such as William Gibson, who argue that the world we encounter in cyberspace is real. Others disagree with that perspective. Not everyone will regard the matrix as a real place populated by real people with real experiences and real issues. Realists abound, who rejoice in their groundedness in the actual, hard, nubby stuff of the material world—yet who see the stuff of cyberspace as representations of that reality at best. This representational view considers Web sites, e-mail, and on-line databases for what they can tell us about reality. Someone who approaches cyberspace as representation would be likely to hold the signs that are found there to the standard traditionally associated with a rhetoric of representation: accurately and faithfully re-presenting the world and material experience to the mind's understanding.

Cyberspace can thus be treated as reality or as representation—and of course, we have seen earlier that many if not most people would see it as being simulation, for better or for worse. This present chapter is, like chapter 5, somewhat perverse in identifying a rhetoric that depicts cyberspace *not* as simulation but as something else—in this case, as representation. A rhetoric of representation views cyberspace as pixels on a screen, but pixels that stand for, should stand for, or are charged with standing for the real world of material experience. In this chapter we explore some strategies used to persuade the observer that certain signs in cyberspace do indeed re-present reality.

Under what conditions would someone expect the stuff of cyberspace to be treated as if it were representations? When would people hold cyberdiscourse to a standard of representing reality? Those questions are likely best answered on a case-by-case basis, but a general principle might be that cyberdiscourse is viewed as representational when it serves the clear rhetorical purpose and intention of reflecting a real state of affairs. A game in cyberspace might have no pretensions to reflect reality. But some discourse may appear in cyberspace largely for the purpose of manifesting real, material activities and objects (or at any rate, to what is claimed to be real). Examples of discourses that fall into such categories would include news groups, or talk groups, that reflect real life interests or occupations that people have.

A newsgroup is a site on the Internet on which people may view messages posted by others on a variety of topics within a general subject heading. The range of subjects is vast, and one may find a newsgroup on practically any interest, hobby, or activity. One way to access such sites at this writing, for example, is www.dejanews.com. At that site one will find current messages organized by *strings*: series of messages in conversation with one another, identified by a shared subject heading (other servers may organize messages differently, for instance, listing messages in strictly chronological order rather than by strings). Some newsgroups are not moderated at all, accepting any posting whatsoever, which tends to create a newsgroup with a great deal of clutter and irrelevance. Other newsgroups are tightly moderated by a designated individual or small group who review all messages and allow only those meeting certain standards to be posted. Other newsgroups range widely in between these two poles. One example of a newsgroup might be rec.guns, in which participants post messages having to do with preeminently real objects and activities: firearms and their uses. That group is tightly moderated by a clearly identified team of individuals. This chapter examines a discursive space in cyberspace that is especially well suited to illustrate a rhetoric of representation: the newsgroup *rec.motorcycles*.

One of many thousands of newsgroups that may be accessed by going on-line, rec.motorcycles follows the pattern of many of those newsgroups. It is only loosely moderated to ensure that completely irrelevant posts, posts that are frankly commercial ("spam"), or posts that are offensive or inappropriate to the topic in some way (pornography) do not appear. Otherwise, discussants send to the group e-mail messages which are posted regularly throughout the day. People may respond to postings, resulting in strings of discourse that are sometimes quite long and complex. Topics discussed vary widely, but they mainly have to do with buying, riding, and maintaining motorcycles. Some names or aliases of posters appear often, others rarely, and inevitably many people are "lurkers"—checking in from time to time to read messages but never creating actual posts.

Rec.motorcycles is nothing but pixels on a screen. Yet those pixels are intended (often passionately) by their creators to represent real exertise and experience. Readers of this discourse likewise hold each posting to that standard of representation and quickly castigate contributions perceived to be made by mere poseurs. Thus, rec.motorcycles is a good discourse to examine as an illustration of the rhetoric of representation. This study is based on forty-six messages posted during a two-day period (obviously only a sample; hundreds of new messages appear daily). These messages comprised three strings during that two-day period at the end of the year 2000. One string concerned the difficulties a poster was having starting his bike during cold weather. A second string concerned a trip that a poster was planning on his motorcycle, for which the rider sought tips and advice. A third string concerned a new rider who was purchasing his first motorcycle and wondered about the odds that he would "drop" the bike; he didn't want to invest a lot if that mishap were likely. My purposes here are not served by keeping the strings separate nor by identifying posters, even anonymously, since all three strings tend to illustrate the same principles of a rhetoric of representation. Therefore, this chapter directly quotes from the postings to illustrate the principles articulated in the following paragraphs. This approach also helps to preserve the anonymity of the postings. The obvious misspellings that occur in the messages have been corrected since they are not relevant to our purposes here; grammatical errors are retained to give the flavor of the discourse.

This chapter examines the discourse of these three strings during that period to identify ways in which a rhetoric of representation is working. It is clear that the posters for these strings, as for the newsgroup in general, are quite eager to demonstrate that their postings do indeed represent a reality of expertise and experience in riding motorcycles. One might say that the ability of postings to point beyond the computer screen and toward a separate, objective reality of bike riding is the guiding rationale of rec.motorcycles. Rec.motorcycles will always remain nothing but signs; within the context of that newsgroup there can never be any objective demonstration of who is right, more expert, or more experienced. The contributors seem to rely heavily on the representations on the screen as a connection to reality; when one poster asks where he can find other real bikers who might join him on a trip, he is told to consult this newsgroup or some local "motorcycle newsgroup or rag," all of them venues of representation only. In an exclusively representational domain, proving the accuracy of a representation is problematic. If you and I disagree in personal conversation about our use of language to represent furred animals that bark (e.g., if one of us claims that such animals also always have scales), one of us may bring a real furred animal that barks into our presence so we may settle the issue of relative representations (the representation of scales will be shown to be false). That means of settling issues of representation will never be available for newsgroups, which are forever locked away within the computer screen. So the question becomes, how are these signs constructed so as to provide their own guarantees of accurate representation? How do signs that claim to represent, but can never be coupled with the realities they represent, pull themselves up by their own semiotic bootstraps to show their fidelity? How do we guarantee accurate representation when representation is all there is? A discourse that meets these challenges will be one that illustrates a rhetoric of representation particularly well.

The key strategy pursued in this discourse to guarantee representation is to situate *the poster, the person creating the posts*, as the guarantor of the fidelity of the discourse. In a sort of cyberCartesian method, one might doubt anything about a posting on rec.motorcycles but not that a real person has posted it. From that foundation the discourse builds upon signs and tokens within itself that argue for the fidelity of the representations. What they represent is the real expertise and the real experience of the poster. Posts are constructed so as to create the sense that the contributor *must* know what she is talking about. Thus, we will organize our examination of the discourse in these three strings around two major categories: (1) tokens of the person (the rider) as having technical expertise, and (2) tokens of the expert rider as having real world experience.

TOKENS OF EXPERTISE

Perhaps the chief way in which the discourse of rec.motorcycles guarantees the expertise of the poster is by featuring specialized, technical language. Posters show a rich command of facts and figures, measurements, engineering terms, references to parts of the motorcycle, and other arcane knowledge. Such nuggets of knowledge are guaranteed by the technical language, or jargon, as if to say that where there is so much discussion of trickle chargers or starter motor brushes there must be a real expertise. The richness of technical detail in the posts thus serves the purpose of guaranteeing that they represent real expertise.

Technically detailed language is representative of real expertise in many posts. Posters will use, without explanation, such terms as "top end job," as did one person in recommending a repair that might fix a nonstarting bike. One person cautions that a car battery charger will work on a motorcycle only "as long as the rate of charge is slow enough to allow the heat generated in the battery to dissipate before it causes damage." Another contribution is full of knowledgeable technical language that seems to represent real expertise:

Many bikes have vacuum operated fuel shut offs. When left setting for an extended period the fuel in the carbs evaporates. When you go to start it, the engine must spin fast enough to create a vacuum to open the petcock or you won't get gas to the carbs. There is usually a position on the shut off that allows you to bypass the vacuum shut off. Try to leave the tank full when you're not going to be riding for a while. The air in a part filled tank expands and contracts. When it contracts it takes in air with water vapor from outside. The vapor condenses to form water in the tank that can cause starting problems and rust.

Detailed technical language guarantees real expertise in this advice:

FWIW, when working with car batteries you still need to keep an eye on them unless your charger automatically switches into a trickle mode and/or limits the charging rate. Even then I'd not leave one hooked up indefinitely unless the charger had an operating mode designed for precisely that.

Giving advice to a new rider about dropping a bike, another poster refers to "engine guards (stock) and the saddle bag guards." Another writes with technical confidence that

The EX500 really has no more plastic than a Bandit or a Seca. The front fairing provides wind protection, and is essentially equivalent to the almost-naked bikes in terms of size, etc. As for the lower ¼ fairing, yes, that is plastic and yes, that can be damaged when dropped.

But heck, if you damage the plastic there, just remove and don't replace: I see many EXs riding around without that belly plastic, and they look and handle normally.

The bike specifically named in the original posting is judged by another writer who displays technical expertise through knowledge of specialized terms: "A Vulcan 800 shouldn't be THAT bad, although it is a little on the heavy side." Some of the advice given to the original inquirer displayed technical expertise related to gaining information from the Internet itself: "This question gets thrashed out here pretty regularly. A Deja search should give you more advice than you can conveniently read before you get the MSF course [Motorcycle Safety Foundation basic course, offered nationally]."

Technical language that bespeaks expertise comes in different fields of knowledge. How much a motorcycle should cost is often a topic of discussion on rec.motorcycles. This poster displays his expertise in giving advice to a new rider who is shopping for a first bike:

$5500 seems high for a used 99 vulcan Classic—I paid $5299 for my Y2K Vulcan 750. I checked on motorcycleworld.com for some comparisons—there was one 800 listed out of Florida for $4600 with 400 miles on it. Of course I don't know what shape that bike is in, or how accessorized your prospective bike is . . . but it does seem pricey.

The use of different figures seems to bespeak technical expertise about several brands and models.

Discussants also display expertise in the technical detail offered in regard to specific merchants or products: "You want a trickle charger made for small batteries like yours—half an amp is about right, and it might take 10 hours or more," says one. The message goes on to show expertise through more detail, keyed to knowledge of specific brands or stores: "If you can't find one, J. C. Whitney sells a variety of them for $10–$14. They have a unit with a plug connector that stay with the bike; there's no need to get to the battery every time to hook up the charger." The original poster was grateful for this brand-specific expertise and replied, "Seeing as I can't get to the bike store for the next week or so, I took your advice and ordered one from JC. Shipping costs stink, but the charger is in the mail, so to speak!" Contributors often show expertise through such knowledge of specific products or components: "I'd recommend getting a Battery Tender by Delkron. They monitor the state of charge of the battery and shut themselves off when the battery is fully charged. Much better for the battery than a charger of any kind, and you don't have to remember to go shut it off after ten hours."

Expertise is signaled by technical terminology outside the message itself. Posters often have signature lines in which they list the bikes they own or have owned, often by model number only or through some other bare designation that seems decipherable only to the cognoscenti. Other signature lines include other, even more mysterious technical information that is so occult that it *must* reflect some reality of expertise. One poster's signature line includes: CWRA #4 SDWL #2 CIMC #1 DoD #2009 LOMP #2. Several riders sign themselves with a DoD

number; the acronym stands for Denizens of Doom, a secretive network of devoted, presumably expert, riders.

The importance of displaying technical expertise is validated by those new riders who are frequently the originators of strings. These original postings often
grovel in displaying their ignorance and inviting the responses of their elders and
betters. "I thank you all in advance for putting up with what is probably a straight-
forward question as I plunge through my first winter of bike ownership," says the
originator of one string, who concludes, "Many thanks in advance." In a later post
he says, "I'll plead ignorance and say that I'm not sure what it means to lap the
valves." Likewise, he gives up any claim to experience by admitting that "the bike,
though a '94, only has 4,000 miles on it." The originator of another string asks for
advice on taking a trip from Phoenix to San Diego, and offers up the disclaimer
that "I am new to these types of trips."

The originator of a third thread is buying a new motorcycle and wants to know
what the odds are of an accident, since he will not invest as much if it is likely that
he will damage the bike. Thus he takes the stance of a novice coming before ex-
perts: "I am close to getting my first bike and I have a question for you guys." He is
asking the question precisely because "I have learned a lot from this group." One
response to his post also emphasizes his lack of experience and expertise: "Even a
dancer can trip from time to time. And a beginning dancer falls a lot." The original
poster returns to the string later, validating the expert advice he has been given:
"Thanks for all the good information again," and praising the experiential wisdom
of his elders in the group: "Someone posted a message here once that ended with a
saying that I am trying to live by: Work on adding life to your days, not days to
your life." A following response validates that wisdom and thus the expertise of
the group in general: "Very true words in this age of all the health and safety hype."

Another important way in which the signs of rec.motorcycles are guaranteed to
represent expertise is in the ways in which strings later in their development so often show posters moving away from the original subject matter to a heated, even
vituperative exchange of insults. Questioning the expertise of others is a widely
accepted (if logically spurious) rhetorical device for the bolstering of one's own
expertise, and is thus a way to strengthen the claims of one's own representations.
When one respondent warns against using a car battery charger, another responds
"Car amps are not bigger or more powerful than bike amps. As long as you keep an
eye on it and don't let the battery boil, a car charger will work fine." One poster is
assailed with this response:

I read your first response. Do you really think the air filter plugged up while the bike sat for a
month? Or that the carbs got out of sync? Do you think he should try to sync the carbs without the engine running? Telling someone you can't diagnose a problem over the internet and
then rambling on about how the old bike might need a top end job is not being helpful!

This poster builds his own expertise by questioning that of his victim.

When one commentator suggests that the fuel in a carburetor may have evaporated, preventing an easy start, another commentator sarcastically dismisses that

suggestion: "If all the fuel in his carbs evaporated in a month, he A) needs to find a better place to buy gas, B) better take the carbs apart and clean them, and C) needs to find out why his carb float bowls have huge chunks missing from them." He similarly dismisses a suggestion that cold weather can significantly reduce the battery current needed to start by saying, "Only if you have a dying battery, a dying starter, or you put straight 50W in your crankcase."

Even when intemperate exchanges do not arise, strings often tend to move late in their life spans toward a level of metacommunication, in which posters are commenting more on other posters than on the original question. Metacommunication puts one in a position of discursive authority, whether one is denigrating another or not. To comment on another, as Foucault reminds us, is to claim authority and status. Thus, even gentle metacommunication is a strategy to guarantee personal expertise. Several postings into a string, one contributor tells the original poster that "R———— B———— gave you good info about a charger," validating not only R. B.'s expertise but his own expert ability to say what is good advice and what isn't. When one contributor suggests that "Many bikes have vacuum operated fuel shut offs," another replies that the bike in the original poster, a Magna, does not: "At least my '97 didn't. The rest of your advice is spot-on though." He gives tokens of expertise not only in referring to his own experience of a Magna but in positively evaluating the contributions of another. Another such positive endorsement of another's expertise is when one poster writes, "R—— K—— paging R—— K————. Where's R—— K————? (R—— is considered to be our ultimate expert on this subject)."

TOKENS OF EXPERIENCE

We have seen that it is important in a rhetoric of representation for posters to demonstrate their personal expertise. If an expert individual is behind a posting, it is that much more likely that the posting accurately and truly represents reality. A second level of strategy in a rhetoric of representation is for the expert poster to demonstrate real life experience. It is good to know about motorcycles, even better to show that one rides them constantly. Thus we find several strategies by which tokens of real life experience are offered on rec.motorcycles.

Probably the chief such strategy is simply to offer anecdotes of real world experience. These "war stories" are ways of claiming accuracy and fidelity for representations. To someone complaining about a bike that would not start in cold weather, one rugged respondent said, "BTW, I was riding around New Hampshire and Vermont two days ago. It was 23 degrees out." To which another even hardier rider replied, "Pussy. That's warm." And the original poster jocularly replies, "Shit. That's about as low as I can go right now. 20 F. :-/" The exchange seems to represent a couple of tough bikers just in from long, cold rides long enough to log on and check in.

Another poster represents his own experiences in starting a difficult motorcycle in the cold: "On my 77 KZ1000 it will crank over fine but not start, just like yours. If I use the kick starter it will usually start on the first or second kick. After that I

can use the electric starter the rest of the day." Sometimes posters anticipate anecdotes by telling of what they plan to do in the future: "With any luck at all, I'm
gonna open things up tomorrow and take a look. I'm thinking it should be pretty
easy to fix. Electrical tape, and wha-bam, I'm back on the road."

Another poster responds to a request for advice on a trip from Arizona to California with this remembrance:

I used to run back and forth between the SF Bay area and Tucson AZ in the early '70s when I
went to school down there. I found the best thing to do was to make the trip at night. If I left
Palo Alto at sunset, I could usually be in Tucson about dawn, pushing it slightly in the desert
along I-10 where there wasn't going to be any traffic anyway. I-10 stopped at the AZ state
line back then, so I had to take US 60 to Phoenix, the I-10 again to Tucson.

Another anecdotal remembrance bespeaks real expertise as well:

It's been a mild winter so far along coastal California. I used to run up from LA to Frisco
along Hwy 1 fairly regularly and my favorite times were Dec and Jan because of less traffic.
You could get nailed with a storm but the heavy rainfall is most likely going to come down
after the first two weeks of Jan, with Feb being the main rain month. But do watch the
weather reports. It's not an El Nino year and we've had day after day of gorgeous weather
lately.

To which another rider from that area replies jokingly, "not really, actually we
have had our third nuclear disaster this week. Just awful. My dog is glowing in the
dark. No use coming out this way."

Sometimes technical advice is directly coupled with a claim of extensive real
world experience that suggests anecdotes that *could* be told:

You can have starting problems long before *all* the gas evaporates. If all you needed was a
little in the bowl then they wouldn't have a spec for the float level. I didn't dream up the
problem that I described. I have experienced the problem on more than one bike, and a
month is plenty long enough to cause it.

Likewise, this contributor suggests a history of real experience which he pits
against that of another contributor whom he is attacking: "Then there is something
wrong with your gasoline, your bikes, or both, because in ten years of owning and
servicing bikes (for myself and many others), I've never seen gas go so bad in a
month of sitting that a bike won't start at all (assuming there's nothing else wrong
with the bike, and the gas was fresh to start with)." The voice of experience also
comes through in this posting which hints at anecdotes of real riding that could be
told: "If you're riding up Highway 1 in January, be prepared for weather from
mid-50s and sunny to barely above freezing with hard rain and heavy winds blowing inland. You're *right* on the coast, and the Pacific can have some nasty
weather patterns. They're quite variable, though." A hint of possible real life anecdotes is evident in another discussant's reply, "Not only that, but Highway 1 between San Louis Obispo and Monterey is often closed due to slides in the winter."

Implied anecdotes are found in a reply to that post: "Yes, and it's not frequently patrolled, either, so good luck to you if you happen to come across a place where the road's fallen out before Caltrans or the CHP gets there. It's a long way down, and a mighty unfriendly surface at the bottom." Dangerous anecdotes are hinted at likewise in this warning: "They get some pretty substantial rockslides and the road washes out fairly regularly. Check your weather report carefully and be prepared to stop or take 101 if it looks risky. Watch out too for strong crosswinds." The hinted anecdote can bespeak real experience more eloquently than a developed anecdote at times, as in the ominous stories evoked by this allusive contribution: "And oh, by the way, make sure to get gas at Gorda or Ragged Point, no matter HOW much it costs. Don't ask why I know this."

Some anecdotes can emphasize the relative lack of experience of new riders. Cast in the tone of the older (perhaps sadder), but wiser, rider remembering his own novice missteps, questioning the ability of new riders is a way of confirming one's own ability through experience. Commenting on the chances of damaging a bike as a new rider, one writer says that

For a newbie the big and heavy bike is something he is not used to handling and balancing. Even with the lighter bikes there are situations when you can't muscle them around but have to rely on keeping the bike balanced. That skill has to be learned, and until you do there is a chance you will drop the bike. This chance increases with the weight of the bike, because the heavier the bike the harder it is to control with sheer muscle and the more you have to rely on balancing.

Even experienced riders can drop a bike, and claiming to do so can be a claim of long experience, as the same writer says, "FWIW I've dropped my Kawasaki 440 LTD (standard/cruiser) twice at 0 mph, with zero damage both times."

Another strategy employing tokens of experience as guarantors of representation is to provide a high level of *detail* in the anecdotes one tells of real life experience. If reality is infinitely complex, complexity of representation indicates fidelity. The originator of one string specifies that his bike is "a '94 Magna 750" and "a 4-cylinder." The weather has been "barely above 35 degrees F" for a month, but it was exactly "31 degrees" on the day he is posting. "After about ten minutes of trying the battery sounds like it's dying," and so he will "wait five minutes." Another contributor says that "a fresh battery will lose 1% of its charge per day of sitting. A bike in a good state of tune will always start after sitting for a month, unless the battery will not hold a full charge, or is weak and discharges more quickly than 1% a day." Notice the detail in this poster's contribution:

Bikes with electronic ignition are actually more likely to have this problem than those with points. On some systems the electronics that read the trigger signal are very voltage sensitive. When the bike has been sitting for a month the battery is probably not at full charge. Combine that with 30 degree temperatures, that will cause 10w-40 to thicken up quite a bit, and the starter can draw enough current so that the voltage drops below the trigger's minimum requirement. The starter will still crank the engine over fine, but there will be no spark.

Such complexity in the posting bespeaks a real, complex reality. So does the detail given by one poster who warns of price gouging along a route in California: "Be prepared for $3/gal gasoline and $8 sandwiches at some of the really remote stops near Gorda." Stories of bad weather likewise lurk in the advice, "Well, you might as well pack your raingear for starters and some long underwear, just in case."

This contributor offers up a finely detailed anecdote that bespeaks expertise grounded in real experience:

Just a counterpoint: yesterday I rode a round trip from Paso Robles through Lockwood to Mission San Antonio do Padua, thence over Nacimiento-Ferguson Road to Hwy 1, south along PCH to Cambria, and then back to Paso Robles by Hwy 46. It was a 140 mile, 4 hour trip. The weather was clear, dry, and sunny, albeit somewhat cold. Wear appropriate gear. The roads through the mountains were dry, in quite good condition, with little sand, leaves, or rock falls. These are some of the finest riding roads along the Central Coast, with a mix of sweepers, straights, and sharp corners and hairpins. You climb from 300 feet above sea level in Paso Robles (about 30 miles inland), to several thousand feet along the spine of the Santa Lucia mountains in Big Sur, and then back down again to the coast in a long series of tight hairpins with no barriers and drops of hundreds of feet if you make a mistake. The views are fantastic, ranging from coastal foothills, to deep redwood canyons, and expansive Pacific vistas. I arrived at the crest just at sunset and stopped to watch the sun set on horizon. The trip back to Cambria, some 30 miles or so south, was fairly slow but nevertheless chal- lenging if only because it was a dark and nearly moonless night. The road was in nearly per- fect condition. No cops in view and if you want to go fast, just pull over, enjoy the view until the road clears, and then go play. Hwy 46 back to Paso Robles is a fast climb east back over the mountains, with long sweepers. It's patrolled during the day, but pretty empty at night.

The string concerning the likelihood of a new rider dropping the bike also re- cited anecdotes that purported to represent real experience by giving a high level of detail. Note how detail is coupled with a claim of real world experience in this con- tribution:

My experience today undoubtedly was typical: 30 degrees (10 degrees with wind chill); no precipitation; light bike (475 pounds); "experienced" rider (2500 miles on my bike in past four months; two MSF courses; third bike owned); low seat height (about 28 inches). What happened? I was exiting a shopping center; I saw a car coming perpendicular to me; the car didn't have a turn signal. Was it going to go straight (hence I should stop); or was it going to turn into the center (hence I could proceed through the intersection)? I smelled a turn with- out a signal, but couldn't be sure that the car wouldn't go straight. What to do? I followed MSF and my instincts, and erred on the side of caution. I stopped! I put my feet flat on the ground; then . . . ! Alas, my left foot went right into a puddle of liquid lubricant, something of a combination of oil and antifreeze. I lost my footing, the bike went down . . . almost in slow motion as I struggled to keep it right.

One writer gives a detailed blow-by-blow account of his beginning days when he says:

When I got my Road Glide (735 lbs), I had basically no road experience with a motorbike (and very little on a dirt bike)—if mopeds aren't included, that is. I knew which bike I wanted. Signed up for the motorcycle course. Passed that and got my license. From there, I went pretty well straight to the Harley dealer, bought the bike and rode it home. No real problem—although the size difference (from the bikes in the motorcycle course) was quite a shift at first, to put it mildly. But no one gets anywhere by being too meek and tentative, so off I went. Rode that bike every day after that. In the first 2 weeks I had the bike, I think I laid it on its side 2 or 3 times. Each time, it was in a stand-still position where I had either placed my foot on a slippery surface or wasn't prepared for the shifting weight dynamics when, on an incline, I turned the wheel to move the bike around. That is where a big bike is a bit of a killer (figuratively) because, once it tips past a certain tip point, there's no way you are going to be able to hold it up. After those initial 2 weeks (and more than 40,000 miles later), the bike never went down again (I don't count 2 episodes goofing around on snow and ice in February).

Another detailed reminiscence of one's early days of riding is:

I paid $300 for a 15 year old trasher with a lot of miles on it, and which took more than three weeks to put back into running condition. That was about 10 years ago, and now I'm going to regret letting it go. It's possible that another motorcycle wouldn't have had this effect, because rattletrap is well suited to the riding I do, and is fairly easy to maintain.

Detailed accounts of dropping a bike can demonstrate expertise, as they give assurance that a rider has paid his dues. This rider says:

I took the MSF course as well, and went out and bought a 2000 Vulcan 750 this fall as my first bike. I've laid it down a few times, mostly in my driveway, all at 0 mph from gravel underfoot, awkward positioning when stopping, etc. Damage done were bent shift/brake levers, and some small scuffs on the muffler and turn signals. In the worst instance though, I had the bike out for 2 hrs in 40 degree weather and was probably a touch hypothermic. When I got home, my brain was so frozen that I forgot to put the kickstand down before dismounting = 1 footrest broken. Total replacement costs for footrest and levers were ~$70, which I replaced myself.

A different perspective on the chances of dropping a bike is also couched in terms of a detailed anecdote of early experience:

Let me add another view. . . . I took MSF (Motorcycle Safety Foundation basic course, offered nationally), and have not dropped at all. That said, I got a lightweight rat bike, in fact, a CB250 that had ALREADY been dropped while doing time at the MSF course. The nice thing about it was, I got it for $1000 off MSRP w/almost no haggle (OK, I haggled for winter riding gloves!), with full 1-yr warranty (never been titled=sold as new), w/option for a 3 year war, with merely 175 miles on it and a few insignificant scratches. I am convinced that, based on my own experience, I'd definitely have dropped a heavier bike. Several times I've caught the 300 lb (wet weight) CB250 leaning too far, say while backing it in the garage, yet I doubt I could do that with a 500 lb one.

Note the explicit invocation of the writer's own experience more than once. He later compares that experience with a novice's inexperience by giving the avuncular advice,

I recommend you get a used standard bike (any entry level 250 will do, and there are always lots to choose from) unless you're certain what features and capabilities you value and what ones you don't. After awhile, you'll learn things you'll only know from actually riding. Good luck—if you haven't changed your mind 10 times by the time you're done with MSF, then you really know yourself well!

A strategy related to detailed complexity of an anecdote is to consider a *range* of possible problems or solutions in discussing topics. Posters often suggest a panoply of answers to the questions and issues posed by original posters. Suggesting a wide range of possibilities indicates real life experience, which is typically of a wide variety of problems and solutions. If reality has many options, then a discourse that represents that reality should present many options as well. Musing on what might keep a bike from starting, a poster considers several possibilities:

Your problem seems to be worse in the cold, which is not unusual for general "old age" related troubles. You could have tired carburetors, they could need synchronizing, you could need a valve adjustment, or have low compression . . . How many miles? When was the last time the valves were lapped? Have you done a compression test? It could be something as simple as running out of gas, or old gas in the tank. Could just need new plugs, or have a dirty air filter.

Another contributor offers this range of suggestions: "Low miles probably means no troubles with top end. My first suspicion would be bad gas, or a dirty air filter. Did you check the plugs? Air filter? Try fresh gas?" Speculating on why a brake light should be burning out, this poster considers a range of options: "Now the brake filament is burning out, too? Or is the parking filament burning out when you hit the brake? If the latter, you probably have the parking and ground wires reversed." His mastery of a range of solutions represents his technical expertise. Complexity is also found in this writer's suggestion of a range of reasons why someone might drop a bike: "Numerous other factors could be noted (e.g. is the seat height too great so that it impedes the ability to put your feet firmly on the ground; how tall is the center of gravity on the bike; etc.)."

Paradoxically, although articulating a wide variety of possibilities in reality is a strategy of representation, so is a dogmatic language. Insisting on one "right" answer to a question is a way of insisting on one's own real life experience that would generate such knowledge. Those who understand that they are not expert hedge their questions with all sorts of hesitancies and contingencies, posing one question after another and offering up only "my guesses," as one string originator put it in regard to why his bike won't start.

One responder to a question about a bike that is hard to start emphatically declares, "Well, you definitely ran the battery down," then more provisionally, "and you may have taken some life out of the starter." Then dogmatic language continues: "There is no way to diagnose a no-start problem over the internet." This poster concludes all his contributions with a signature line that dogmatically says, "The only way I'll stop riding is if I stop breathing." Another discussant flatly declares, in response to another suggestion, "The worst thing to do is use a car charger."

Giving advice on a trip route, a poster dogmatically instructs a questioner, "Use the freeway. That's what it's there for," and is directive in saying, "If it's winter time, you won't want to be driving a motorcycle over the Sierra crest." Other dogmatic advice takes this form: "If you're riding 1 through Big Sur in January–March you really really don't want to ride when there's an incoming storm system." However, "In clear weather with no Winnebagos, it's a really fine ride." To a rider who complained of the cold, a responder insists that "this means you definitely need to invest in some better riding gear!"

Dogmatic language appears in a string concerning the likelihood of a new rider damaging his bike: "As so often elsewhere has been noted: there are two kinds of bikers; those that have dropped their bike, and those that will." Dogmatism is expressed as rates of probability: "Probability is fairly high," or "The probability of dropping is pretty high," while yet another poster put certainty on a sliding scale: "I would say the probability increases with the weight of the bike." A logic for calculating high probability is given by this poster:

So some things to consider—the Vulcan isn't as light as the range bikes, so it's going to be much harder to catch if it starts going over. The Vulcan's also got a hell of a lot more power than those range bikes. I got used to that very quickly, but the first few times out the bike scared the sh** out of me. Add the two up, and the odds of it tipping on you become high.

One writer dogmatically asserts that "the probability that the bike will not be dropped sometime in the first year is vanishingly small." Another puts the chances of a drop at "99.9% but most likely drop (drop meaning falling over while standing still or very slow parking maneuver) damage will be minimal like a bent turn signal or broken mirror." The likelihood of dropping a bike is presented dogmatically as a general rule: "Sure, there probably are people out there who started with a Wing or a Valkyrie as their first bikes and never dropped them. However, even they themselves will agree that this is the exception rather than the rule." Another rule-like statement is, "If you end up on oil, you're gonna slip."

CONCLUSION

It would appear to be a matter of pride among many contributors to rec.motorcycles that what they say on that newsgroup represents them as expert riders with long experience on the road. Representation rules on rec.motorcycles, since few of its contributors will ever confront each other in the flesh to compare representations of riding with the reality. If the ferociously bad Harley rider on the screen is actually an eight-year-old child, other readers and contributors of the group will never see that reality in the flesh. Exclusively textual strategies must therefore arise to present representations that guarantee themselves as accurate and faithful indicators of reality.

The problem of representations that must guarantee themselves *as* representations is especially widespread in a culture that depends so heavily on mediated communication. Chat room participants want to know if they really are speaking to the paragons of physical perfection that their messages represent them to be. Consumers wonder if the Help Desk consultant for their new computer is really as expert as she seems. On-line shoppers want to know if the goods they buy look as wonderful in reality as they do on the Web. Even people who will *eventually* confront a reality to compare with Internet representations may want to know of the fidelity of the representations *now*; all manner of business transactions that are computer mediated may depend upon such assurances. In a digital world in which the representational epistemic standards of accuracy and fidelity can rarely if ever be confirmed, an urge to guarantee unverifiable representations can be as pressing as it is poignant. Rhetorics of representation, rhetorics that assume that signs *do* represent, may thus become increasingly important as mediation among communicators increases.

Chapter 7

The Simulational Self in *Groundhog Day*

Clouds roll across the sky, taking shapes in which one can see dogs, elephants, or what you will. Clouds are among the earliest venues of simulation for us, pictures that are not pictures, shapes that morph into other shapes. These instruments of fantasy stream by in fast motion, animated by cinematic technology.

What better way to begin *Groundhog Day*, a film that depicts and critiques the never-ending loop of a life into which a self-centered denizen of postmodern culture has magically fallen. This film suggests that many of us are Narcissus and in danger of falling into that pool. Using the rhetoric of simulation (although never using that term), the film is a metaphor for a life of social disconnection and self-absorption. A simulational culture is built upon, and builds, the simulational self, the film tells us, and until we can break out of that self-referential loop, we are doomed to the same old, same old every day.

Pittsburgh television weatherman Phil Connors makes clouds his business. We find him doing a weathercast with animated gestures in front of a totally blank blue screen. His demeanor suggests a fascination with high pressure systems and a comradely bonhomie that seasoned television audiences have been taught to wink at. He stands in profile and talks about things that the audience, in reality, cannot see. It is not until the film screen fills with another smaller screen, that of a television, that we see the technologically created fantasy in which he works. A map of Pennsylvania appears where once we saw only blue, and it is busy with moving weather symbols. Connors mimes blowing, and clouds move in response across a map of the Northeastern region, an approaching storm in microcosm. An icon for a cold front appears, which he refers to as "one of those big blue things." Phil knows he is in a fantasy world. It doesn't matter to him, nor to us, for we are used to this simulation, we understand this world and its larger context: "Coming up next: sex and violence in the movies," says the news anchor. The media report on the media. This "news" will be no more real than the clouds.

The anchor reveals that Phil and a technical crew will travel to Punxsutawney, Pennsylvania the next day, Groundhog Day, to report on the annual emergence of Punxsutawney Phil, *the* groundhog of Groundhog Day. Phil has done this several times, he tells her, and a hint of leaden desperation is clear in his voice. He has a running start on the running loop that the next day will become—and we may recall that endless, closed repetition is a characteristic of simulation. Phil will wake up the day after Groundhog Day and discover that it is still Groundhog Day—and similarly the day after and the day after. That is the whole premise of the movie: How do we live a day—a life—that is a never ending copy?

Off camera, Phil's good humor dissipates like a cloud, showing him to be bad tempered, ironic, and cruel. He insults the anchorwoman. Phil's assistant weatherman promises him "excitement" in his trip to Punxsutawney, especially since he will be going with Rita, a new producer at the station: "You guys are gonna have fun," the assistant says, to which Phil sarcastically replies, "She's fun, but not my kind of fun. I won't be there for fun." Whether he has fun or not, the valorization of entertainment as the main issue in anticipating their trip is characteristic of a world of simulation.

Phil and his crew pile into a high-tech van loaded with the latest equipment. Simulation often depends on today's advanced technology, and they have plenty of it—they are an ark of simulation. On the way, Phil complains bitterly about their assignment, and says, "Someday somebody will see me interviewing the groundhog and think I don't have a future." That, of course, is precisely what will happen; Phil's confrontation with the groundhog will bend time from a straight march into the future to a circle turning back upon itself. Besides being a closed loop, a simulation is endless repetition, and so are both the annual emergence of the groundhog and Phil's pilgrimage to cover the event. The technician in the van fondly recalls earlier assignments in which he covered the yearly return of the swallows to Capistrano, which he compares to the groundhog's yearly emergence. A template of endless return has been established, and Phil is going to join it.

Who is this Phil Connors, weatherman, who is heading toward a day that will cycle and recycle for what may well be decades, even centuries? He is the groundhog, Punxsutawney Phil, who comes back year after year. Punxsutawney Phil is, of course, a fantasy, a simulation. He is the "same" groundhog, and has been the same groundhog, for decades as well. The occasional deaths of the real, material groundhogs involved are irrelevant. There is no Phil IV, Phil V, or Phil XXIII. Every year, the reset button is hit on this particular video game, and the simulational rodent emerges from his den. This fate is awaiting Phil Connors. In case the film's audience doesn't get this equation, on the first day of repetition Rita will call a bewildered Phil by name, which prompts the response by two local men nearby, "Phil?! Like the groundhog Phil?" Another sign that Phil is the groundhog is that on the first, "real" Groundhog Day, as the officials prepare to open Phil's den, the film audience can barely hear the crowd chant "Phil! Phil! Phil!" But the next day, the first day of the repetition, the film audience hears that chant much louder—for now the crowd in the movie is calling to Phil doubled, man and rodent merged.

The Phil Connors who is about to enter the loop is a thoroughly unpleasant person. He is completely self-absorbed. All his conversation is about himself, his career, his prospects in life. He cares little for others and insults people habitually, carelessly. If he approaches women, it is for his personal gratification. The dominant trope in his life is irony, which detaches and distances him from others. This is the kind of life the film comments upon. Showing the dangers of such a life is the point toward which a rhetoric of simulation is directed. *Groundhog Day* will depict self-absorption as simulation, and simulation as bad. It is only as Phil learns to turn out of himself that he escapes the cycle at the end.

Comes the dawn of Groundhog Day, and the camera shows the digital clock at Phil's bedside click over to 6:00 A.M. "I've Got You Babe" swells up from the radio, and two jolly, chatty radio DJ's banter about the day and the weather. We are seeing the props for the temporary eternity that Phil will spend here, and intimations of an endless cycle emerge early: "It's cold out there," says one announcer, to which his partner replies, "It's cold *every* day; what is this, Miami Beach?"

Phil, lodged in a large bed and breakfast, goes downstairs to eat. Mrs. Lancaster, the kindly old landlady, says, "There's talk of a blizzard." Phil goes right into his television act, standing at right angles to an imaginary screen and gesturing, running through his spiel, the gist of which is to deny that there will be a blizzard. It is a telling act, for it highlights both the technological, simulational nature of Phil's professional life and the disconnection that his constantly ironic demeanor brings to his life. He is mocking the bewildered Mrs. Lancaster's well-meant social comment on the weather. Refusing that social connection, he then asks her if she *really* wanted to talk about the weather. She asks if he is departing that day, and he replies within the frame of his television discourse to tell her the changes are one hundred percent, as if giving a prediction of rain. We see the link between an age of simulation and an age of irony in the distance both create from real connection with others.

As Phil begins to move through the day, we encounter more of the pieces of the scene in which he will be trapped. Insurance salesman Ned Ryerson, who knew Phil in high school, accosts him on the street. Phil's first and instinctual response is to assume that people relate to him not at a personal level but in terms of his fame within the simulational world of television: "Thanks for watching," he tosses out, and keeps on walking. Ned will not be put off and begins ticking off reasons why Phil should remember him, punctuating each reason with "Bing!" Ned, like many members of the television public, like the film's audience, is so accustomed to living within a simulational world of special effects and video that he must provide sound effects for his discourse.

Arriving at the scene of the groundhog's emergence, Rita greets Phil with, "This is fun!" expressing a dominant value of simulation. Phil is rude to all and sundry. He behaves himself on camera: "Once a year, the eyes of the nation turn to this tiny hamlet in western Pennsylvania to watch a master at work"—as if it were the same groundhog, over and over, year after year. And off camera Phil the weatherman grumpily expresses that very sentiment: "Then it's the same old shtick every year." Back on camera, he lapses into his habitual, detaching ironic mode: "This is one time when television fails to capture the true excitement of a large squirrel predicting the weather."

The high technology van heads back to Pittsburgh, but the scene quickly grows colder and snowier as they proceed. Eventually they are stopped just outside of town by state troopers who tell them that the road is closed and they must return to Punxsutawney. "Haven't you listened to the weather?" asks the officer? An outraged Phil replies, "I make the weather!" and once again goes into his on-camera act, gesturing at a nonexistent weather map and predicting that the storm will blow over, despite the fact that he is shaking with cold and dusted with the falling snow. He simply cannot escape what is clearly professional engrossment in a simulation, disconnected from the real blizzard that rages around them. Back in town at a gas station telephone, Phil gradually gets closed off from any outside reality: "Come on—all the long distance lines are down? What about the satellite? Is it snowing in space?" Technology cannot free him from the closed world he is entering, nor can his manufactured celebrity. Pleading that the phone company must keep *some* lines open for celebrities and emergencies, he declares, "I'm a celebrity in an emergency."

At this point, a passerby with a snow shovel whacks Phil on the head; is this his entry into simulation? Is this the window blowing in on him that will send him to Oz? The film never says, and there is never a point of awakening from a coma late in the film that would bracket the endless cycle of Groundhog Days as a hallucination. The film gives a nod to this standard cinematic/televisual convention of putting a character into a simulation, but refuses to separate that entrance into fantasy from everyday experience. In this way the experiences of Phil Connors that are about to unfold become a commentary on all our everyday experiences, and a warning to be alert for their simulational dangers. Back at his bed and breakfast, a grumpy and ironic Phil is last seen heading for his room after a cold shower—which should have awakened him from unconsciousness if anything could.

Comes the dawn and the bedside clock is seen ticking over to 6:00 A.M. "I've Got You Babe" awakens Phil. Is the song speaking to his childish ego now? "They say we're young and we don't know, won't find out until we grow." He notices the similarity in this morning's radio patter to yesterday's, and expresses it in technological terms: "Hey, storm boys, you're playing yesterday's tape." He clearly doesn't think much of their dramatic inventiveness. Phil anticipates their lines already and calls them out: "chapped lips!" But he soon starts to recognize the scenes he sees as yesterday's tape: "What the hell?" he cries upon seeing a snowless street from his window. "Didn't we do this yesterday . . . what day is this?" he asks a man on the stairs whom he encountered the day before. Mrs. Lancaster asks him the same questions and makes the same comment on the weather. In reply he asks, "Do you ever have deja view, Mrs. Lancaster?" On the first, real Groundhog Day he told her that his "chances for departure" were one hundred percent. Today he is not so sure, and responds to her query about his plans by downgrading it to eighty percent.

As he moves toward the broadcast site of the groundhog's home, he meets the same people—a bum, Ned Ryerson—and he steps in the same puddle of water. He tells Rita, "Something's going on, I don't know what to do." Rita asks, "Are you drunk or something?" Phil says, invoking The Value of simulation, "Drunk's more fun. . . . I'm having a problem—I *may* be having a problem." His on-camera monologue begins more tentatively, with dawning awareness of his fate: "Well, it's Groundhog Day . . . *again*." The film quickly cuts to Phil back in his room that evening, still trying to phone out and being told that service will be restored tomorrow. "Well, what if there's no tomorrow?" he replies. "There wasn't one today." Any character in a video game might say the same.

The bitter truth is made clear to Phil as he awakes the next morning to the same day. Arriving at the groundhog site, Rita tells him, "You've got work to do." "No I don't," he replies, "I've done it twice already." He tries to explain the situation to Rita later in a restaurant: "Rita, I'm reliving the same day over and over. Groundhog Day. Today." Nobody understands him. He goes to a psychologist who says, "I think we should meet again. How's tomorrow for you?"

This day will be pivotal in Phil's understanding of his simulational circumstances. Later, drinking in a bowling alley with Gus and Ralph, two down and out locals, Phil recalls an idyllic day he once spent in the Virgin Islands with a beautiful woman. "That was a pretty good day. Why couldn't I get that day over and over?" His stance toward his recurring day, just like his stance toward life, is entirely selfish and hedonistic. Fun is the only value by which he judges life. Phil poses a question to his drinking buddies: "What would you do if you were stuck in one place and every day was exactly the same and nothing that you did mattered?" Ralph burps, stares into the middle distance, and says, "That sums it up for me." It sums it up for many in the film's audience as well, who may be as detached, self-absorbed, and caught in a pointless loop as is Phil.

The conversation leads Phil to pose what may be the key question for the whole movie to these friendly philosophers: "What if there were no tomorrow?" One of his new friends gives the key answer: "No tomorrow . . . that would mean there would be no consequences, there would be no hangovers, we could do whatever we wanted." And one truth about what simulation really means dawns on Phil: "That's true, we could do whatever we wanted." Before long, he takes a first step in exploring this hypothesis by leading the local police on a merry, drunken chase in Ralph's car.

Why should a simulation appeal to people? Why would it be "fun" to live in a world without consequences, in which pushing the reset button or waiting for 6:00 A.M. makes all things new? What prompts the film's *audience* to escape real life and sit for two hours in a simulation? Careening around town in Ralph's car, Phil articulates a vision of control and order from which one might well flee into simulation's total freedom: "It's the same thing your whole life: clean up your room, stand up straight, pick up your feet, take it like a man, be nice to your sister." He runs the car onto the railroad tracks, police in hot pursuit. "I'm not gonna live by their rules any more! You make choices and you live with them"—and in this last assertion he must be referring to real life because, as he will discover, you make choices in simulation and you need not live with them at all. Swerving off the tracks in front of an oncoming train, Phil knocks over a giant plywood groundhog on his way to crashing into some parked cars. If he is the groundhog, he has knocked any firm foundation out from under himself in his decision to live life without rules and consequences. He enters simulation in spirit as well as in fact. The police descend upon Phil and his friends, and his stance is still ironic: he orders hamburgers as if the officer were a waiter. Predictably, control and order reassert themselves. The final scene of this day is of a forlorn, doubting Phil behind iron bars.

But he awakes the next day to an awareness that his recklessness of the night before indeed has no consequences. "Yes!" he cries, pumping his arms as he springs out of bed and launches into a day of pure piggish indulgence, which at a spiritual level is exactly what he has been doing all his "real" life. The obnoxious insurance salesman Ned Ryerson gets punched out cold. We see no evidence at all that he showed up to give his on-camera monologue. Phil sits in a café behind a table groaning with piles of fattening, greasy food and tells an astonished Rita, "I don't worry about anything any more." He begins a recurring pattern of asking women for information about themselves that he can use the "next day" to make it seem as if they have some connection from the past—all this in aid of seducing them. His only approach to relationships with others, given his new freedom, is selfish and manipulative.

The next day Phil puts his plans for seduction to work, approaching a woman (Nancy) as if he knows her. He uses the information he got the day before to act as if they were in high school together. His strategies work. But we see his real desire; as they tumble about on the sofa, he calls her Rita both before and after he offers up this lie: "Nancy, I love you. I've always loved you." When he *does* make human connection, it is with the "wrong" person.

So for a while we pursue this rake's progress beginning with the alarm at 6:00 every morning. The film never indicates that Phil dreams. Instead, he seems called from a sound sleep into wakefulness. But perhaps by beginning each new/old day by pulling Phil from sleep, the film presents its action precisely as if it were a dream; it is only on the last day that 6:00 brings a true awakening.

The film ceases to document each specific day's pattern of recurrence (for he will be here for years and years) and instead points to the fruits of his piggish labors: He robs an armored car because he has had days to study its patterns and pick the right moment of lapse in security. With the proceeds from this theft he plunges even deeper into simulational fantasies: He buys a Rolls Royce and emerges from it dressed as, and imitating, a Clint Eastwood cowboy character, with an attractive woman in tow. Phil is playing out other simulational fantasies within his simulation, and perhaps the audience envies him. He is in a cycle of complete self-absorption and indulgence, which is the fate of those in simulations, the film would seem to say.

Turning his attentions to the real object of his desire, he asks Rita, "Rita, if you only had one day to live, what would you do?" She doesn't know how to respond, so he asks her an important question: "So what do you want out of life, anyway?" It is a question he needs to ask himself, since never-ending life is all he has, but he is squandering this opportunity to pursue personal gratification and sexual seduction instead. He is seeking information about her personal preferences and longings as he did with Nancy, and will use them in an attempt to get Rita into bed.

We begin to see one iteration after another of Phil's gradually improving strategies with Rita. He takes her to a bar and discovers her favorite drink, and so we see the same scene the next day in which he surprises her with ordering her favorite drink, but then he must discover her favorite toast, which he offers up the next day—and on and on. The audience, as is Phil, is treated to one copy after another of the same scene, each one altered only slightly as he attempts to get it right. We see calculating looks in Phil's eye as he salts away one new revelation after another about what will please and seduce Rita, to be used the "next day." At one point, ironically, Rita asks Phil, "There is something so familiar about all this. Do you ever have déjà vu?" Is the power of his simulation leaking over into her real life? Ever distanced by irony, Phil replies, "Didn't you just ask me that?" When, back in his room, she says that she should go, he applies to her the standards of his own life: "Where would you go? Why?" But sooner or later she detects his strategy every day and in each repetition: "Is this what love is for you?" Phil relies on a false rhetoric of reality: "No, this is real, this is love." Rita replies with the main truth: "Stop saying that! You must be crazy. I could never love anyone like you Phil because you'll never love anyone but yourself." We are shown a long, long series of failures for Phil to achieve his goal of seduction, metonymized by a quick series of slaps she gives him at the end of each day. Rita has named the very problem that keeps Phil in a simulational loop, and that may well trap a narcissistic audience as well: he loves only himself. The simulational closed loop of self-centeredness is clear to Rita, but it may be something experienced by many in the audience as well, and the film warns us of its consequences.

What would count as success for Phil in his pursuit of Rita? Even sexual triumph would not be the love, the personal connection, that would spring him from his prison. The burden of endless repetition with no real consequences weighs heavily on Phil. A closeup of the digital clock's clicking over to 6:00 makes the stroke of that hour seem like a massive wall falling, with appropriate sound effects. Phil looks haggard and desperate. Unable to orient his life to any meaningful purpose, and unable to seduce the woman he really wants, he spends his days watching endless television, participating in the pointless cycle of recurring shows to which so many in the audience subject themselves. Sitting in a forlorn living room with a group of aged pensioners, he appears to know every answer to the quiz show *Jeopardy*—which earns him polite applause.

Anger at his simulational prison begins to take over. He tries smashing the bedside clock, to no avail. He gives his on-camera monologue in rage and bitterness, speaking of his own eternal repetition: "There's no way that this winter is ever going to end. As long as this groundhog keeps seeing his shadow, I don't see any other way out." What is it, to see one's shadow? In the context of this simulation, it is a preoccupation with the self and the self's representation. Note that the legend holds that if the groundhog sees its shadow, bleak winter will continue for six more weeks. Only if the groundhog does not see its shadow, is not given a token of itself, and can thus look to other matters in the world around it, will there be an early spring.

But both Phils are still locked into the eternal contemplation of their shadows, so Phil Connors decides to take matters into his own hands. "He's gotta be stopped," Phil says of Phil, "and I've gotta stop him." Phil kidnaps the groundhog, steals a pickup truck, and leads the police on a chase to a quarry outside town. Phil Connors is still in the simulational world of fantasy, television, and entertainment, for he tells his victim, "Well, we mustn't keep our public waiting, huh? It's showtime, Phil"—and drives into the quarry's abyss, plunging to the bottom in a fiery explosion. The rest is silence. But Phil has only ended until the tape can be played again. Phil despairs when he awakes, alive and well and back from the dead, the next morning at 6:00. There follow several ingenious attempts at killing himself, by electrocution, stepping in front of a truck, and leaping from an upper story. These suicides have no more consequences than do anything else he has ever done in this simulation.

So Phil tells Rita, "I'm a god . . . not *the* God, a god . . . I'm immortal." He shows her that he knows each detail of what will happen in the café they sit in, who people are, their sexual orientations and life histories, who will say what, when a dish will fall, and so forth. He knows *her* in detail, and tells her all about her own life and hopes. But it all seems like yet another show, an artifice, to Rita: "How are you doing this?" she asks in wonder, as if viewing a magic trick. Phil replies, "I told you, I wake up every day right here, right in Punxsutawney, and there's nothing I can do about it." They spend the day together discussing his plight. Rita has a naïve view of how to see simulation: "Maybe it really is happiness," she says tellingly, for who in the film's simulation-sodden audience would not grasp for the same irresponsible existence? Who in the film's audience did not delight at Phil's ability to stuff himself without shame or to pursue seduction like a single-minded goat? It seems as if it ought to be happiness, but the film is showing us it is not; it is pointlessness because it is simulational.

Phil begins to feel some genuine closeness to Rita. As they sit companionably on his bed, Phil tries to teach Rita how to toss cards into a hat, and lets it be known that he has spent six months, four or five hours per day, doing nothing but perfecting this dubious virtue. "Is this what you do with eternity?" she asks. What else would he do, having tried self indulgence and death? His greatest sadness, Phil tells Rita, is that she will not remember this day tomorrow, but "it doesn't make any difference. I've killed myself so many times, I don't exist any more." Rita replies, "Maybe it's not a curse, just depends on how you look at it." It's an offhand comment, but key. She is inviting him to live his recurring life in a way that will break the simulational loop. She prepares to leave, saying it was a nice day. "Maybe if it's not too boring, we could do it again some time," she says, not quite having understood Phil's situation. But tiredness overtakes her. She falls asleep next to him in bed, but for once he does not try to seduce her. It is an important first step in his recovery. He tells her sleeping form that she is the "kindest, sweetest" person he knows, and he expresses love to her, but she is asleep and does not hear. Awaking suddenly, she asks, "Did you say something?" But he only replies, "Good night." Phil has come close to breaking away from his self-preoccupation. But the words he has spoken that can take him out of simulation and into real relationship were spoken to a sleeper, perhaps one in a dream; he could not say them to a real person, fully awake.

The next morning he awakes again in the same day, but he has turned a corner. He walks through life with a new purpose, keyed to helping others, to reaching out of his loop into the lives of those around him. He gives money to a beggar he has passed thousands of times. He buys his crew coffee and pastries, is helpful and kind to them. He reads literature and takes piano lessons, learns Italian, masters ice sculpture and is generally pleasant to everyone. We see the new Phil getting better and better at his piano lessons and sharing that skill with others.

The hard realities of the actual world begin to draw Phil out. He discovers that the beggar he has helped is doomed to die in the evening of that day from old age and long dissipation. He pursues many strategies to help the man, feeding him and even giving him mouth-to-mouth resuscitation when he finds the man dead in a trash heap. He takes the beggar to a hospital, but nothing helps; the Great Reality is too strong. "Sometimes people just die," says a nurse, consoling him. "Not today," Phil replies bitterly, although his resolve is still not enough to save the man. This confrontation with a reality beyond himself changes Phil even more. He delivers a stirring, eloquent on-camera monologue on life and winter that draws the entire assembly at the groundhog's den to gather around him in profound respect and admiration.

Phil now spends his days helping people, being on the spot to change tires for elderly women in cars, catching children falling from trees, giving the Heimlich maneuver to a man who chokes on steak every night, and playing the piano for parties. We know he has studied the pattern of the city and its residents for a long time so as to know when to be on the spot with a helping hand. Phil's new way of living is entirely selfless, for he cannot benefit from any of his actions. To some extent he is still stuck in a simulational loop, though, for his actions cannot ultimately benefit those he helps, either. The boy will fall from the tree again tomorrow, the tire will go flat, the diner will choke. Phil has not taken that last step out of himself to establish true connection with others. His simulational self helps but then moves on. He is a hit-and-run philanthropist. He has emerged from his own preoccupations but has not yet crossed over deeply into others' lives. It is clear that he has lived in this limbo for a long time, as he shows mastery of medicine, foreign languages, and arts to a degree that bespeaks decades or more of study.

Then comes yet another iteration of the dance held on the evening of Groundhog Day, and this time he dances with Rita as many people come up to thank him and praise him for the help he has rendered them that day; two of them call him "Dr. Connors." An astonished Rita asks, "What did you do today?" To which he replies, "Oh, same old same old." A bachelor's "auction" ensues, and Rita bids all the money she has in her wallet to "buy" Phil. As they leave the hall, Ned Ryerson runs up to gush about all the insurance Phil has bought from him. "This is the best day of my life," he says, and both Phil and Rita respond, "Me, too." This particular Groundhog Day *has* been the best of Phil's life, for he is finally learning to reach out in real love to others. Phil tells Rita, "No matter what happens tomorrow, or for the rest of my life, I'm happy now, because I love you." This time he means his expression of love, and she responds, "I'm happy, too."

The next morning the clock ticks over to 6:00 and "I've Got You Babe" comes on as usual. The DJ's inside the radio are stuck inside that musical loop. But Rita is lying in the bed with Phil! He's *got* her, his Babe. "Something is different," he says slowly. "Anything different is good. This could be real [pause] good." He is right, it is *real* good, and good because real. He turns to Rita: "You know what today is? Today is tomorrow. It happened. You're here." Her being there, the human connection he made and maintained, has pulled him over into February 3. Rita says that last night he just fell asleep; even his old plans for seduction were set aside. He asks her, "Is there anything I can do for you—*today*?" He is oriented toward another person and her needs now. And what he does for her today will be real, it will make a difference. They go out and he says, "It's so beautiful. Let's live here." And then thinking again: "We'll rent for starters."

Groundhog Day enacts a rhetoric of simulation, showing the audience Phil Connors and his life as a mirror for so many of us. People today are preoccupied with self and selfish interests, obsessed with entertainment and its technological underpinnings, unable to make real human connection. *Groundhog Day* is this predicament carried to its logical conclusion, a simulational paradise of no consequences in which total selfish piggishness is *possible*. But the film uses the most negative meanings of simulation to advise its audience that such a life, if possible, is not desirable. The real harm of simulation, it argues, is loss of real human connection through inauthenticity of being, refusal of love, ironic detachment. And for a culture lost in simulation, the film advises a recovery of that connection and authentic being.

Bibliography

Arnheim, Rudolf. "Foreword: Visual Thinking in Overview." *Perception and Pictorial Representation*. Ed. Calvin F. Nodine and Dennis F. Fisher. New York: Praeger, 1979. xix–xxix.

Balsamo, Anne. "Forms of Technological Embodiment: Reading the Body in Contemporary Culture." *Cyberspace/Cyberbodies/Cyberpunk*. Ed. Mike Featherstone and Roger Burrows. London: Sage, 1995. 215–37.

Baudrillard, Jean. *The Ecstasy of Communication*. Trans. Bernard and Caroline Shutze. Ed. Sylvere Lotringer. New York: Semiotext(e), 1988.

——— . *For a Critique of the Political Economy of the Sign*. Trans. Charles Levin. St. Louis, MO: Telos P, 1981.

——— . *Simulations*. Trans. Paul Foss, Paul Patton, and Philip Beitchmann. New York: Semiotext(e), 1983.

Beckmann, John, ed. *The Virtual Dimension: Architecture, Representation, and Crash Culture*. New York: Princeton Architectural Press, 1998.

Benjamin, Walter. *Illuminations*. New York: Harcourt, Brace, & World, 1968.

Berger, John. *Ways of Seeing*. London: BBC/Penguin, 1972.

Berger, Rene. "Re-Enactment and Simulation: Toward a Synthesis of What Type?" *Diogenes*. 147 (1989): 1–22.

Boggs, Carl. *The End of Politics: Corporate Power and the Decline of the Public Sphere*. New York: Guilford, 2000.

Bois, Yve-Alain. "Painting: The Task of Mourning." *Endgame: Reference and Simulation in Recent Painting and Sculpture*. Ed. David Joselit and Elisabeth Sussman. Cambridge, MA: MIT P, 1986. 29–49.

Boorstin, Daniel J. *The Image: A Guide to Pseudo-Events in America*. 1962. New York: Atheneum, 1973.

Brummett, Barry. *Reading Rhetorical Theory*. Fort Worth: Harcourt, 2000.

Burke, Kenneth. *A Grammar of Motives*. Berkeley, CA: U of CA P, 1962.

——— . *Language as Symbolic Action*. Berkeley, CA: U of CA P, 1966.

Cassirer, Ernst. *Language and Myth*. Trans. Sysanne K. Langer. New York: Harper & Brothers, 1946.

Clark, Nigel. "Rear-View Mirrorshades: The Recursive Generation of the Cyberbody." *Cyberspace/Cyberbodies/Cyberpunk*. Ed. Mike Featherstone and Roger Burrows. London: Sage, 1995. 113–33.

Critical Art Ensemble. "Utopian Plagiarism, Hypertextuality, and Electronic Cultural Production." *CyberReader*. Ed. Victor J. Vitanza. Boston: Allyn and Bacon, 1999. 339–50.

Croce, Benedetto. *Aesthetic as Science of Expression and General Linguistic*. 2nd ed. Trans. Douglas Ainslie. 1st Italian ed. 1902. London: Macmillan and Co., 1929.

Crow, Thomas. "The Return of Hank Herron." *Endgame: Reference and Simulation in Recent Painting and Sculpture*. Ed. David Joselit and Elisabeth Sussman. Cambridge, MA: MIT P, 1986. 11–28.

Currie, Gregory. "Imagination and Simulation: Aesthetics Meets Cognitive Science." *Mental Simulation: Evaluations and Applications*. Ed. Martin Davies and Tony Stone. Oxford, UK: Blackwell, 1995. 151–69.

Danto, Arthur C. "Pictorial Representation and Works of Art." *Perception and Pictorial Representation*. Ed. Calvin F. Nodine and Dennis F. Fisher. New York: Praeger, 1979. 4–16.

Davies, Martin, and Tony Stone, eds. *Mental Simulation: Evaluations and Applications*. Oxford, UK: Blackwell, 1995.

Day, Larry. "Painting as Paradigm." *Perception and Pictorial Representation*. Ed. Calvin F. Nodine and Dennis F. Fisher. New York: Praeger, 1979. 42–54.

Dukes, Richard L. *Worlds Apart: Collective Action in Simulated Agrarian and Industrial Societies*. Dortrecht, The Netherlands: Kluwer Academic Publishers, 1990.

Dyson, Frances. " 'Space,' 'Being,' and Other Fictions in the Domain of the Virtual." *The Virtual Dimension: Architecture, Representation, and Crash Culture*. Ed. John Beckmann. New York: Princeton Architectural Press, 1998. 27–45.

Edelman, Murray. *From Art to Politics: How Artistic Creations Shape Political Conceptions*. Chicago: U of Chicago P, 1995.

Eliade, Mircea. *The Myth of the Eternal Return, or, Cosmos and History*. Trans. Willard R. Trask. Princeton, NJ: Princeton U P, 1954.

——— . *The Sacred and the Profane: The Nature of Religion*. Trans. Willard R. Trask. New York: Harcourt, Brace, and World, 1959.

Featherstone, Mike, and Roger Burrows, eds. *Cyberspace/Cyberbodies/Cyberpunk*. London: Sage, 1995.

Fiske, John. *Media Matters*. Rev. ed. Minneapolis: U of Minnesota P, 1996.

Foster, Hal. "The Future of an Illusion, or the Contemporary Artist as Cargo Cultist." *Endgame: Reference and Simulation In Recent Painting and Sculpture*. Ed. David Joselit and Elisabeth Sussman. Cambridge, MA: MIT P, 1986. 91–105.

Fuller, Gary. "Simulation and Psychological Concepts." *Mental Simulation: Evaluations and Applications*. Ed. Martin Davies and Tony Stone. Oxford, UK: Blackwell, 1995. 19–31.

Gabler, Neal. *Life the Movie: How Entertainment Conquered Reality*. New York: Alfred A. Knopf, 1998.

Gergen, Kenneth J. *The Concept of Self*. New York: Holt, Rinehart and Winston, 1971.

————. *Realities and Relationships: Soundings in Social Construction*. Cambridge, MA: Harvard U P, 1994.

————. *The Saturated Self: Dilemmas of Identity in Contemporary Life*. New York: Basic Books, 1991.

Gibson, William. *Count Zero*. 1986. New York: Ace Books, 1987.

————. *Mona Lisa Overdrive*. New York: Bantam, 1988.

————. *Neuromancer*. New York: Ace Books, 1984.

Goldman, Alvin I. "Empathy, Mind, and Morals." *Mental Simulation: Evaluations and Applications*. Ed. Martin Davies and Tony Stone. Oxford, UK: Blackwell, 1995. 185–208.

Gordon, Robert M. *The Structure of Emotions: Investigations in Cognitive Philosophy*. Cambridge, UK: Cambridge U P, 1987.

Gray, Chris Hables. *Cyborg Citizen*. New York: Routledge, 2001.

Gregory, Richard L. "Space of Pictures." *Perception and Pictorial Representation*. Ed. Calvin F. Nodine and Dennis F. Fisher. New York: Praeger, 1979. 228–45.

Gunkel, David. "Rethinking Virtual Reality: Simulation and the Deconstruction of the Image." *Critical Studies in Mass Communication*. 17 (2000): 45–62.

Gunn, Joshua, and David E. Beard. "On the Apocalyptic Sublime." *Southern Communication Journal*. 65 (2000): 269–86.

Gup, Ted. "The End of Serendipity." *CyberReader*. Ed. Victor J. Vitanza. Boston: Allyn and Bacon, 1999. 250–53.

Hayles, N. Katherine. *How We Became Posthuman: Virtual Bodies in Cybernetics, Literature, and Informatics*. Chicago: U of Chicago P, 1999.

Heim, Michael. "The Design of Virtual Reality." *Cyberspace/Cyberbodies/Cyberpunk*. Ed. Mike Featherstone and Roger Burrows. London: Sage, 1995. 65–77.

————. "The Essence of VR." *CyberReader*. Ed. Victor J. Vitanza. Boston: Allyn and Bacon, 1999. 20–35.

————. *Virtual Realism*. New York: Oxford U P, 1998.

Helmreich, Stefan. *Silicon Second Nature: Cultivating Artificial Life in a Digital World*. Berkeley: U of California P, 1998.

Hjort, Mette, and Sue Lauer. *Emotion and the Arts*. New York: Oxford U P, 1997.

Hochberg, Julian. "Some of the Things That Paintings Are." *Perception and Pictorial Representation*. Ed. Calvin F. Nodine and Dennis F. Fisher. New York: Praeger, 1979. 17–41.

hooks, bell. *Black Looks: Race and Representation*. Boston: South End Press, 1992.

Irwin, Robert. "Some Notes on the Nature of Abstraction." *Perception and Pictorial Representation*. Ed. Calvin F. Nodine and Dennis F. Fisher. New York: Praeger, 1979. 217–27.

Johnson, Steven. *Interface Culture: How New Technology Transforms the Way We Create and Communicate*. New York: HarperCollins, 1997.

Joselit, David, and Elisabeth Sussman, eds. *Endgame: Reference and Simulation in Recent Painting and Sculpture*. Cambridge, MA: MIT P, 1986.

Landberg, Alison. "Prosthetic Memory: *Total Recall* and *Blade Runner*." *Cyberspace/Cyberbodies/Cyberpunk*. Ed. Mike Featherstone and Roger Burrows. London: Sage, 1995. 175–89.

Langer, Susanne K. *Mind: An Essay on Human Feeling*. Vol. I. Baltimore: The Johns Hopkins U P, 1967.

————. *Philosophy in a New Key: A Study in the Symbolism of Reason, Rite, and Art*, 3rd ed. Cambridge, MA: Harvard U P, 1957.

Levinson, Jerrold. "Emotion in Response to Art: A Survey of the Terrain." *Emotion and the Arts*. Ed. Mette Hjort and Sue Lauer. New York: Oxford U P, 1997. 20–34.

Locke, John. *An Essay Concerning Human Understanding*. 1690; Cleveland: Meridian Books, 1964.

Lupton, Deborah. "The Embodied Computer/User." *Cyberspace/Cyberbodies/Cyberpunk*. Ed. Mike Featherstone and Roger Burrows. London: Sage, 1995. 97–112.

Massumi, Brian. "Live Parable for the Virtual (On the Superiority of the Analog)." *The Virtual Dimension: Architecture, Representation, and Crash Culture*. Ed. John Beckmann. New York: Princeton Architectural Press, 1998. 305–21

Negroponte, Nicholas. *Being Digital*. New York: Alfred A. Knopf, 1995.

Negrotti, Massimo. *Theory of the Artificial: Virtual Replications and the Revenge of Reality*. Exeter, UK: Intellect Books, 1999.

Nichols, Bill. *Representing Reality*. Bloomington: Indiana U P, 1991.

Nodine, Calvin F., and Dennis F. Fisher, eds. *Perception and Pictorial Representation*. New York: Praeger, 1979.

Norton, Anne. *Republic of Signs*. Chicago: U of Chicago P, 1993.

Ogden, C. K., and I. A. Richards. *The Meaning of Meaning*. New York: Harcourt, Brace, and World, 1923.

Parenti, Michael. *Make-Believe Media: The Politics of Entertainment*. New York: St. Martin's, 1992.

Perrella, Stephen. "Hypersurfaces: Socius Fluxus." *The Virtual Dimension: Architecture, Representation, and Crash Culture*. Ed. John Beckmann. New York: Princeton Architectural Press, 1998. 235–40.

Poster, Mark. "Postmodern Virtualities." *Cyberspace/Cyberbodies/Cyberpunk*. Ed. Mike Featherstone and Roger Burrows. London: Sage, 1995. 79–95.

Prietula, Michael J., Kathleen M. Carley, and Les Gasser, eds. *Simulating Organizations: Computational Models of Institutions and Groups*. Menlo Park, CA: AAAI Press; Cambridge, MA: MIT P, 1998.

Punday, Daniel. "The Narrative Construction of Cyberspace: Reading *Neuromancer*, Reading Cyberspace Debates." *College English*. 63 (2000): 194–213.

Rheingold, Howard. "Introduction to *The Virtual Community*." *CyberReader*. Ed. Victor J. Vitanza. Boston: Allyn and Bacon, 1999. 63–77.

Richards, I. A. *The Philosophy of Rhetoric*. London: Oxford U P, 1936.

Richardson, John Adkins. *From Pure Visibility to Virtual Reality in an Age of Estrangement*. Westport, CT: Praeger, 1998.

Robins, Kevin. "Cyberspace and the World We Live In." *Cyberspace/Cyberbodies/Cyberpunk*. Ed. Mike Featherstone and Roger Burrows. London: Sage, 1995. 135–55.

Roetzer, Florian. "Outer Space or Virtual Space? Utopias of the Digital Age." *The Virtual Dimension: Architecture, Representation, and Crash Culture*. Ed. John Beckmann. New York: Princeton Architectural Press, 1998. 121–43.

Romm, Celia T. *Virtual Politicking: Playing Politics in Electronically Linked Organizations*. Cresskill, NJ: Hampton Press, 1999.

Rorty, Richard. *Philosophy and the Mirror of Nature*. Princeton, NJ: Princeton U P, 1979.

Rushkoff, Douglas. "Seeing Is Beholding." *CyberReader*. Ed. Victor J. Vitanza. Boston: Allyn and Bacon, 1999. 36–48.

Schenk, Ronald. *The Soul of Beauty: A Psychological Investigation of Appearance.* Lewisburg, PA: Bucknell U P, 1992.

Shapiro, Michael J. *The Politics of Representation: Writing Practices in Biography, Photography, and Policy Analysis.* Madison: U of Wisconsin P, 1988.

Slouka, Mark. *War of the Worlds: Cyberspace and the High-Tech Assault on Reality.* New York: Basic Books, 1995.

Stenslie, Stahl. "Flesh Space." *The Virtual Dimension: Architecture, Representation, and Crash Culture.* Ed. John Beckmann. New York: Princeton Architectural Press, 1998. 19–25.

Stephan, Michael. *A Transformational Theory of Aesthetics.* London: Routledge, 1990.

Stewart, John. *Beyond the Symbol Model: Reflections on the Representational Nature of Language.* Albany: State U of New York P, 1996.

Stone, Allucquere Rosanne. *The War of Desire and Technology at the Close of the Mechanical Age.* Cambridge, MA: MIT P, 1995.

Taylor, Mark C. "Stripping Architecture." *The Virtual Dimension: Architecture, Representation, and Crash Culture.* Ed. John Beckmann. New York: Princeton Architectural Press, 1998. 195–203.

Thieme, Richard. "Stalking the UGO Meme." *CyberReader.* Ed. Victor J. Vitanza. Boston: Allyn and Bacon, 1999. 49–58.

Turkle, Sherry. "Identity Crisis." *CyberReade*r. Ed. Victor J. Vitanza. Boston: Allyn and Bacon, 1999. 78–94.

Virilio, Paul. *The Art of the Motor.* Trans. Julie Rose. Minneapolis: U of Minneapolis P, 1995.

————. "Speed and Information: Cyberspace Alarm!" *CTHEORY* [On-line]. http://www.ctheory.com/a30-cyberspace_alarm.html. 1995.

Vitanza, Victor J., ed. *CyberReader,* 2nd ed. Boston: Allyn and Bacon, 1999.

Wagner, Roy. *Symbols That Stand for Themselves.* Chicago: U of Chicago P, 1986.

Walton, Kendall. *Mimesis as Make-Believe: On the Foundations of the Representational Arts.* Cambridge, MA: Harvard U P, 1990.

————. "Spelunking, Simulation, and Slime: On Being Moved by Fiction." *Emotion and the Arts.* Ed. Mette Hjort and Sue Lauer. New York: Oxford U P, 1997. 37–49.

Wartofsky, Marx W. "Picturing and Representing." *Perception and Pictorial Representation.* Ed. Calvin F. Nodine and Dennis F. Fisher. New York: Praeger, 1979. 272–83.

Wertheim, Margaret. "The Medieval Return of Cyberspace." *The Virtual Dimension: Architecture, Representation, and Crash Culture.* Ed. John Beckmann. New York: Princeton Architectural Press, 1998. 47–60.

Woolley, Benjamin. "Cyberspace." *CyberReader.* Ed. Victor J. Vitanza. Boston: Allyn and Bacon, 1999. 7–19.

Index

Advertising, 68–69
Aesthetics, 25, 34–44, 61, 68, 77, 83–94, 120–21
African American, 4, 87–88
Art, 4, 20, 28, 30, 34–41, 48, 50–52, 55, 68, 79, 83–94, 100, 120
Authorship, 79

Baudrillard, Jean, 6, 10–11, 14–15, 20, 40–42, 46, 49, 53, 56–61, 65–67, 80, 82–83, 89, 91–92, 94
Benjamin, Walter, 15, 48, 63, 68
Body, and the physical, 49, 56, 72, 75, 77–78, 80, 100, 106–109, 113, 117
Boorstin, Daniel, 6, 8, 10, 41–42, 48, 55–56, 58, 61, 67, 82, 92
Burke, Kenneth, 5, 33–35

Capitalism and capital, 48, 62, 66–68, 73, 91, 110
Cassirer, Ernst, 6, 17, 32
Commodification, 62–69, 110–14
Computers, 10, 12–13, 23, 50–51, 59, 77, 82, 97–122
Construction, 25–44, 50

Croce, Benedetto, 27–28, 35–36, 38, 51, 85, 88
Cyberspace, 7, 11, 23, 56–57, 67, 74, 79–81, 89, 93, 97–124

Democracy, 73
Derrida, Jacques, 20
Dewey, John, 35
Disneyland, 10
Dualism, 2–3, 30, 43, 49, 57–60, 69, 72, 87

Eliade, Mircea, 16–18, 48–50
Epistemology, 5–6, 38–39, 50–54, 86–88
Exchange and use values, 62–69, 73, 76, 110, 113, 120

Film, 22, 35, 39–40, 50, 56, 61, 67, 76, 78, 87, 92, 137, 140
Fiske, John, 9–10, 12, 22–23, 30, 51, 53, 68
Folk psychology, 21
Form, 84–85, 89, 91, 93–94
Foucault, Michel, 53, 129

Gabler, Neal, 12, 29, 39–40, 42, 61, 69, 82, 93–94

Games, 7, 15, 21–22, 58, 60, 67, 72, 78–79, 91, 97, 125, 138, 141
Gergen, Kenneth, 30, 33, 53-55, 57–59, 72–75, 78–79, 83
Gibson, William, 97–122; *Count Zero* synopsis, 99–101; *Mona Lisa Overdrive* synopsis, 101–103; *Neuromancer* synopsis, 98–99
Gunkel, David, 7–8, 14–15, 20, 57, 59

Heim, Michael, 7–8, 12, 19, 23, 26, 47–49, 61–62, 84, 90, 93

Identity, 79
Images, 5–7, 13, 23, 29, 51-52, 58-59, 65, 74-76, 87-88, 102
Internet and the World Wide Web, 11, 65, 68, 97, 103, 105, 109, 116, 118, 121, 123–24, 135–36

Kant, Immanuel, 92

Langer, Susanne, 4–5, 8–9, 16, 26, 30–33, 51, 85–86, 88–89, 93
Language. *See* Signs and symbols

Matrix. *See* Internet and the World Wide Web
Mind, 2–3,
Music, 93

Narrative, 129–35
News and reporting, 13, 16, 42, 138
Newsgroup, 124
Norton, Anne, 6, 10, 43, 52, 64, 66, 74, 76, 90

Orientation, 79–80

Painting. *See* Art
Perception, 26–32, 35–36
Permanence and change, 115–62, 103–109
Photography, 15, 24, 34, 65, 90
Plato, 84, 86
Pleasure, 83–84, 139, 141
Politics, 41–44, 53–54, 64, 78, 87
Pornography, 65
Power, 2, 6, 41, 49, 52–54, 61, 66, 94, 110

Prostheses, 77–78, 98–99, 101, 116–20

Reagan, Ronald, 28
Reality, 1–3, 18–44, 46–50, 63, 72–73, 84–85, 97–122
Reality, representation, simulation as rhetorical claims, 1–2, 24, 43–44
Relationships, 78–79
Representation, 1–6, 11–12, 18–44, 50–54, 63–65, 73–76, 85–88, 123–36
Rhetoric, 2, 46, 59–61, 63, 72–73, 95, 98, 102–103, 113–15, 122–23, 125, 129, 135–37, 139, 146
Richards, I. A., 4, 7, 26–27, 31–33
Ritual, 16–18

Saussure, Ferdinand de, 31
Schenk, Ronald, 35, 38, 48, 83, 87–89, 92
Science, 27, 38, 47, 93
Self. *See* Subject and subjectivity
Signs and symbols, 2–7, 11–12, 25, 27, 31–35, 47, 50–54, 57–58, 61, 63–67, 69, 75–76, 87–88, 90, 92, 124–25, 128, 135–36
Simulation, 1–3, 6–11, 18–44, 54–62, 65–69, 76–83, 88–94; as copies, 14–18, 137–38, 143; as signs without representation, 11–15, 137–38, 141
Slouka, Mark, 3, 9, 11, 14, 46–51, 53–58, 61, 65, 68, 73, 82–83
Subject and subjectivity, 2, 30–31, 36–38, 44, 49, 71–83, 115–20

Technology, 6–7, 23, 40, 56–57, 60, 74, 79–80, 97–122, 126–29, 139–40
Television, 9–10, 13, 15, 22, 40, 42, 47–48, 51, 57, 68–69, 76–77, 79, 83, 88, 137, 139, 143–44

Virilio, Paul, 6, 10, 13, 15, 28, 30, 40, 48, 53–54, 56–57, 59, 75, 79–80
Virtual reality, 8–9, 12, 14–15, 19, 23, 28, 30, 56, 59, 81–82, 91
Voodoo, 99–102, 104–105

Walton, Kendall, 4, 7, 23, 37, 54–55, 60, 86, 89, 91

About the Author

BARRY BRUMMETT is Charles Sapp Centennial Professor in Communication and Chair of the Communication Studies Department at the University of Texas at Austin. He is the author of several books and articles, including *Contemporary Apocalyptic Rhetoric* (Praeger, 1991) and *Rhetoric of Machine Aesthetics* (Praeger, 1999).

Rec